Canada: Is Anyone Listening?

CANADA: Is Anyone Listening?

Rafe Mair

KEY PORTER BOOKS

Canadian Cataloguing in Publication Data

Mair, Rafe, 1931–
Canada: Is anyone listening?

ISBN: 1-55263-000-5

1. Canada—Politics and government—1980–1984.*
2. Canada—Politics and government—1984–1993.*
3. Canada—Politics and government—1933–   .*
4. Nationalism—Canada. I. Title.

FC635.M34 1998	971.064	C98-931418-9
	F1034.2.M34 1998	

NOTE: Some photos were taken by Norman Tarnow and provided by Melvin H. Smith,QC.

Key Porter Books Limited
70 The Esplanade
Toronto, Ontario
Canada, M5E 1R2

www.keyporter.com

Text set in Minion

Electronic formatting: Rena Potter

Printed and bound in Canada

98 99 00 01 6 5 4 3 2 1

To Kenneth, Kevin, and Ashleigh Mair;
Tyrel and Trent Mair-Valin;
and Robert and Karyn Leigh Armstrong,
in the hope that there'll be something left for them.

Contents

Introduction: My Case

I'm going to tell you about my life, about British Columbia and Canada, and about politics and freedom of speech.

Is what I'm about to tell you true? I don't honestly know. What I do know is that this is what I think. Winston Churchill was once asked if his Nobel-Prize-winning six-volume book *The Second World War* was accurate. He replied, "It's my case." So be it with this book. It will be for readers to judge its credibility.

I do not speak for British Columbia nor British Columbians. However, I do believe that much of what I have to say does represent, at least in part, what most British Columbians believe. There are different shades of importance, of course, and some will hold similar views but perhaps not so strongly. On the other hand, I believe that for everyone who thinks I overstate the case, an equal number will believe that I don't go far enough.

I've been around for years and have had some involvement in the country's public life, both as a politician and a journalist. Throughout the latter half of the 1970s I served in B.C.'s provincial Social Credit government, under Premier Bill Bennett. Since the early 1980s, I've been a talk-radio broadcaster based out of Vancouver, first with CJOR and then with CKNW. I am a lawyer by training, now armed with a pen and a microphone. I practise advocacy journalism, as do many "real" journalists—except they don't admit it.

This is a book of advocacy journalism. My political career included stints as British Columbia's minister of environment and minister of health. You won't be surprised to hear that I have strong opinions in both of those areas. In my years in politics, and for much of my time in broadcasting, I have also been immersed in Canada's seemingly endless constitutional soap opera and the unity crisis.

Before we get to the advocacy, though, I'd like to provide some context, by telling you about myself and my province.

CHAPTER ONE

My Canada Includes B.C.

My province has been part of Canada virtually since the beginning. We are not latecomers. Yet we have endured 127 years of being ignored by the Canadian establishment, because Canada has a bankrupt political system: there is no need for anyone seeking political power at the national level to pay the slightest attention to people in B.C.

While I express myself as a Canadian from British Columbia, I have no need to speak for the people of B.C. They have, when given the chance, spoken loudly and clearly on their own behalf.

I also cannot and do not speak as a "Westerner." There is no such thing any more, if indeed there ever was. Jean Barman's wonderful book *The West Beyond the West* demonstrates beyond any doubt that British Columbia has never—geographically, demographically, historically or economically— been part of "the West."

However, the notion of "the West" has always been convenient for Ottawa. That it's nonsense has never occurred to them as relevant, and they continue to assume that there is some sort of geographical and cultural association between thought in The Pas, Manitoba, and Ucluelet, British Columbia. What this notion does is confuse issues, marginalize the concerns of those from provinces arbitrarily included in the "Western" designation, and anger people west of the Lakehead, especially people in British Columbia.

Nothing is more annoying to most British Columbians than to be lumped in with the other three Western provinces. This is not because of some sense of superiority. Not at all. To treat the four Western provinces as one region does as little justice to Alberta, Saskatchewan, and Manitoba as it does to British Columbia. And it must be quickly added that even within the Prairie region substantial differences are developing. Alberta, despite the lack of a natural boundary with Saskatchewan, is developing quite a distinctive character of its own.

When I was in school, many of the kids were originally from other provinces. The ones from the Prairies were just as different as those from other parts of Canada. For one thing, they could skate and play hockey, but they couldn't swim. In B.C., none of us could skate, because there was no natural ice—but we all could swim. Prairie children clearly had a heritage which, while as Canadian as mine, was different. Not better or worse, but different.

When I see polls in the Toronto *Globe and Mail* dividing the country into four regions—Ontario, Quebec, Atlantic Canada and the West—I bristle. I know that there are also bold differences within Ontario and Quebec, but to stretch an opinion poll from Lake of the Woods in Manitoba to the Queen Charlotte Islands in B.C. is inaccurate and condescending. Worse, such ridiculous samplings inevitably lead to erroneous conclusions.

The Toronto *Globe and Mail*, which passes itself off as "Canada's national newspaper" (which makes as much sense as my claiming to be Canada's national broadcaster), has two West-themed weekly columns. One, by David Bercusson and Barry Cooper, is called "The West." Bercusson and Cooper, both bright, excellent writers whom I like and respect, live in Calgary. The other column, by whomever is currently running the paper's tiny Vancouver bureau, is called "Western Voices." Neither column has any particular resonance in British Columbia, though according to the Toronto *Globe and Mail*, B.C. is part of "the West." And this from the very paper that holds itself out as Canada's newspaper of record.

I am often called upon to do radio and TV commentary as a "Westerner" and, in the interests of both my own province and the other provinces that are west of the Canadian establishment, I must waste a couple of minutes explaining that I am not a "Westerner."

I was asked, a few years ago, to write a column for the Toronto *Globe and Mail* on "views from the West." I refused, at least in part because I have no hands-on idea how people in oil country or wheat country feel about national issues. I've seldom even visited places like Calgary, Regina and Winnipeg, much less the smaller communities that always make up the backbone of the larger political unit. I have far more personal and professional contact with Ontario than I do with any of the Prairie provinces. How could I know what those in the Prairies are thinking? I would be much better qualified to give "the view from Seattle."

In saying all this I'm not merely exposing the sensibilities of a Lotuslander (though I'm doing that as well), but trying to make a point to the rest of my country: You simply cannot understand Canada if you think in the antiquated terms so comfy to Ottawa, the CBC, *Maclean's* and the Toronto *Globe and Mail.* It's like saying that Newfoundland is part of "the Maritimes"—if you believe that, you are betraying an ignorance of this country that is appalling and, worse yet, dangerous.

Is this all that important? Does it really matter if many Canadians feel left out both emotionally and politically? Aren't we all just Canadians who should get on with our lives?

It is critically important. A nation is much more than just territory bounded by lines on a map. It must provide a sense of belonging for all.

There is a curious thing about British Columbia—it never seems to produce a Canadian of note. Notorious yes, but seldom, if ever, important. B.C. has far fewer Order of Canada members than its proportion of Canada's population would seem to warrant, for example.

If you look in the classic major history texts, from which most English-speaking Canadians learned about their country, you won't find out who British Columbia's first premier was. No big deal, I suppose, but it probably explains why a Canadian author confidently asserted that it was Amor de Cosmos (William Smith by birth)—who in fact was the second. I tried my best to tell her that it was John Foster McCreight, but she insisted that she had her facts right. The importance of this example is not just to historical accuracy but to national perception. British Columbia is simply seen as an asterisk in Canadian history. It's trivialized in the minds of other Canadians, simply because of the historians' silence.

It is not my position that all Canadians—or even all British Columbians—should know the name of B.C.'s first premier. In May 1998, Ontario Premier Mike Harris was stumped by schoolchildren who asked him to name Ontario's first premier. He couldn't, and neither can I. But at least Harris and I can *find out* the name of the Ontario premier, by looking in a standard Canadian history text; the same text would not include the name John Foster McCreight.

A few years ago *Maclean's* put out a small almanac which, amongst other things, listed the most famous living Canadians by birthplace. As I recall, there were about 150 names, so based on population proportions one would assume that about twenty would be from British Columbia. In fact, only two were: former premier Bill Bennett and—are you ready for this?—Margaret Trudeau!

W.A.C. Bennett—Bill's father, who served as B.C.'s premier for twenty years (1952–1972) himself—is a good example of how prominent British Columbians are ignored or put down by the Eastern-run media. He was a towering figure in Canadian politics, unless one exempts British Columbians from that description. Yet he was dubbed "Wacky" by the Eastern-run press—considered notorious but certainly not important.

His son Bill is another example. When I served in Bill Bennett's cabinet in the late 1970s and early 1980s, I was constantly twitted by Central Canadian colleagues about the goofy politics in British Columbia. Yet I would come to Ottawa to see a chain-smoking scatterbrain leading Quebec, a smug pipe-smoking platitudinous bore leading Ontario, one of the strangest cats in Christendom running New Brunswick and, in the days before Brian Peckford, a perpetual hangover, at best, leading Newfoundland. I'd then wonder, often aloud, how a thoughtful and strong leader like Bill Bennett was considered goofy.

Perhaps there's something in the air in British Columbia that depresses the intellect and other skills, so that curious mediocrity is the ultimate to which a Lotuslander can aspire. Or perhaps it has something to do with how the Eastern establishment, which controls the country's media, presents British Columbians in Central Canada. It might be argued that unless something happens in Ontario or Quebec, no one with a national printing press or television network notices.

British Columbians are used to being treated by the Toronto *Globe and Mail* (I will never stop using the modifier Toronto because that's what fairly identifies it) and by *Maclean's* as if they were some rare pygmy tribe in darkest Africa.

It must surely be the same for other regions, but British Columbia in general and Vancouver in particular are invariably "reported on." It would be unheard of for *Maclean's* or the Toronto *Globe and Mail* ever to have their minuscule bureaus manned by British Columbians, or even by people who have the faintest inkling of what British Columbians think. In fact, the Toronto *Globe and Mail* often uses one person, located in B.C., to report on all of Canada west of Ontario, assuming, as it has from the beginning, that there is but one "West."

"Bureaus" are usually composed of one or two reporters who read Vancouver's Southam-owned papers, the *Sun* and the *Province*, and then paste some words together and file their stories. I have been in the eye of most of B.C.'s political storms for the past twenty-five years, and have often been called by prominent members of the local media and national radio and television; however, I have been called by a Toronto *Globe and Mail* bureauperson only once: during my outspoken stand on the 1992 referendum on the Charlottetown Accord. In my reasonably seasoned view of the media, "bureaus" are only here in Vancouver to meet their publications' self-imposed mandate of appearing to be national media outlets. They are not, of course, national media outlets at all, as a quick glance at the letters to the editor and the obituary page of the Toronto *Globe and Mail* will readily demonstrate. The utter cheek these two Toronto publishers show in presenting themselves as "national" is only exceeded by the CBC's assertion—based, in fairness to the "Mother Corp.," on its enabling statute—that it has a mandate to further national unity. If the CBC is responsible, even in part, for the state of this country's unity, it ought to be disbanded forthwith while there's still time.

I have no hope for Conrad Black and David Radler's proposed national newspaper either. It will report on B.C. through the eyes of *The Vancouver Sun* and *The Vancouver Province*, which are Central-Canada-owned and -operated papers, and hire accordingly.

The evidence of the Central Canadian establishment's reporting bias is overwhelming, but doubters may wish to watch hockey games and see how it is assumed in Toronto that, deep down, all Canadians outside Quebec are Maple Leafs fans. For my checkmate move I need only refer to the 1994 Stanley Cup semi-final match between Toronto and Vancouver, when the announcer (Bob Cole) and the "colour" people (Harry Neale and Don Cherry) were so pro-Maple Leafs that even the odd Torontonian was embarrassed. (Have you ever noticed how Torontonians have never understood that the plural of "leaf" is "leaves"? But I digress.)

Let me illustrate this very real Central Canadian media bias by way of a personal anecdote. A few years ago, I was scheduled to be the mystery guest on CBC's *Front Page Challenge*. My appearance was cancelled at the last moment. Why? Because the story was about my involvement in the defeat, in British Columbia, of the 1992 referendum asking Canadians to ratify the Charlottetown Accord. (You'll remember that the referendum was also defeated throughout the rest of the country.) The producers decided that this was not a politically correct story.

At the risk of sounding like a philandering husband whispering to his secretary, British Columbia is not understood by the rest of the country. It is especially not understood by Central Canada.

British Columbia *is* different. Very different.

For one thing, it's geographically unique. Not only is it vast, it is mountainous. The mountains don't begin and end at the Rockies by any means, though this immense chain does provide a huge psychological barrier. Much of the rest of the province, especially the most inhabited part, is also mountainous—not in the sense of what are considered mountains in, say, Ontario or Quebec, but in the sense of *real* mountains. B.C.'s proportional amount of arable land must surely be the smallest in Canada.

The province is dominated by three rivers (much as many central and southern American states are dominated by the Missouri and Mississippi), all of which rise within a few miles of each other: the Columbia, the Thompson and the soul of the province, the Fraser. These rivers—at least the Fraser and the Thompson, though sadly no longer the Columbia—carry with them salmon: seven species now that Pacific salmon are deemed by biologists (though not, I might add, by fishermen) to include the steelhead (rainbow "trout") and cutthroat "trout." While salmon is no longer the economic factor it once was, it's a huge part of B.C.'s culture and heritage, especially its Native culture. One has to live in a province where rivers dominate to understand the importance of the Pacific salmon and the waters in which they run. Indeed, one of the best books ever written on British Columbia, by the late Bruce Hutchison, is simply called *The Fraser*.

With such a huge and diverse geography, much of British Columbia also differs from the rest of Canada in a very important respect: climatically. Whether it be on the coast, where it rains a great deal, or in the lower third of the interior, where most of "inner" B.C. resides, British Columbia does not have severe winters. On the coast there may be no winter at all, at least not one comparable to that of other parts of the country. A snowfall in Vancouver will, because of inadequate snow-clearing equipment, jam all the streets and even close the airport. When I was a kid we would pray for at least one snow-fall each season, so that we could make some money shovelling driveways. Often our prayers went unanswered. In Victoria the havoc of a snowfall is even greater, because they have no snow-clearing equipment at all. Even in the southern interior, winter is a short, relatively mild affair starting around the beginning of December and ending by the middle of February.

In Vancouver the Japanese cherry trees start blooming in early February, and daffodils and crocuses pop at about the same time the East is pondering the question of shadows on Groundhog Day.

Of course, there have been cold winters on the coast. Back in the sixties there were a couple in a row. But even then, we're talking a duration of a few weeks, not months.

The weather—principally the lack of a "Canadian" winter—has a couple of effects.

First off, there's a feeling of remove from traditional concepts of Canada. If you ask most non-Canadians what immediately comes to mind when they think of Canada, "cold winters" invariably tops their list. I visit London frequently and have a devil of a time explaining to taxi drivers that Vancouver has the same climate as London, and really is an ice-free port. Most Canadians themselves think that we have universally harsh, not to say entirely unenjoyable, winters. After all, our main game is played on ice.

Second, because most native British Columbians are terror-stricken at the thought of a snowy and frigid "Canadian" winter, they are reluctant to take on any jobs in "the East" (which to their minds commences at Golden, B.C.)—very much including Member of Parliament.

Let me drive home this last point with a personal anecdote. In 1984 I was, as we say in my business, "between engagements," having been quite suddenly let go by CJOR radio in Vancouver. It was a federal election year and in June I was approached by Jacob Brouwer—an old personal friend and one of the Tory bigwigs—to run as a P.C. candidate in Capilano, then a very safe Tory seat. (This offer was made on the direct instructions of Brian Mulroney—ironically, in light of our later battle over the Charlottetown

Accord.) This was not just an idle offer. He knew I was out of work and part of the deal was that a job in a law firm could be found for me to keep the wolf from the door until the expected fall election.

"Jake," I said, "if you will guarantee that the Tories will win and I will lose, thus gaining for me all the advantages of being a losing candidate in a winning cause, I'm your man. But you know and I know that not only will the Tories win, but so will I. And there is no way in the world I'm ever going to live in Ottawa. I'll stay here and starve first."

Jake pointed out that I, as a former senior cabinet minister in the B.C. government, might well be in line for a cabinet post in Ottawa if the favoured Tories won. His eloquence was in vain. There simply was no way I was going to willingly relocate to a city that had such a deathly cold winter.

I must say that I was influenced in this by an experience Mel Smith and I had one February in Ottawa, during one of our many constitutional jaunts. (Over a twenty-year period, Mel was a constitutional advisor to five B.C. premiers; in the late 1970s, Bill Bennett had assigned him and me to spearhead B.C.'s role in constitutional affairs.) Staying at the Inn of the Provinces, we decided one morning to walk down to the convention centre by the Chateau Laurier, perhaps a kilometre away.

Like typical Lotuslanders we were dressed for the minus-thirty-degree weather (not to mention the wind chill) in our two-piece suits and raincoats—no hats, scarves or gloves, of course. We literally had to duck into three stores *en route*, or we would have certainly perished of exposure. (Vancouverites are amazing. If you look around in a typical Vancouver rainstorm you will see folks with umbrellas, raincoats and galoshes. In all likelihood, they're from Toronto or the Prairies. The Vancouverites will have no overcoats, though their sport or suit jackets will be turned up at the collar, and they will be wearing suede shoes and carrying newspapers over their heads. A big part of being a Vancouverite is persistent denial of reality.)

One look at the parliamentary guide over the years will reveal that the bulk of B.C. MPs are born elsewhere—most often in the Prairies, where a winter in Ottawa does not hold the terrors it does for a Vancouver native.

All this means, of course, that British Columbia loses twice. Its voice is not heard in business, because of the well-known predisposition of Lotuslanders to refuse anything but the most temporary transfer elsewhere, nor in councils of state for the reasons stated. Perhaps even more serious,

British Columbians and other Canadians are therefore unlikely to meet and know one another.

What is little known east of the Rockies is that British Columbia has a very different history than that of the other Western provinces. We were not populated, for the most part, by an east–west migration, but from the south and the far east, or directly from the United Kingdom: first round the Horn or across the United States by rail, later through the Panama Canal and finally across Canada by rail.

British Columbia was not "discovered" by Canadians. Rather, it was first "discovered" by Sir Francis Drake in 1579, then by the Spanish, then by Captain James Cook in 1778; it was finally extensively charted in 1792 by Captain George Vancouver. It was also well known to the Russians, who occupied Alaska and had settlements in California. All of these "discoveries" happened before Alexander Mackenzie's amazing overland voyage, which reached Bella Bella in 1793, and the explorations of the fur traders Simon Fraser and David Thompson in the early nineteenth century.

Most Canadians do not realize that, unlike the other three Western provinces, British Columbia was, to all intents and purposes, self-governing when it negotiated entry into Confederation with Canada. British Columbia was *not* the result of the Canadian Pacific Railway, though that undertaking did change the province dramatically. The province came into Canada in 1871, fifteen years before there was even a suspicion of a "Vancouver," much less a completed transnational railway. To this day, the old pioneer families of Victoria and New Westminster look down their noses—with good reason—at people from Vancouver who claim to come from pioneer stock. Vancouver, the jewel of the Pacific, is a British Columbia Johnny come lately, and its overblown status is often much resented by other British Columbians.

Early on, British Columbia was a fur-trading colony and, for a mad time in 1858, a gold colony. It was full of Americans, as well as lots of Chinese and East Indians, mostly Sikhs, and attracted pioneer spirits from all over the world, including such great characters as Matthew Baillie Begbie, the so-called "hanging judge" who dispensed justice by horseback throughout the interior of the province. And Amor de Cosmos (William Smith), our second premier and the prime mover of B.C.'s entry into Confederation (which, with all the political sensitivity of the day, took place without any contact at all, much less consultation, with "lesser breeds" like miners, workers, women or Natives).

When I was in school we learned about Natives, as well we should. We learned, however, about Iroquois, Algonquins and Hurons, and not one word about Haida, Shuswap or Musqueam. That deficiency goes a long way to explaining why negotiations over Native land claims in B.C. are so difficult.

Of course, Canadians need to learn about Cartier, Champlain and La Verendrye. It's trite to observe that this is essential Canadian history. But why did it take until 1991 for Peter C. Newman to write *Merchant Princes* (part of a trilogy about the Hudson's Bay Company, and also an excellent source of B.C. history)? I'm not complaining about Newman, mind you— it's a great book. And ever since Peter moved to B.C., there has been a remarkable broadening of his Upper Canada College education.

Politics have always been edgy in this province. Unlike Quebec and Ontario, where relations with Ottawa have been about exercising influence, and unlike Atlantic Canada and the two eastern Prairie provinces, which were the creatures of the Canadian Parliament and are characterized by need, British Columbia has from the beginning fought Ottawa tooth and nail. (There are dangers in such generalizations, of course. All provinces have sometimes begged from Ottawa, fought with Ottawa and schmoozed with Ottawa. But for most of the last 127 years, governments of B.C. have fought with Ottawa.)

British Columbia's entry into Canada was a controversial question amongst the province's establishment, who mostly lived in Victoria and Nanaimo, on Vancouver Island, or in New Westminster (the original capital, near Vancouver). The catalyst for B.C.'s entry was a dispute over the province's boundary with the United States. British Columbians had long felt that the Columbia River should mark the border (if this had happened, incidentally, it would have provided B.C. with another city named Vancouver). The Americans, after the voyage of Lewis and Clark (fifteen years after Mackenzie's expedition), began to see all the West Coast—from the Mexican border to Russian Alaska—as theirs. In 1838 a U.S. Senate bill called for annexation of everything up to latitude 54–40. In fact, the rallying cry of James Polk, in his successful run for the U.S. presidency, was "54–40 or fight."

In 1846 Britain and the U.S. agreed that the 49th parallel should be extended to the British Columbia mainland, and that Vancouver Island—a good portion of which, including Victoria, is below the 49th parallel—should remain outside American territory. Still unresolved was the ownership of the San Juan Islands, and an incident on the main island of San Juan, where an American farmer shot a pig owned by the Hudson's Bay Company, nearly provoked a war between Britain and America.

In 1867 the U.S. purchased Alaska from Russia, reviving American cries of "manifest destiny" and "54–40 or fight." Now British Columbia had Americans to the north of them as well as the south. And Britain had made it clear that it was no longer willing to insure British Columbia's political integrity. The options were to join the United States, join Canada, or tough it out as a Crown colony and hope for the best. With annexation bills popping up in the American Congress, the last option—which was the natural preference of many—seemed fraught with peril; it was either the U.S. or Canada.

While the general population, namely the "lower classes," may have had other ideas, the establishment—meaning old Hudson's Bay men—were British to the core. They were also practical enough to know that union with Canada was the only hope of maintaining their colony's British connection. The capital had been moved from New Westminster to Victoria in 1868, so the colony's business community was now cheek by jowl with the legislature. A small band of Canadians also pressed the case for Canada.

A three-man delegation headed to Ottawa and negotiated a deal that had little if anything to do with a yearning to be Canadian, and a great deal to do with a desire to avoid American absorption. There were two major considerations: a railway link with Canada, and money. Both were provided, and on July 20, 1871, British Columbia joined Confederation.

From the start, then, B.C.'s support for Confederation has been less than whole-hearted. Despite the large legislative support for a deal with Canada, many British Columbians were dubious about the whole idea. Much of the population of B.C. had come from the United States, especially during the 1858 gold rush. Many of these people would no doubt have supported American dreams of extending the Oregon territory up to the Alaska panhandle.

Then the completion of the CPR railway was five years late, bringing a move for secession into the legislature. Over the following decades, British Columbia's feeling of alienation began to mount—a feeling occasionally expressed with a more-than-faint odour of the ridiculous. For instance, in August 1914 Premier Sir Richard McBride, having failed to convince Ottawa of the need to defend the Pacific Coast, bought two Chilean submarines, which had been built just below the border. The subs arrived in Esquimalt two days after the First World War was declared. Three days later, Ottawa—in a huff—hastily bought them from the B.C. government.

There is a straight line running from that event to the "Captain B.C." stance of Premier Glen Clark in the August 1997 salmon dispute, when—much against the wishes of the federal government—he cancelled an underwater lease with the U.S. government. This cocking a snook at both Ottawa and Washington brought shrieks of outrage from the editors of the Toronto-owned local press—but played very well indeed with most British Columbians.

In fact, the salmon fishery is a common thread holding the decades of discontent together—as a highly emotional issue, it survives and flourishes to this day. There is not space in a dozen volumes to cover this issue, but suffice it to say that British Columbians, to a person, believe that Ottawa has from the start screwed up the salmon fishery. This clearly held view was fortified by the perceptions of the B.C. government and many of its citizens that in the summer 1998 treaty negotiations, the province was once again "sold out" by the feds.

The first mistake was giving Ottawa jurisdiction over the offshore fishery in the first place. From the beginning this was deemed a federal power; I suppose there was no alternative, because the East Coast fishery was already Ottawa's responsibility, but the decision was a bad one, mainly because it meant that decisions would be made a great distance from the area that those decisions would affect. Ottawa bureaucrats had difficulty understanding that they were not dealing with the Atlantic salmon, but with their distinct and unique cousins.

The intricacies of the various salmon species, each with different feeding habits and lifespans, are difficult for bureaucrats to comprehend. For example, different stocks often share the river for spawning, making it difficult to protect one stock while allowing another to be fished. And unlike the East Coast cod, the Pacific salmon—especially the large chinooks and the wonderful coho—are superb sports fish, which are caught in the ocean, not exclusively in rivers.

Also, the West Coast resource is shared with three United States: Alaska, Washington and Oregon. Fish do not respect political boundaries, and huge coho stocks spawned in British Columbia traverse Alaska waters to be caught. However, the bargaining table is set up with chairs for Alaska, Washington state, Oregon, Washington D.C. and Ottawa. You will notice who's missing. No treaty can be struck unless the three states involved agree; British Columbia, however, is left as an observer.

The salmon fisheries in B.C. and Newfoundland are as unalike as chalk and cheese save in one respect: both fisheries have developed coastal communities that utterly rely on the fishermen and the nearby canneries. For seventy-five years or more there have been royal commissions investigating overfishing and habitat destruction (though the latter problem has only been fashionable to contemplate in recent years). Every decade or so there has been a statement that "Too many fishermen are chasing too few fish." Buy-back schemes to put fishermen out of business have been devised, and millions of dollars have been spent redeeming licences. But while the number of boats has been reduced, new boats, much bigger and complete with all manner of fish-finding devices, have gone into action. The real problem is that too much capacity, not too many fishermen, are chasing too few fish.

The major problem with the fishery issue, though, is that with one exception—John Fraser in 1984—we haven't had a federal minister of fisheries and oceans who knew anything about the *Pacific salmon* fishery. The concentration has always been on the Eastern cod fishery; while no doubt understandable on a political basis, this has been disastrous for B.C. Most ministers have been more interested in rivers as opportunities for industrial development than as fish habitats. (Although at this writing there seems to be some hope that the current minister, British Columbian David Anderson, does understand our fishery.)

In British Columbia, you see, the Pacific salmon is something approaching the sacred. It's one of our distinguishing features. The great rivers into which the huge runs spawn are in everyone's backyard. Our respect for our salmon runs isn't just motivated by money—in fact, you can make a lot more money by damming rivers than by leaving them for the fish—but goes to the very soul of the province. The federal lack of appreciation of what the salmon means to all British Columbians (and especially to Natives) lies at the root of British Columbia's alienation from Ottawa.

In the 1930s, the ever-present and ever-increasing spats between Victoria and Ottawa led Gerry McGeer, the colourful then-mayor of Vancouver, to say, "It's only 2,500 miles from Vancouver to Ottawa but it is 25,000 miles from Ottawa to Vancouver."

By the time Liberal T.D. Pattullo became premier in 1933, relations with Ottawa had become permanently testy. Pattullo, with his never ending squabbles with Mackenzie King, tested to the ultimate the cohesion of the federal and B.C. wings of the Liberal Party—a test that continues to this day. Indeed, in the 1950s and 1960s W.A.C. Bennett was able to make the Social Credit Party into a great provincial force largely because it was a B.C. party with no allegiance to Ottawa. This establishment of a B.C.-only party (though Bennett did for a brief period flirt with the national Socreds), had a profound effect on B.C. politics. It painted the provincial Liberals as "Ottawa boys," an image which they still have not been able to shuck.

While T.D. Pattullo may have been the father of B.C. bitching—though a case can be made, some historians say, for Sir Richard McBride and John Oliver—William Andrew Cecil Bennett was the patron saint. As a Conservative backbencher in the 1952 provincial legislature, Bennett sensed the pending collapse of the Liberal–Tory coalition government (formed in 1941 as an uneasy alliance against the CCF-cum-NDP) and began casting about for a new political vehicle. He selected the rather strange Social Credit movement. The Socreds were in power in Alberta but no more than a minor source of amusement to most British Columbians. The party would never be the same; nor would B.C. politics. The Socreds would govern British Columbia from 1952 until 1991, interrupted only by the NDP government of 1972–75.

W.A.C. Bennett marched to his own drummer. For example, when the Columbia River Treaty between Canada and the United States became necessary for Bennett to implement his "Two Rivers Policy" to dam both the Peace and the Columbia, Bennett simply overrode federal objections with stubbornness, guile and brass. Bennett's biographer, David Mitchell, described the scene when the treaty was signed on September 16, 1964, at the Peace Arch (at Blaine, Washington, on the Canada–U.S. border): "President Lyndon Johnson and Prime Minister Lester Pearson attended to symbolically seal the agreement, yet those heads of state both seemed like stage-hands compared to the obvious star of the show, W.A.C. Bennett."

Pearson later wrote, "While I was head of the Canadian government and Mr. Johnson was head of the American government, in British Columbia Mr. Bennett was head of all he surveyed."

It's interesting to note that B.C. political mavericks like Pattullo, McGeer and W.A.C. Bennett were all born *outside* the province, proving again, if proof be needed, that the convert is more zealous than the faithful by birth.

Let me return to geography. British Columbia is on a north–south axis. That's the way the mountains run. So do the major rivers and lakes. A flight over the Gulf Islands in the Strait of Georgia dramatically demonstrates this geographical, and thus psychological, truth. British Columbians take their vacations in Seattle, Portland, San Francisco, Los Angeles, San Diego and, of course, Hawaii. There is no massive, annual holiday exodus of British Columbians into Alberta, Saskatchewan and Manitoba.

Many British Columbians go to university south of the border.

Much of our sports interest—including the University of Washington Huskies, the Seattle Mariners, the Seattle Seahawks and, until the arrival of the Grizzlies, the Sonics—is focused to the south.

Many old Vancouver families are American lumbering families. Our lumber industry has long been connected to the corresponding industry below the border—not always happily, but connected nevertheless.

The United States has always been a huge customer, especially for B.C. lumber and pulp products. Since the Free Trade Agreement was implemented, as tariffs protecting Central Canadian industries have abated or disappeared, we've become more of a buyer of American products.

The past fifteen years or so have seen the rise of an interesting idea called "Cascadia," whose supporters include former Vancouver mayor Art Phillips and his equally prominent wife, Carole Taylor, a B.C. convert with all the enthusiasm that entails.

It's the notion that British Columbia and its neighbouring American states—Alaska, Washington, Oregon, northern California, and to some extent Idaho and Montana—have so much in common that they should work much more closely together. The "common interests" are economic, of course, but there are social and environmental considerations as well.

The idea of Cascadia is probably not the prelude to some political union. The United States, never mind Canada, is not about to surrender territory to some newly defined entity. But the notion is becoming an increasing force of distraction, focusing B.C. attention onto north–south relationships. It doesn't directly weaken the political bonds between B.C. and Canada, but it very much does so indirectly, as more and more of Ottawa's social and economic policy seems irrelevant on the West Coast.

A major event of the past couple of decades has been the shift in economic importance from east to west. This is not to deny the enormous economic clout of southern Ontario, but it can no longer be ignored that the economic line is ultimately moving—slowly, unevenly, but moving—westward. Much of that, of course, is due to the importance of Asia, not only in terms of our exports, but in terms of Asian investment in Canada as a whole.

Vancouver has become the Canadian beneficiary of this enormous new shift—temporarily stalled by the so-called "Asian flu" and the NDP government—and looking ahead, especially as markets in the old Soviet Union begin to open up, the future is brilliant for B.C. What, then, is the present general attitude in B.C.?

Up until about fifteen years ago, British Columbia in its relations with Canada was like a little boy running away from home with his little sack on his back. He knew in his heart that he really didn't want to go and that he couldn't long survive if he did. Mummy—Canada—would put her arm around him, take him back into the house, say, "There, there," and put out some chocolate milk and cookies. Reality would carry the day.

Things have changed. Now British Columbia *could* go it alone as a country and do so very easily. Larger in population than New Zealand, it has rich natural resources. Besides being the major North American port for shipping to and from Asia, Vancouver is well located in relation to eastern North American markets, as well as the European community. There is a new spring in British Columbia's step: confidence.

It's not that many British Columbians want to leave Canada: a 1997 poll put that figure at ten percent (which some say is still a lot). But that number could easily grow dramatically in a short time. And looking at Ottawa policies, the shift will likely come about as stupid, Central Canadian-dominated thinking steadily becomes a serious provocation to British Columbians.

CHAPTER TWO

Youth and Apprenticeship

I first saw the light of day at Grace Hospital, Vancouver, on December 31, 1931, at about 2:00 P.M. My mother was urged to postpone my birth and try for all the prizes that came with being the first mother of the year, but apparently she'd had enough of me. Some have since claimed that my father wanted me for the tax year 1931, but since he wasn't working at the time this is probably apocryphal.

My parents were, I suppose, of slightly upper middle-class stock, with not enough money to match their pedigree. My father came to Canada as a youngster with his mother, father and two sisters in 1913. Apparently my great-grandfather, Dr. Coates, had heard that the streets of upstart Vancouver were paved with gold, and he convinced his son-in-law—my grandfather, Leslie Mair, a bank clerk—to move to this city with his family (which included my father). Doctors are reputed to have poor business judgment, and Dr. Coates was no exception. Those first few years in Vancouver were pretty tough for my grandfather and his young family.

In those days Vancouver's West End was the fashionable place to live and there my father was raised, although I suspect the family income came more from family help than honest toil.

My father claimed he went to nearly every school in Vancouver, including Lord Roberts, King George and Prince of Wales. He never boasted of a matriculation certificate, however, so I assume he didn't graduate.

My mother was born in Vancouver to Leonard and Jane Leigh. Leonard was an American by accident of birth to his English parents in Minneapolis, Minnesota, while Jane was a Macdonald from Cape Breton Island who spoke Gaelic before she spoke English. I therefore have the distinction of having one grandparent born in Auckland, New Zealand; one in Salisbury, England; one in Cape Breton Island, Nova Scotia; and one in Minneapolis. Mom's family also lived in the West End (though my parents didn't know one another until their early twenties) and their summer home was at Jericho Beach, where the Royal Vancouver Yacht Club now has its clubhouse. In those days it was most of a day's trip: the streetcar to Granville and Broadway, then a horse and wagon the rest of the way. Later their summer place was at Langford Lake, now part of metropolitan Victoria. The road to their cabin, built by my grandfather and called Leigh Road, is still very much in use (though considerably upgraded).

I was fortunate to know all my grandparents. My dad's father, Pop as we called him, was a truly lovely, gentle, man. Though I was only seven when he died I well remember the hours he spent with me and my cousins, playing his banjo, smoking his pipe and singing Maori songs to us. My grandmother, his wife (called Nan-Nan), often suggested that these songs were not suitable for young ears, but since they were in Maori the adverse influence was much minimized.

My maternal grandfather, Leonard, also had a great influence on my life. A businessman throughout his working life, he was also an outdoorsman who, by the time I came along, had retired to a small farm in what is now smack in the middle of highly populated Burnaby. He taught me about moss on the north side of trees and neat stuff like that.

He had a bantam rooster named Jiggs who used to chase me all over the farm. I hated that bird and I was genuinely afraid of him. Gandi, as Leonard was called, took me into the woods, cut a slingshot for me from a maple tree and fitted it out with an elastic band and a sling. At his urging I armed the slingshot with a piece of coke from the main pathway and nailed Jiggs square in the ass. Jiggs never bothered me again and I'm bound to say that I think the lesson learned stayed learned—for both Jiggs and me.

I also learned more about chickens than I've ever found useful since— for one thing, Gandi told me, it's better to throttle them than cut their heads off when you want roast chicken. It's far less messy than the hatchet, and strangled chickens don't run around with their heads cut off, further aggravating your troubled conscience.

Of my four grandparents, though, Leonard's wife Jane, my Gram, had far and away the most influence upon me. She was a beautiful woman, but made of very stern stuff indeed. A Scot through and through (though she was third-generation Canadian) she always maintained (truthfully, I believe) that she had never met a Campbell that she liked or trusted. The Campbells had massacred Gram's ancestors, the Macdonalds, at Glencoe in 1692, and the scars were slow to heal in Cape Breton Island.

When Gram was in her late eighties, she went to the U.K. for the first time and stayed with a cousin of mine in London. When she returned I asked her how she liked Scotland.

"I didn't go, my dear," was her reply.

Astonished, I asked her, "Why not?"

"I was afraid it wouldn't be like I thought it would be," was her reply—contorted but quite comprehensible. Scotland as related to her by family oral history was the Isle of Skye, and she didn't want to be disappointed.

About three or four years later, now in her nineties, she went back to the U.K. and upon her return I again asked her if she had been to Scotland.

"Yes, my dear," was her reply. "I went over the sea to Skye and it was just like I thought it would be."

In 1992 I went to Glencoe myself, to do a story on the three-hundredth anniversary of the Clan Macdonald massacre. It's a long and interesting story, full of the politics of the day, and it's widely held that the greatest crime of all was not the massacre itself but Clan Campbell's betrayal of highland hospitality. I had been steeped in the story, of course, by my grandmother.

I interviewed the head of Clan Campbell, who I thought, even three hundred years after the event, was a tad defensive about it all. Then I interviewed the oldest Clanranald Macdonald, who was in his nineties.

I asked him, "Mr. Macdonald, are there any bad feelings left?"

"Och, noo," he replied. "That's all behind us noo."

After the interview, Old Macdonald and I walked up the street from his house to the cairn commemorating the slaughter. It was May and the anniversary had been the previous February, but there were still some tattered wreaths on the monument.

"Look, Mr. Macdonald," I said, "there's a wreath from Clan Campbell!"

"The bastards," he muttered, "the bastards!"

So much for all behind us noo!

My great-great-grandfather on my father's side, Gilbert Mair, was a seafaring man from Peterhead, Scotland. He went to New Zealand in 1818 and married a vicar's daughter, Elizabeth Puckey, in 1827. He settled in Paihia in the Bay of Islands, and subsequently built his trading post across the bay at Wahapu, where the studs for his wharf, the first in New Zealand, are there to this day. He took an active part in the affairs of that very early white colony and, along with a number of other settlers, petitioned William IV to bring British justice to what was then a pretty rough part of the world. This petition was the New Zealand equivalent of Canada's Durham Report, and led directly to the appointment of a British governor and to treaty negotiations with Maori leaders. Gilbert, his wife and their children were present in 1840 when the Treaty of Waitangi was signed with a number of Maori tribes, thus spawning the country of New Zealand. A visit to the Treaty House at Waitangi discloses a number of displays in which the Mairs are featured, including, at my last visit, a spinet given to Gilbert and Elizabeth for their wedding.

In 1840, Gilbert and his family moved a few miles south and helped found the city of Whangarei (pronounced "Fongeray" in Maori), and there is a Mair Park, a Mair Street and a district called Mairtown in this modern, middle-sized New Zealand city. The Anglican Christ's Church is also on land deeded it by Robert Mair, my great-grandfather.

As you might suppose, I grew up with New Zealand as part of my life and, thanks to my father's birth in Auckland, have New Zealand citizenship, which I cherish. I didn't travel there until 1981, but I have been back virtually every year since, sometimes twice a year, and if I wanted to retire I would cheerfully move there for my dotage. I love it there, as does my wife Wendy.

I had a happy childhood growing up in Kerrisdale—now a very tony neighbourhood, but then a very new area. In fact, behind our house were two square blocks of woods that were heaven for me and my youthful pals.

There were still working farms in the area. One was owned by Baroness Van Steenwyck, a Dutch noblewoman who looked a lot like Queen Victoria. She was visited during the Second World War by the Dutch princess (later queen) Juliana. It was great excitement as all us kids lined up at 47th and McCleery to cheer her on. Where we got the Dutch flags from, I'll never know.

Growing up during the Second World War was captivating to my active and curious mind. I was always keenly interested in what was happening in the world, a curiosity sparked by both my mother and father. In my bedroom I had a huge map where I daily charted the advances and retreats of the Russian and North African campaigns. I well remember listening to Churchill and Roosevelt on the radio. I listened to Churchill's stout-hearted "give us the tools and we will finish the job" speech, and the strong impression this great man made upon me has lasted ever since.

On my birthday in 1941 I heard Churchill address the Canadian House of Commons with his famous "some chicken, some neck" speech. It's strange what sticks in a child's mind but I remember two things vividly about that speech. First that the CBC announcer, in a bit of trivia that should have won a gold medal, told us that since sound travelled by wire at the speed of light, we at home would actually hear Churchill's voice a split-second before those in the Commons chamber. I also remember hearing, for the first time, the banging of desks as applause—something I was to do myself thirty-four years later in the B.C. Parliament.

My schooling started at home. My mom, who read to me from infancy on, had me reading and writing while I was still in play school. Had I been born before December 1, I would have been able to go to school in 1937, but as it was I had to wait until 1938. My mother, afraid I would fall behind my peers, was keen to see that I learned as much as I could and for that, and so many other things, I am eternally grateful to her. In fact I skipped grade five, so I ended up where my mom thought I should have been all along.

I went to Maple Grove School, which I still remember with great affection. I can still easily visualize my teachers and the sternly presented but most kindly Oliver Lacey, our principal.

Much later, when I first went into radio, I reminisced on-air with a fellow student about those days.

"Do you remember Miss Dunlop, our grade one teacher?" my guest asked.

"Sure do," I replied, "but she must have gone to her reward long ago."

Not so, I quickly learned. Miss Dunlop, who seemed so old when I was in grade one, was in fact about my mother's age and very much amongst the quick, as she informed me by the promptest of posts. The memories of children are, notwithstanding what psychiatrists tell us, more than a bit unreliable.

When I was ten I was sent to a private school, St. George's, largely I suspect because my bosom pal Denis Hargrave had gone there a year earlier. It was an interesting experience and one I am glad to have had. That I did not send any of my own four children to private school reflects not only my relative poverty at the time but my uncertainty about the wisdom of education for the elite.

Wartime St. George's was different, I'm sure, from anything since. The best "masters" were in the armed forces at the time, and we were taught by what many would see as a pretty motley crew—but that was true for all kids of that time. For all that I have some wonderful memories.

Captain B.O. Robinson (whose initials, in those days when ads for Lifebuoy soap promised to do away with your BO, brought ribald laughter behind his back) was truly a memorable character. His lasting influence is attested to by all he taught. An English public school boy (Blundell's), Robinson was very badly wounded in the First World War. He lost an eye and was left with a steel plate in his head. His injuries made him subject to monumental headaches with resulting terrible temper tantrums. But could "Cappy"—as we knew him, behind his back, of course—ever teach, especially English literature!

Cappy was very big on stiff-upper-lip British stuff, of course. His great heroes were Drake and Nelson—and along with Churchill, they remain mine, too. I can still recite many verses of Sir Henry Newbolt's "Drake's Drum" and "Vitae Lampada," and Tennyson's "The Revenge." Cappy's version of Nelson at Trafalgar was stirring stuff indeed, but somehow we never did get the full story on Lady Hamilton! (Cappy's two sons both went on to sparkling careers—Geoffrey in medicine and Basil as a senior mandarin in the federal public service.)

I played rugby and cricket at St. George's and especially liked the latter. My father, being a Kiwi, also played cricket, so I was steeped in the game. Though my interest waned when I went to a public school, I still follow the game today.

I was a baseball nut, though I never played much of it other than sandlot and high school stuff. To this day I love the game and very much enjoy its literature. In fact baseball is one of the few games around which a legitimate literature has grown. Some of America's finest writers have done baseball stories.

Starting very early in childhood I began a lifelong love of fishing and, in later years, fly fishing. I started out on the pier at Granthams Landing fishing for shiners (which are a type of small wharf perch) and out in Howe

Sound with my parents, who fished for salmon, and left me with a handline for "trout," as we called the small younger salmon.

In later years I would develop this hobby to the point where I became a competent fly tier and the author of a book on fishing. Every year since 1981 I have made a pilgrimage to the Lake Taupo area of New Zealand to fish wonderful rivers like the Waitanahui, the Hinemaiai, the Tongariro and my favourite, the Tauranga–Taupo.

Besides a passion for fishing, another major legacy of my childhood is a profound interest in matters of religion. I am a recovering Christian—or perhaps I should say a recovering agnostic who would like to return to the faith of his fathers, which was altered when my great-great-grandfather, a Presbyterian, married the Anglican vicar's daughter in the Bay of Islands in New Zealand in 1827.

I'm by no means born again. I'm sure I disappoint my Christian friends, whether mainstream or not, because I continue to ask questions that were answered for them many years ago in Sunday school. The one distinction I have been able to make is between the church and the "corporate church." I've finally understood that God cannot be held responsible for the short-comings of the "corporate church," ranging all the way from killing people for heresy and forcing people to accept its faith, through to the mindless meanderings of ministers (so wonderfully parodied by the classic British comedy troupe of yesteryear, Beyond the Fringe).

After a traditional Anglican upbringing, which included Sunday school and a stint in the choir at St. Mary's Church in Kerrisdale, fortified by my four years at St. George's—veddy, veddy British—School for mostly Anglo-Saxon Church-of-Englanders, I lapsed into a nether region somewhere between agnosticism and atheism. Never scholarly enough to get formally philosophical about these matters, I found myself troubled for about forty years by the question, "Who made God?"

Being a slow-thinking philosopher at the best of times, it took me a long time to figure out that man's mind is finite and that one might better ask the question, "If there is a universe, as demonstrably there is, who made *it*?" Despite the big-bang theory and the incomprehensible (though best-selling) notions of Stephen Hawking, the scientists were no closer to answering the basic questions of life than the creationists, who simply stopped asking questions sooner. Even the "discovery" that our universe, pre-big bang, was no bigger than a pea doesn't answer the basic question: "If that's true, who made the pea?"

In any event, in my advancing years I decided that I would settle the question, once and for all, in favour of God.

This left the question of whose version.

I re-read the New Testament and decided that I believed in Jesus but was dubious about what the high muckamucks decided about dogma—such as the Trinity, the meaning of Communion, and the like—at the Council of Nicea in AD 325. So I have decided that it's the message that's important, not the dogma. I only hope that God is of the same view.

In 1946 I left St. George's and enrolled in grade ten at Prince of Wales High School, then situated at the intersection of 25th (King Edward) and Marguerite.

I have wonderful memories of Prince of Wales and I made many long-time friends there, including John Fraser, former Speaker of the House of Commons and now Canada's ambassador for the environment.

I was a good but not distinguished scholar, quite frankly because I took things too easily. I started a lifelong interest in the female of the species at Prince of Wales, which proved to be a distraction as well as a pleasure.

My athletic career wasn't much in high school. I played football for a couple of years but frankly wasn't good enough to play much, and I was handicapped by not having played the game previously. I never did understand a play book, and the chalk marks on the blackboard might just as well have been hieroglyphics.

I started to play golf at the old Quilchena Golf Club at 33rd and Pine Crescent, sold in the late 1950s by the CPR to developers. By the time I was in my thirties I was a scratch player with a foul temper. At my best, I was very good indeed—but I had precisely the wrong temperament for the game. My temper turned many otherwise decent rounds into nightmares.

I entered the University of British Columbia in 1949 and was off to a bad start. I had picked up two first-year university courses in high school and loafed through first year, just writing exams in the three courses I needed to complete the year. The next year was, from the start, lost.

I had enjoyed female companionship at Prince of Wales but at UBC, even though the student population's huge gender imbalance then favoured women looking for men rather than the other way around, it was like I'd died and gone to heaven. A new crop, you might say, of young ladies every fall. It was amazing how those "little kids" of a few years before had grown up! New golfing buddies appeared and to this heady mix I added bridge and a fraternity, Zeta Psi. With all these distractions, I simply attended no classes and failed the year. It was not a class act—not at all. I am still, to this day, thoroughly ashamed of myself and how I let down my family.

I then completed second and third year Arts and would like to say that my failure in second year spurred me on. It didn't. Apart from the occasional decent mark in history or international studies, I squeaked by with a bare second-class average.

After third year, my father told me I had to make some sense out of university or find a job, so I entered the UBC law school and joined a truly unique group—what would become the famous Class of '56. This class had everything from brilliant scholars, who made it into the top ten without ever going to a class, to regulars at the old Georgia Beer Parlour, who just scraped through. I was in the latter group. Probably the best known of our class were Tom Berger and Ron Basford, both of whom had sparkling careers. I consider my relationship with my law classmates to be even stronger today than that with my high-school class or my fraternity. It was one of those classes that comes along every decade or so, which for some reason has an extraordinary number of characters in every sense of the word.

In those days there was no LSAT to take—you needed three years of arts with a sixty-percent average. The winnowing process didn't happen with a test before entry but through a huge (in our case fifty percent) failure and drop-out rate. Law school, even for the casual and the bright, was a harrowing experience, especially if you were married—as I was.

I married Eve MacInnes, the sister of one of my fraternity brothers, just before I started my third year of law at UBC. The story of our meeting is a tale with a twist.

I had been dating a lovely lady named Molly Lou. There was a big fraternity dance coming up at the old Commodore Cabaret, and Molly Lou told me she couldn't go out that night. I asked my friend Dunc MacInnes if he thought his sister would go with me. He suggested that I ask her—which I did. She accepted.

We arrived at the Cabaret, and who should be there but my pal Dunc with my soon to become ex-girlfriend Molly Lou! They married and had four kids, as did Eve and I. We all remained great pals for many years. Indeed, I think I can say that we still are.

On the MacInnes side, Eve came from an old Montreal family, though her father had been educated at Eton and had served in the British Army during the Second World War. Eve herself was born in the Channel Islands, from which the family was evacuated in June 1940, her father going to war and her mother moving the kids to Peterborough, Ontario, where Eve's two brothers attended Lakefield School. When Duncan senior came back from the war the family moved to Vancouver. I was very fond of my in-laws and used to have great spirited debates with my father-in-law about all manner of things political.

By the end of my third year of law school we had a son, Kenneth Rafe, who now, at 42, has a lovely family in Toronto, including the eighteen-year-old Kenneth Rafe III.

When I graduated from law school, I had no money and my father had fallen on sorry times. The going rate for articling students was $150 to $200 per month and I couldn't support a family on that, so I decided to become an oil tycoon by moving to Edmonton with Imperial Oil.

I lasted about four months before I knew that Edmonton was not for me. When we came in by train on May 15, 1956, the ice was just breaking on Wabamum Lake. On Labour Day it snowed. I was a Vancouver boy and I knew it, so by October we were back there, where I landed a job as an assistant safety supervisor in a sawmill at $350 per month, just what I had been making in Edmonton.

I lasted two months and I was fired for good reason: I hated my job and it showed.

I was given two weeks' severance pay. As luck would have it I immediately landed a job as a claims adjuster at Allstate Insurance, without ever losing a day's work. In effect I came out of the deal $175 to the better. That was a lot of money in those days, and to Eve and me it was a hell of a big windfall. I stayed with Allstate from the beginning of 1957 until May 1960, when I decided that I really had to get back to law.

I had some luck there. I had turned pro in golf in order to make some money, giving lessons at a driving range—this supplemented my meagre income while I looked for more meaningful work. Also, with my experience in automobile claims, I was worth a little extra to lawyers in that field. The best of the lot, prominent Vancouver lawyer Tom Griffiths, started me at $100 per week, an unheard-of sum in those days, moving to $125 after three months.

Articling for Tommy Griffiths and his amazing "clerk," Max Wrixon-Becher, was a great experience. Max was a former insurance claims manager who had seen a bit of life. An Aussie through and through, he had served in mainland Greece and Crete in the Second World War during the terrible battles there, and had no great love for the British, who he felt (probably rightly so) gave all the dirty jobs to the "colonials." Max chain-smoked Camels (he is alive today in his mid-eighties in California, though I'm told he has forsaken the weed) and was an investigator of the old school. It didn't matter who the witness was—Max demanded, and always got, a signed statement. He was great fun.

The best part of the articling year was that because Tommy didn't know anything except personal-injury claims, I got to do everything else that came into the office. I had to learn by the "sink or swim" method. It might not have been what the Benchers of the Law Society approved of, but I was called to the Bar on May 15, 1961. By this time I had added Cindy and Shawn to my family, and Karen was a couple of months away.

I practised with Tom for a few months after I was called but then was asked to join a young, two-man firm as counsel. They customarily sent all their personal-injury claims to Tom where they often landed on my desk, and thought it would be a better idea if I joined them. I did, spawning the new firm of Lambert, Kroll, and Mair.

I stayed in Vancouver with the same firm, though there were a couple of additions and deletions, until July 1969. We had done reasonably well but certainly weren't setting the world on fire.

Back then, Vancouver was very much dominated by half a dozen old law firms. It was very difficult to break their hold on lucrative corporate clients. I had refused to even contemplate joining a large firm, although with my father's connections that would have been easy. My dad was a great pal of Walter Owen, QC (later lieutenant-governor of B.C.), who headed a large firm. M.M. McFarlane, QC (later a distinguished judge of the B.C. Court of

Appeal), was "uncle Med" to me and, in addition to encouraging my legal studies, taught me to cast a fly line. (The latter was by far his most important contribution to my life!) My mother was a great friend of the Farris family, which spawned a chief justice of the Supreme Court, a chief justice of the Court of Appeal and the famous Senator J. W. de Beque Farris, who had run the governing B.C. Liberal Party for years. Forgive the name dropping—all of it is by way of saying that I had, early on, a great loathing for the "establishment" to which I was born (but not necessarily for the individuals in it, by any means). I was and remain a rebel.

By 1969, tired of the humdrum of my practice and concerned by what I saw in the schools my children were attending, especially the dope, I put the word out that I would love to relocate to the interior of B.C. To my great and happy surprise I was contacted by one of my classmates, Jarl Whist, a Norwegian immigrant. (An encyclopedia of his escapades could be written.) His firm in Kamloops needed counsel. Would I be interested?

Eve and I went to Kamloops, a city I had always loved, especially for its wonderful fishing, and in two days put our house in Richmond (a Vancouver suburb) on the market and bought a house right on the Thompson River on Ridgeview Terrace.

I found Kamloops very much to my liking. I think it enabled me to branch out a bit. While there were old established firms there too, there were also a lot of newcomers who needed lawyers and weren't impressed by stuffiness.

After about a year with the firm of Whist, Wozniak, Webber, Meikle and Mair, I left to go out on my own. Jarl, still a good friend, could be insufferable—and so could I. The firm wasn't big enough for two large egos, so I opened K. Rafe Mair and Co. down the street, in the new seven-storey "skyscraper," the Klapstock Building.

It was, looking back on it, a gutsy move. I had no "network" in Kamloops and no reason to expect much business. As it turned out, business was brisk from day one and the firm had grown to include four partners by the time I left Kamloops. Mair Jensen Blair is now, I'm told, the biggest firm in the interior, with more than thirty lawyers.

In 1973 the NDP government amalgamated the city of Kamloops and a number of municipalities. I ran for alderman and was elected by a landslide of fifty-seven votes! I was now in politics—and things would never be the same again.

CHAPTER THREE

Social Credit Days

I suppose my political career really started with golf. During the 1960s I belonged to the then-ragtag Quilchena Golf Club, which had moved from Vancouver (where it was quite upmarket) to the Vancouver suburb of Richmond when the CPR, its lessor, sold the land for development. The new club was, from the beginning, teetering on bankruptcy. I was elected to the board of directors in 1960 and was its president in 1962 and '63, during some hair-raising times. Somehow my colleagues (an amazingly competent bunch as I look back) and I kept what should have been a bankrupt outfit going until happier times arrived.

I take great pride in the fact that under my leadership (very unpopular in some quarters, on the following issue especially), we opened the club to all races and creeds. Amazing though it now seems, this club, for all its financial grief, still would not accept Jews or people of colour.

Integration happened in a curious way. We were having one of our many membership drives when we received an application from a chap named Ken Lee. We thought nothing of it and were later amazed to see, one bright day, a Chinese chap out on the practice fairway. It was Ken, who became the Jackie Robinson of Quilchena Golf and Country Club.

All hell broke loose as several Japanese Canadians from nearby Steveston put in their membership applications. I decided to clear the air with an Extraordinary General Meeting of the membership. Prior to the meeting, in quick order, I received two phone calls at home. The first was from a lady who had been prominent in club affairs for years; if I permitted "Japs" and "chinks" into the club, she would leave and take forty members with her. The next caller, a younger but popular woman, informed me that if her Japanese friends couldn't join the club, she would quit and take with her— you've guessed it—forty members.

At the packed meeting I looked down and there in the front row was an old Scotsman, Bill Campbell, who had spent the war under horrible conditions in a Japanese prison camp. He looked grim. It was going be a tough night.

I made what I must in all modesty say was a barnburner of a speech on civil rights. When I was finished there was, for the longest time, dead silence.

Then Bill Campbell stuck up his hand. This was, I supposed, it.

"Mr. President," he asked, "when are you going to cover that horrible ditch on the seventh and eighteenth holes?"

I could have kissed the old bastard. Everyone laughed, the tension was broken, the club was integrated and not a soul quit.

Quilchena Golf and Country Club survived splendidly and is now one of the finest in the area. When I last checked, it cost $25,000 to get in. In 1961, when I joined, it was $250. Later, in Kamloops, I became president of the Kamloops Golf and Country Club. Golf clubs, like universities, have red-hot politics—mainly because most of the issues are so trivial—and thus are marvelous places to start one's political career.

I had a strange career on Kamloops City Council (where Nelson Riis, the present Kamloops MP, was a colleague). I became very unpopular with much of the real-estate community, and associated lawyers, because of what I saw as a conflict of interest through which you could have driven a Mack truck.

When I was elected, the city was formulating a community plan called "Kamplan." The people chosen to spearhead this scheme and chair the committee were Stanley and Associates, who also happened to do most of the engineering work for the city. Stanley and Associates also acted for potentially the biggest developer in the city, and much of that potential work would depend upon what the committee recommended.

Surprise, surprise: Stanley and Associates, as head of Kamplan, recommended development in the southwest quarter of the city, where their client, Dominion Construction, owned all its property! Their fall-back plan, if you didn't happen to like the first one, also included all Dominion-owned land.

I screamed blue bloody murder for a year and a half and got precisely nowhere with officials and council colleagues. Kamplan, with all its many warts, was approved by council despite my stonewalling, public objections, and vote. I did, however, get a taste for politics and an ambition to go further. In politics, being known is critical, and this certainly got me known.

Let me add here that I imply no criticism of Stanley and Associates. There was no evidence whatever of any wrongdoing by them, nor do I mean to so imply. My criticism was of the city, for permitting such a conflict to arise and then remain unresolved.

On matters political and economic I'm pretty orthodox. I'm a small-l liberal who detests the Liberal Party—because I once belonged to it.

My Liberal affiliation probably started because my parents always voted for the Conservative MP for the Quadra riding, and, being of that sort of temperament, I wanted to be contrary.

As a young boy, I followed politics keenly and my initiation into political argument came with the great Second World War debate over conscription. (I was for it.)

I never had a communist period, though not for lack of indoctrination. One of my classmates at St. George's, a chap named Clark (who incidentally always had the highest grades in the class), was a communist and quite ready to argue the virtues of his position. Even at university I stayed away from both the communists (or the Labour Progressive Party, as they called themselves in those days) and the CCF, which was the forerunner of the NDP. In those Cold War days, the LPP was looked upon with some amusement at UBC. The highlight of one year was when someone threw a dead cat onto the stage while LPP leader Tim Buck was speaking.

I suppose my problem with developing a recognizable political philosophy was that I was, and remain, undisciplined. I simply could not say, "Here is a political dogma I can mostly live with, therefore I'll go along with the dodgy parts." I watched friends pursue hopeless causes for a lifetime; I admired their political integrity and all that, but for me I saw no sense pursuing politics unless you could actually get elected and thus do something. This less than admirable tenet is, no doubt, what initially attracted me to the Liberal Party, which puts getting elected ahead of all other political virtues.

From childhood I've always had a deep sense of justice and a built-in rage against what I consider unfair. I've always asked myself why things were the way they were and have always stuck up for the underdog. I carried with me a deep shame that during the Second World War my father had bought a Japanese-Canadian-owned paper box company at fire-sale prices from a family sent to one of our internment camps. I think I also probably felt hurt that my father had not gone to war, which was most unfair on my part since he was well past draft age when the war commenced. Had he gone to war, I certainly wouldn't have been in any private school—but kids don't always think things through.

Both my parents were bigots and I rebelled. The Chinese were "chinks," Japanese were "Japs," Blacks were "niggers" and Jews were "kikes." That's the way things were in WASP Vancouver when I grew up. I realize I'm being very hard on my parents; they were really only representative of their times and station in life. Such language was common, and carried with it no real hatred or violence—just intolerance and condescension.

However, I believed the propaganda that the war fed us. The "Four Freedoms" that my two heroes, Winston Churchill and Franklin Roosevelt, affirmed with their Atlantic Charter were important to me. I thought that they meant it, and that after the war there would truly be a worldwide brotherhood of man. When I was a teenager, Jackie Robinson broke the colour barrier in baseball. My parents' generation was *passé*. It was a new era dawning.

Translated into political terms, that meant I supported the Liberals because they were for all Canadians (as I saw it), while the Tories were only for rich Anglo-Canadian people, especially if they lived in Ontario. That impression, in the late 1940s, was pretty accurate.

This even affected my view of sports. I detested the Toronto Maple Leafs because they were so anti-French; Foster Hewitt was a bigot and Conn Smythe was a bigger bigot. I became a rabid Montreal Canadiens fan and *still* have trouble with my loyalties when they play the Canucks, so deep was my commitment. (I must say, I was lucky in my emotions, considering how many Stanley Cups the Habs were to win in the days after I joined their fandom back in 1942. Still, one of the worst moments of my life came in 1967, when I was in Maple Leaf Gardens to see the hated Leafs win the Cup from my beloved Canadiens.)

My political activity was minimal in my early adult years. A member of the Liberal Party, I did work on their 1962 and 1963 campaigns and, after moving to Kamloops in 1969, worked for the Liberals in that year's provincial campaign.

One thing I never did, until December 1975 when I voted for myself, was vote Social Credit. I always voted Liberal.

I left the Liberal Party while I was living in Kamloops. It was 1970, the time of the October Crisis: the Front de Liberation du Quebec, a fringe group of separatist extremists previously known for bombing mailboxes, had kidnapped British diplomat James Cross and murdered Quebec's minister of labour, Pierre Laporte. Pierre Trudeau responded by implementing the War Measures Act, essentially placing the entire country under martial law.

In Kamloops, the local Liberal Party cell wanted to send a telegram of unanimous consent to Trudeau's totalitarian decision. I could never consent to such Draconian measures being meted out for such trivial reasons. Yes, there had been a murder and a kidnapping, and some mailboxes had been bombed. But as far as I was concerned the only evidence of real political instability was in the government and person of Robert Bourassa.

When John Turner, then federal justice minister, took to television and assured Canadians that there was a national crisis and that in the fullness of time he would explain all, I knew it was bullshit—as indeed it proved to be.

(Even if there had been a crisis, it was in Quebec, not British Columbia. However, Vancouver mayor Tom Campbell, showing authority, Canadian style, at its best, wanted to use the War Measures Act to throw hippies in jail. Actually, Tom Terrific had a point: it made as much sense to jail B.C. hippies as it did to jail Quebec separatists. In both cases, the only crime had been to hold a then-unpopular viewpoint.)

I had also been disillusioned to see the Liberal organization move from the party of King and Saint-Laurent to one that cared only about getting elected, quite prepared to put the unity of the country at risk to gain that end. Under Trudeau, the party's backroom boys—led by Keith Davey and Jim Coutts—concentrated all their efforts on winning seats in Ontario and Quebec. As a political strategy this was flawless. For national unity, it was a disaster. A government elected solely from Central Canada was not likely to care much about the rest of the country.

I officially left the Liberals over the October Crisis. I then supported the Tories nationally—if a hundred dollars into the treasury of the local P.C. candidate in 1972 and 1974 constitutes a commitment—and, after looking at all the options, went for the Social Credit Party provincially.

Politicians who seek out parties in order to get elected are always deemed "opportunistic," apparently a bad thing to be. Surely if you think you have something to offer you ought to look for the best place to make your mark. That means finding a party where you feel moderately comfortable that membership can help you get elected.

In August 1972, the long reign of W.A.C. Bennett came to an end, at the hands of Dave Barrett's NDP, which Bennett described as "socialist hordes at the gate." There were many reasons for this. For one, people had become environmentally aware, and Bennett was historically a dam-builder who cared little, if anything, about environmental consequences. Many other social issues also needed attending to—there was a growing feeling that public servants, especially those in the health field, were not treated properly, and that the labour sector was also hard done by—and the NDP were seen as the ones to do it. Mostly, though, Bennett and his colleagues seemed to have all grown old at once. It was simply time for a change, many felt.

However, not long after the NDP swept to power, it became clear to me that the sooner we were rid of Barrett and his bunch, the better. These feelings were shared, or would be shared, by a majority of British Columbians. At first there had been hope, even from a non-socialist like me, but this withered in the face of uncontrolled social experimentation. The NDP did institute some good policies, such as the Agricultural Land Freeze, but these were more than offset by one financial catastrophe after another. A royalty on production in the mining industry was imposed, which curtailed development and all but eliminated exploration. The government bought a restaurant in Victoria (dubbed Barrett's Beanery, naturally) and a poultry processing company called Panco Poultry (thereafter called Pinko Panco), and also purchased an entire town, Ocean Falls, to keep the antiquated and badly supplied pulp mill alive.

Most of all, the NDP simply looked incompetent. When the human resources minister (that's a euphemism for "welfare minister") was short some $160 million (and we're talking 1972 dollars here) and could not account for it, the die was cast. W.A.C. Bennett was right: the NDP couldn't even run a peanut stand.

After the 1972 election, the Socreds had been left with only ten members of the legislative assembly (MLAs) out of fifty-seven. There were five Liberals and two Conservatives, and it was by no means certain which party would be the force to dislodge the NDP. Indeed, it wasn't clear that *anyone* could, given the bickering amongst the non-socialist parties.

In 1973, W.A.C. Bennett, who had taken little part in opposition affairs after he lost, resigned his leadership and his seat to make way for his son, Bill. The younger Bennett was a successful Kelowna businessman, but apart from what he may have learned at his father's knee, he was inexperienced in politics. However, the only political card he did have was the ace of spades—he was W.A.C.'s son. He was to prove a very worthy one.

At the time, though, I thought Bill Bennett's appointment as Socred leader was looney tunes. The Socreds had always seemed a bit strange to me—one sort of pointed them out on the street as if they were oddities. They started out as a movement rather than a political party, and one had the feeling that Social Credit was like some mystic offshoot of an offbeat fraternal order—not bad people, but to the more conventional, perhaps a bit strange. That W.A.C. would turn the reins over to his son—whoever he was—and expect the party to revive was preposterous.

In 1973 my former law partner, Jarl Whist, who had long been very active in Kamloops Liberal affairs, started an organization (of one, I think) called "Stamp Out Socialism" (SOS) and began flooding newspapers with letters. The choice of words was unfortunate and the NDP started to portray Jarl as a Nazi jackbooter. This didn't sit too well with Jarl who, as a kid in Norway, had spent five years suffering under the Nazis.

One Sunday I was invited to Jarl's house. Along with half a dozen others, we started what we called the Majority Movement. What followed was quite amazing. The idea spread like a grass fire—an apt simile because while there was lots of smoke and fire, not very much was burnt.

The next thing we knew the Majority Movement was taken over by Vancouver non-socialists and spread to Victoria. In a matter of a few weeks it was a spent force, but the movement had concentrated people's attention on the fact that to get rid of the NDP they had to unite behind one of the three forces (Socreds, Liberals or PCs) available.

As expected, Bill Bennett was crowned head of the Socreds. Early in 1974 I met Bennett at a cattle sale in Kamloops. He asked me to visit him in Victoria the next week, which I did. Bennett struck me as a sourpuss—austere, serious, and unfriendly—but a sourpuss with a very strong will to win. He recruited me without offering me a damn thing—indeed, he made it clear that no one had a cabinet seat until after the election was won. I'm not really sure what drew me to Bill, but I was prepared to follow him as the logical route to defeating the NDP.

Others felt the same way, and the stampede to Social Credit really started when Grace McCarthy became the president of the party and went to work to build it. A very successful businesswoman, Grace had long been politically active. Having served in Vancouver city politics, she became an MLA in the later years of W.A.C. Bennett's reign. After losing her seat in the 1972 election, she dedicated herself to restoring the apparently dead Socreds to power. She would succeed gloriously.

Grace was and is a woman of boundless energy and stubbornness. She could make you do things you swore you would never do, like going door to door with political flyers. I hated it, but I did it.

The real secret of the 1974–75 success of the Socreds was, in my opinion, that they made memberships available at $5 a year. This was ridiculed by journalists (including Allan Fotheringham and Marjorie Nichols) but Grace knew what she was doing. A membership card, no matter how cheap, was a commitment. It meant that when politics came up in the beer parlour or at the church social, there was a Socred in the house, if only by reason of a $5 card in the wallet or purse.

This also permitted the Socreds to get into a numbers game. They could point to the number of membership cards sold and tout having the 65,000, or 75,000, or whatever number of members it took, to put them way out in front of the Liberals and Tories. It was a simple idea but a brilliant one.

By the end of 1974, I had decided that I would seek the provincial Socred nomination for Kamloops, and accordingly did not seek re-election to the city council. I was never really comfortable as an alderman and found it a terrific waste of time. In addition, I had gotten into the land business, and though there were no conflicts of interest, there would surely have to be in due course.

At about that time I met a man who was to become a very close friend. Dick Lillico had been a highly regarded radio journalist who, toward the end of W.A.C. Bennett's term, had worked for the Socreds. He was a brilliant political strategist, a Saskatchewan Liberal who had unsuccessfully run for Parliament and had worked with Ross Thatcher—before, during and after Thatcher's time as premier of Saskatchewan.

To this day I don't know whether or not Dick came to Kamloops to help me personally, or for the stated reason that he wanted to get the constituency organization up to snuff. It doesn't matter, really. I monopolized his time, learning how to win a nomination.

The formula is easy to know but not so easy to implement. You must sign up more party members than anyone else and also—and this is critical—be the second choice of as many of your non-supporters as possible.

My campaign manager, Garnet Lineker (later B.C. Amateur Golf Champion), and I met in my boardroom. Garnet was an old friend and golfing buddy from my days as a junior member of Marine Drive, a fairly tony Vancouver golf course; Garnet had been a young assistant to the Marine Drive pro Stan Leonard, a pioneer and successful Canadian on the American Tour. While a political neophyte (who wasn't in those rebuilding days?), he was loyal and had a very strong competitive edge. Like me, he wasn't overly fond of losing. We selected a committee of about eight supporters, who were each given two tasks. First, they were to sign up as many members as they could. Second, each of them was given a weekly list of people signed up by rivals, and it was their job to "rush them"—to put Rafe Mair's case to them and seek their outright support or their second-choice support.

There were two other serious contenders for the crown: a young man named Pat Desmond, who was "old Kamloops" and seemed to be related to everyone in town, and a fellow about my age from Barriere, about forty miles north of Kamloops, named Dave Kozoris. Dave, while not well known in Kamloops, could bus in a hell of a lot of supporters to the convention from the North Thompson River area. Both were very fine guys and, for the most part, the campaign was aboveboard and decent. My people worked their tails off. There were no slackers and when any of them were sent to do a job, it was done.

The nomination meeting was on St. Patrick's Day, 1975, and was held in the gymnasium of Kamloops Senior Secondary. It drew a huge crowd, estimated at about one thousand people. Many of them had to stand outside in the schoolyard and listen to the proceedings through speakers.

Grace McCarthy chaired the meeting. When she surveyed the crowd and saw all the Kozoris people with noisemakers and the Desmond supporters singing, she asked me where my supporters were. I told her, "Grace, the quiet ones waiting to vote are mine."

One of my supporters, local businessman Ted Smith, was one of the scrutineers. He agreed to give me the high sign if I had won on the first ballot.

Well, the votes were counted. Grace rose to speak. I looked at Ted and he simply turned away. My heart sank. Grace went on and on as only Grace could when in fine fettle, which was most of the time. I just wanted to get it over with, congratulate the winner, and go home.

Finally Grace said, "You have selected a man to carry the Socred banner in Kamloops, and that man is . . . Rafe Mair!"

It was bedlam. For the first time in many weeks I indulged myself in a couple of well-earned beers. I saw Ted Smith later and asked him what the hell had happened. He just laughed and said, "I knew you had won but I just wanted to see you suffer a bit." I forgave him—I was in a very forgiving mood.

A couple of days after the nomination I took the three defeated candidates (another had campaigned at the last minute in an "anybody but Rafe" movement, but was not a factor) to lunch. All of them wanted to know what senior role they would play in the campaign. I was nothing if not blunt as I told them that they would not have any senior role. I had listened to Dick Lillico very closely and knew that each of them had, however much they might not realize it, a death wish for me. Each one thought that my nomination was a mistake, so I told them that I would dance with the one who brung me—that Garnet Lineker would be my campaign manager and my team would be the one that had won me the nomination.

As it turned out, Garnet declined the job because he didn't think he was up to it, and after a rather difficult opening of the campaign—Garnet's first replacement had a stroke—Bud Smith (later a Socred attorney general) became my campaign manager. Bud's wife Daphne, now a B.C. Supreme Court judge, was then an articling student at my law firm in Kamloops, and Bud and I had met socially—which meant we had also traded a lot of political talk. Though only in his late twenties, Bud had had considerable experience in federal Conservative campaigns. He was and is the consummate political animal. When he offered himself as my campaign manager, there was no one else obviously available, so I agreed. It was one of my better decisions.

I went into the election campaign as a naive bumpkin. I had some vague awareness of the idea of party discipline, but I truly thought that if I was elected, I would be expected to make my individual contribution to the governance of the province in daily sessions in the legislature, where I would try to persuade and perhaps be persuaded. Accordingly, when I began to "campaign," I really meant what I told people: these were things I would do.

For example, one of the things I promised was to remove from the city of Kamloops a portion of the Kamloops Native band's land that had been placed there by the NDP government when they created the new amalgamated city in 1973. Fortunately for me, after the election my new colleague, Hugh Curtis, the new minister of municipal affairs, agreed to do this immediately. I was thus able to establish an excellent relationship with Chief Mary Leonard, one that stood me in very good stead with her and her band in days to come.

For the campaign I was assigned a lovely man named Don Duncan, then in his sixties, as my driver. Kamloops was a big constituency, going as far as Blue River on the North Thompson, down to Logan Lake in the south and to Savona in the west. It required a lot of mobile campaigning.

Don Duncan was one of those great confidence builders. He had been the driver for Davie Fulton, who had represented the federal constituency of Kamloops for the Tories for many years. Don would always say to me, no matter where we had been and no matter how paltry the crowd, "Rafe, that was the biggest crowd I have ever seen in this town, and you got a better reception than Davie Fulton ever got!" If I had twenty-two people to a meeting in Blue River, Don would put the crowd at seventy-five and assure me that he had made a full count, including the many women in the kitchen making the coffee and cakes. He was a tremendous boost to the morale. Politicians, like broadcasters, live on ego—and Don always kept mine well fed.

What Don could not do was drive. He was a hideous driver and I used to arrive back in Kamloops with my nerves shattered after one of his hair-raising drives down the Yellowhead highway. But he was a lovely guy whose positive attitude and confidence in me far outweighed his driving deficiencies. All politicians praise unsung heroes and I fear that this praise, because it's uttered by a politician, is often thought of as phony. It usually isn't. My praise of Don Duncan is unstinting.

I often campaigned in the North Thompson area, because Bud Smith's method of getting a candidate elected was to keep him, as much as possible, out of harm's way. Whenever I got angry at one of my opponents' statements about me, I would want to immediately retaliate. Bud would holler, "Don, take Rafe to Blue River," and away I would go!

There were three of us in the race. The incumbent, Gerry Anderson of the NDP, had beaten the famous Flying Phil Gaglardi (more about him shortly) in 1972. Gerry was a decent sort but deadly dull. He had been a backbencher in the Barrett government and had no record of achievement to speak of. The Liberal candidate, Don Carter, was a travel agent and a glib part-time talk-show host. He was backed by the considerable Liberal organization that had propelled Len Marchand to the federal Parliament, over longtime Conservative MP Davie Fulton in 1968.

I never doubted that I would win. I don't know why I was so confident but for some reason I was. I suppose a lot of it had to do with the superb team Bud put together, and their splendid spirit.

Bud was a master of subtle political action. At about the two-week mark I was very concerned at the absence of Socred lawn signs compared to the number of signs advertising my opponents. Bud had an explanation. "Rafe," he said, "in storage we have four times the number of signs as your opponents combined. During the last twenty days of the campaign they will start going up all over the riding and it will look as if a giant tidal wave of support for Rafe Mair has taken over." And that's exactly what happened. I am also proud to say that thanks to my sign man, whose name to my embarrassment now escapes me, we had every sign down the morning after the election.

Bud was also the master of the little things. At an all-candidates meeting in a school, the teacher in charge had arranged things so that I was on the right, Carter in the middle and Anderson on the left. This, to him, was the reality of our political positions. After Bud had got through with him, I was seated in the middle and gave off the subtle but real impression that my opponents were both radicals and I was the voice of sweet reason.

During this meeting, a young girl in the audience kept poking away at Anderson about the Insurance Corporation of British Columbia (ICBC), the disastrous government automobile-insurance company the NDP had set up. This young lady did a superb job and clearly rattled the NDP incumbent with informed questions that one might not expect from a high-school student. After the meeting Gerry asked the teacher who the young lady was.

"Why, she's Shawn Mair, Rafe's daughter," he replied. (My rabid supporter, my lovely, darling daughter, would be dead in less than a year from a car accident—the biggest tragedy of my life by far.)

Once Bud Smith and I went up to Clearwater, a lovely town on the North Thompson, mainly to scout around and to satisfy Bud's curiosity about how recognizable I was. We went into the local café for a bite of lunch. I have a full beard and Bud is clean-shaven. While we were sitting there a man came up to the table and looked us both over. He then turned to Bud and said, "I know who you are—you're Rafe Mair. But don't you usually wear a beard?" As they say, go figure.

One of my main fears was the former Socred MLA, the famous Flying Phil Gaglardi, who was definitely not of the new school of Socreds. Phil, an evangelical preacher who went into government with Bennett Sr. in 1952, was a larger-than-life character who was as famous for getting into scrapes as he was for building hundreds of miles of new highway. He was a collector of speeding tickets as he "tested the curves." Phil was a great pal of Ben Ginter, the nearly as famous and controversial beer baron and construction millionaire from Prince George, and it was often said that the province was run by the three "Gs"—Gaglardi, Ginter and God, in that order. Phil finally met his Waterloo when he flew members of his family to Dallas in a government jet after depositing himself in San Francisco to give a government speech that was never scheduled or delivered. Phil was demoted from his high-profile highways post in 1971 and lost his seat altogether in the NDP sweep of the 1972 provincial election. Out of power in 1975, he was still not without influence, both good and bad.

At about day five of the campaign, Phil flew in from Terrace, where he was supervising the building of a motel. "Rafe," he said, "you've messed up this campaign and so has Bill Bennett. I'm here to turn it around for you."

I gulped because Phil still had quite a following. "Phil," I said, "I don't need your enemies and your friends have nowhere else to go. I'd be grateful if you just went back to Terrace and let us muddle through."

Phil took it with a smile and went back to Terrace.

On the Sunday before the election I was told I should listen to Phil's gospel program on the radio. I shuddered when I heard that famous Gaglardi roar, "Friend of mine!" It was followed by a sermon that put God and me onside against the works of the devil—that is to say, the NDP. I was not surprised that Phil supported me—he would have supported a fence post with hair if he thought it could defeat the NDP—but I was quite uncertain about just how his formal endorsement would be received. In the end, though, it did no harm.

Early in the campaign I went on the local "talk-back show," which, as I recall, was hosted by CFJC's news director, Doug Collins (no relation to the right-wing North Vancouver writer). Doug asked a couple of predictable questions and then opened the lines. I was hit with everything but the ring-post. I was beaten up on call after call and when I lurched back into party headquarters, I asked, "Where the hell were all my supporters?" Everyone just shrugged their shoulders.

Bud Smith had heard the broadcast and was horrified. He read the riot act.

Although the other Kamloops radio station at that time, CHNL, did not do a regular talk show, they had, and indeed still have, the very able Jim Harrison as news director. He set up an *ad hoc* talk show one early afternoon. This time things were different.

In our campaign headquarters we had a bank of about twenty-five phones. In those days you could jump the queue on a talk show by dialling the first six digits of the phone number, waiting until a caller hung up, and then dialling the seventh to get connected.

Miracle of all miracles, this time every call was delightful. At one point Jim said, "My God, your popularity has sure improved!" It was all I could do to keep from bursting into laughter.

One lady came on the air and in a breathless voice allowed that she "had been driving in her car and just had to run to the nearest phone" to tell me what a wonderful man I was and how lucky Kamloops was to have me. It was Emily Latta, one of my supporters, and I could visualize just where she was. It sure as hell wasn't in a phone booth! She was third from the right, row two, in the phone bank in our campaign headquarters!

There was only one hitch. Callers were supposed to give me slow pitches that I could bat out of the park. However, one of my crew, a delightful miner named Bert Forster, got through and asked a real question! Not only was it a real question, it would have taken a doctor of mining engineering to begin to answer it. *Goddamn it, Bert,* I thought, *you're not supposed to ask me real questions!*

In any event, the score was even and NDP supporters were left complaining to the station that somehow it had kept the "real" people from getting to me.

This all became very amusing to me and my supporters when, after the election, the NDP cried foul because of what became known as "Lettergate." On the advice of party officials, some Socreds had written letters to the editors of local papers badmouthing the NDP and signing them with the names of prominent NDPers. As the screams of anguish poured into the legislative chamber accusing us of having stolen the election with these fake letters, I had to chuckle a bit and think what fun they could have if they knew what one Socred cabinet minister and his supporters knew about a certain open-line show in Kamloops!

I'll never forget election night. From the earliest returns it was clear that Bill Bennett's forces had won a very big victory and that I had carried Kamloops by a handsome majority. Neither of my rivals took the time to come and congratulate me that night, nor did I ever hear from either of them again. The big question now was whether or not I would be in cabinet and, if so, in what portfolio.

I really owed my election to two people. Dick Lillico taught me how to win a nomination, and Bud Smith showed me how to win an election. I frankly don't believe I would have won either without this lucky combination. It also goes without saying that I had a superb organization, which very much stayed together between elections and supported me during those rough times that come to all politicians.

I was now off to Victoria.

I must add a footnote. Art Redman, now lamentably no longer with us, was a devout supporter in Logan Lake who had a mobile-home park, which was itself a polling station. When it transpired that the thirty-six voters therein had voted thirty-four for me, zilch for the NDP and two for the Liberals, he was most upset.

"Rafe," he said, "I'll find those two fucking Liberals if it takes me a year!"

A few days after the election I received a call from my friend, the defeated Socred candidate Peter Hyndman, saying that the premier-in-waiting, Bill Bennett, wanted to see me in his suite in the Harbour Towers Hotel in Victoria the following afternoon. Was I to be in cabinet? I demanded of

Peter. He was coy in his answer but left me with a pretty good feeling.

On the seaplane flight from Vancouver harbour to Victoria harbour the next day, I was seated next to Don Phillips, the Socred MLA from South Peace known as "leatherlungs" for his formidable ability to filibuster debates. Don was and is one of the characters of the world. He was the quintessential caricature of the Socred—a successful car dealer, of which the new caucus was to have half a dozen.

As we flew I asked Don where I could get a parliamentary rule book.

"What in hell would you want a rule book for?" he demanded in quite obvious distress.

"So I can learn the rules of the legislature," I rather lamely replied.

"Look," said Don, "what you do is this. You stand up and when the Speaker recognizes you, you start to talk. You talk right over the heckling of the opposition, and you keep on talking until you are finished. Keep your back to the Speaker so you can't see if he stands up, which is the signal for you to sit down. Because I'm a little deaf, that also helps me not hear the Speaker if he is warning me. When you have said your piece, sit down. That is the only rule."

I was to find out that Don was bang on. About the only thing the rules seemed to be for was creating opportunities for the opposition to make points of order and thus make the government's life a little harder.

The following day, at the appointed hour, I went to Bill Bennett's suite, where I found Jack Davis waiting as well. This was a good omen, for Jack had been a cabinet minister in the federal Trudeau government (when he had opted for B.C. politics, he had known that the road to power lay with the Socreds) and would surely be part of Bennett's inner group.

After Davis spent about fifteen minutes with Bennett, he came out and it was my turn.

Bennett was brief and, I thought, distinctly unfriendly. I was to be his minister of consumer services; it was the smallest of the ministries. That was, he made clear, the best he had to offer at this time, take it or leave it. I took it. He shook my hand perfunctorily and headed me out the door.

I was ecstatic. Small ministry or not, I was in!

On December 22, along with some seventeen others, I was sworn into cabinet by my Dad's old friend Lieutenant-Governor Walter Owen. My legs shook so much I was afraid I wouldn't survive the ordeal—but I did, and many others to come besides.

This turned out to be a very interesting day. We went to the Empress Hotel for lunch and our first cabinet meeting, about which I recall very little except the sternness of now Premier Bennett. He seemed angry at everybody, though I now know this was mostly shyness, caused by the fact that he was junior in legislative experience to many of his ministers and was the son of the great W.A.C. Bennett. In the end, Bill would become, in my view, a better premier than his dad had been, and a man his colleagues—especially me—would have done anything for.

After lunch we went over to the cabinet room in the legislature, where we held our first regular meeting. We were guided in by Laurie Wallace, who was deputy provincial secretary and senior bureaucrat.

"Mr. Premier," said Wallace, "the seating is optional, of course, but your father always had the provincial secretary on his left and the attorney general on his right." In a flash of stubbornness for which he was to become rightly famous, Bennett sat *his* attorney general, Garde Gardom (later lieutenant-governor) on his left and his provincial secretary, Grace McCarthy, on his right. Bill Bennett, like a male dog, was peeing on his trees and leaving no doubt in the mind of his senior civil servant as to who was now running the show.

I don't recall much about that first meeting except for this—Bennett announced that in a couple of hours three ministers would be leaving, by government jet, for Ottawa. There they would meet with federal ministers and senior bureaucrats to show the Trudeau government that we meant business on the serious question of ongoing inflation. Those ministers were Allan Williams, the minister of labour, Evan Wolfe, the minister of finance, and Rafe Mair, minister of consumer services, who would go as minister in charge of B.C.'s price freeze.

I had forgotten for the moment that the NDP had brought in a price freeze and, until then, had no idea that it was now my baby. But it was, and I was off to Ottawa to meet the redoubtable Beryl Plumptre, the lady in charge of Prime Minister Trudeau's wage and price controls of November 1975. (We abolished the freeze a few months later, but as of day one we were bound to show that our commitment to fighting inflation was no less strong than that of our predecessors.)

After the briefest introduction to my office staff, including Patti Ballard, my secretary (whom I would subsequently marry), I went to the airport. In the years to come, I would get my share of flak for use of government jets. What the public never did realize was that they were horribly uncomfortable with quite a limited range. They had no toilet and certainly no bar or food facilities. In fact, Jim Matkin (one of the deputy ministers along) had thoughtfully provided a large basket of food, mostly consisting of limburger cheese sandwiches. I remember this because the remains of them were left on the plane in Ottawa and when we left for home the cabin smelled to high heaven. Such are the great perks of political power!

We left at about 5:00 P.M. and, after stops in Calgary and Winnipeg for refuelling, made Ottawa by about 5:00 A.M. the following day. I do not recommend this mode of travel.

I really can't tell you what happened that day in Ottawa. We were all very weary and we went from office to office, meeting dozens of people and talking about God only knows what. What I do remember was returning in the plane, with its reek of limburger cheese, and an even longer trip home because we required an extra stop for fuel in Thunder Bay.

The day we arrived back, December 23, I had hoped to be dropped off in Kamloops. But no, the premier wanted a debriefing, so we duly repaired to his office before heading back out to the airport for the trip home. It was quite an initiation into the world of government.

Speaking of government jets, some years later, Bill Bennett, Don Phillips and I were returning by government jet from Yorkton, Saskatchewan, where there had been a meeting of Western premiers. As we journeyed, a bottle of rye came out. I wasn't drinking at all at that time but Bill and Don had a couple of drinks and soon the premier had to take a leak—badly. Don suggested that he go to the back of the plane and pee into a mixer bottle. Bennett tried that and it just wouldn't work. Something had to be done. The pilot radioed ahead that we would be making an unscheduled stop in Cranbrook, which we duly did. The local press must have been monitoring the airwaves, for when we arrived, there were three or four scribes waiting on the tarmac as Premier Bennett, doubled over in agony, got off the plane to relieve himself. Happily, the Cranbrook media, being more understanding than their big-city brethren, made nothing of this, but the incident conjured up many images of horrendous headlines in the minds of Bennett's colleagues!

In February 1976, the new government was in its first crisis. The Insurance Corporation of British Columbia (ICBC) had been formed a year and a half before by the NDP to have a complete monopoly on car insurance. Even with a monopoly and compulsory insurance, the corporation, under direct political control, managed to lose $183 million in its first year. Bennett determined that the bleeding should stop and he set up a cabinet committee under Patrick McGeer, the education minister, to see what could be done.

Pat McGeer had a double doctorate, including medicine, and was a research scientist at UBC when he won a provincial seat as a Liberal in 1963. He would later lead the provincial Liberal Party, but in August 1975, along with two other prominent colleagues, he crossed the floor to join Bill Bennett and the Socreds. This had a decided impact on Socred credibility and momentum, and probably went a long way toward the party's victory in the subsequent election.

After considerable outside consultation on the ICBC matter, it was decided that we couldn't disband the corporation, as much as we all would have liked to—at least not then. We determined that it must be made to pay its way, and that meant a massive increase in rates, which had been fixed nice and low to help the NDP's election campaign the previous December.

It hit the fan all over the province and many of my supporters, when they computed the damage to their wallets, resigned from the party and looked for ways to impeach me. The Concerned Citizens, a recyclable NDP group that sprang up whenever events demanded that the legislature be stormed by the left, got into high gear. They set a date for a massive demonstration on the legislature lawn.

The day before this event was to occur, Pat McGeer and I had lunch in the Union Club, perhaps a thousand metres from the Parliament Buildings. After lunch we ran into W.A.C. Bennett coming into the club. I had not, of course, served under W.A.C. Bennett. Though I'd met him at party conventions, I was just one of a sea of faces to him. But I did meet him after I became a member of his son's cabinet. I don't believe for a moment that he ever influenced his son politically, if only because Bill was not one for being influenced.

"Mr. Bennett," asked McGeer, "there's to be this huge demonstration on the legislature lawns tomorrow—what should I do? Should I speak to them? Should I have an official speak to them? What do you suggest?"

"Water the lawns! Turn on the automatic sprinkler system," replied the Old Man.

"But Mr. Bennett"—even though McGeer had been in the legislature with W.A.C. for a dozen years, W.A.C. was very much "Mr. Bennett"—"it's only February!"

"Turn the sprinklers on, Pat—that's my advice," the ex-premier said as he walked on to the dining room. McGeer didn't take that advice, though I'm sure he was later sad that he hadn't.

ICBC was eventually taken into the black, where it remained until Bill Bennett evolved the so-called "FAIR" plan, which forbade the company to set rates according to the age of the driver. Bennett was anxious to shake off the old Socred image of being an old-folks party and thought that this would be a good way to win over young voters, men especially. (Males under twenty-five were the single biggest contributors to car accidents, and thus paid the highest premium by far.) After that decision, ICBC began to lose money again, and the governments that followed also played political games with the rate-setting. In the end, the 1976 efforts to make ICBC a self-sustaining corporation were for naught.

Having served in his government for five years, I am and will remain a great fan of Bill Bennett's, regardless of a stock-market case that somewhat tarnished his image. I still regard him so highly that I don't believe he was directly involved in selling shares in Doman Industries on inside information from Herb Doman, and that's that.

Bill was tough—tough as steel. And while he was never much liked by the public, he gave off a strong aura of competence for the good reason that he was, in fact, competent. And he brooked no nonsense about the question of filling his father's shoes—he was his own man.

During his time as Official Opposition leader (a role he detested), Bill Bennett was a ferocious alley fighter. He would mellow considerably as premier but even then, when he made a rare entry into debate, he took no prisoners. One day a certain member of the NDP government was taunting Bill about being daddy's boy. "At least I know who my father is," Bennett shot back, knowing that the member opposite was a bastard literally as well as figuratively.

Once while in government, Bennett had had a bellyful of a well-known NDP MLA who had, in his youth, done time in jail. The member kept on at

Bennett about his record as premier. "I'll match my record against yours any day" shouted the premier at his tormentor. It was not a good idea to heckle Premier Bill Bennett!

Early in his premiership Bill Bennett unveiled a statue of Captain Cook, who had explored the B.C. coastline in 1778, on Government Street, a few hundred yards from the Parliament Buildings and right across the street from the Empress Hotel. I was in the general crowd and when he pulled the curtain, I could see Bennett's muscles tighten and that look of anger—which I'd later come to recognize quickly—come over his face. On the plaque that identified the statue and credited Bennett with the unveiling, the premier's middle name was listed as Richard — not Richards, which was his mother's maiden name. The unveiling occurred at about 1:00 P.M.—and there was a redone plaque on the statue by nightfall.

As for Grace McCarthy, the lady who brought the Socreds back from near-extinction in 1974, I greatly admired Grace and still do to this day. No one worked harder than Grace and her contributions to the province are in the very top percentile. I owe her a lot personally, too: she had helped me enormously in my political career—and she's my friend.

Grace was a very powerful minister, especially in the early days when she carried, if I remember correctly, three portfolios including provincial secretary, house leader and deputy premier. I was a raw rookie who knew bugger all about what I was doing—as were many others—and Grace was not above some solid interference in other people's ministries from time to time, including mine. And when I became minister of consumer and corporate affairs in November 1976, I was in a position to get very substantially in the way of Grace McCarthy, political animal extrordinaire. I was the bane of her existence and we had some dandy fights.

On one occasion I received a visit from a very prominent liquor-company executive informing me that his 1778 Captain Cook Rye Whiskey was all ready to go on the shelves. Since I was responsible for booze in the province he thought it only courteous to let me know.

"Have you got your listing through?" I asked.

"Well, not yet, but Grace said that if I came to see you, everything would be fixed up without any red tape."

I told him, "Listings in liquor stores are just like shelf space in any other kind of store. If one product goes on, something else must be taken off. If I shove your new booze in, I'll have to get rid of one of your competitor's and then they'll be in the office demanding to know why they, who have done all the right things, have their product de-listed because someone is close to the minister."

A day or so later, Grace's executive assistant, scion of a very prominent Vancouver family, paid me a visit on the subject, and while I didn't toss him out, I gave him short shrift. Then Grace phoned. I made it clear that I wouldn't budge. She made it clear she was going to the premier, with whom I naturally thought she had great influence. Moments later the red phone on my desk, the premier's direct line, rang. I was, frankly, terrified. He asked me what had happened. I told him. "You're right," he said, and put the phone down.

Grace and I had a number of other tiffs and I'm sure she had her wins. She wanted to look after the government's political ass, and if that meant bending a rule for a neighbourhood pub licence, seeing a Howe Street rogue in a private dinner, or changing the new Residential Tenancy Act to suit her friends in the landlord community, she would demand, unsuccessfully, that I do so. On these and other occasions I refused her blandishments and was supported, sometimes in front of colleagues, by the premier.

Grace should have been premier. When she ran to replace Bill Bennett as Socred leader in 1986 I didn't support her, because I didn't think we should renew the party with the "old guard." I also worried that Grace would be seen by voters as too close to Bill Vander Zalm. In the race for delegates, there was almost no hostility between the two rivals; the media picked up on this and virtually had them twinned. (Not for the first or last time, the media were dead wrong, as demonstrated when, two years later, McCarthy quit then-Premier Bill Vander Zalm's cabinet.)

I should have supported Grace, and I'm sorry if I adversely affected her campaign. In any event, to the sorrow of all except the far right, Vander Zalm won the 1986 leadership race and subsequent election. It's worth noting that at the convention, only one of the cabinet ministers he had served alongside supported Vander Zalm. There was a reason: mostly incompetent as a minister, he carried the additional political burden of being incapable of reaching a consensus agreement. Indeed, his instinct was always to *break up* a consensus; "my way or the highway" seemed to be his motto.

To make matters worse, Vander Zalm consistently paid heed to the religious right. Though a Catholic, he was from the "Bible Belt" in the Fraser Valley and his policies showed it. To top it off, he could not separate his business interests from his public duty; throughout his term in office, he was embroiled in a number of conflict-of-interest scandals centring on "Fantasy Gardens," a theme park he owned. In 1991 he was forced to resign as Socred leader.

In one of those delicious moments one savours, I appeared on CBC television during the 1986 leadership convention, and predicted that if Vander Zalm won he would destroy the Social Credit Party within two years; he did just that. I need not trouble you with the litany of scandals that characterized the Vander Zalm era, but suffice it to say that the Socreds were all but obliterated in the 1991 provincial election. The party's once-massive annual conventions have now been reduced to a size that a phone booth could easily accommodate.

When Grace McCarthy ran for Socred leadership again in 1991 and lost to the sitting premier, Rita Johnston, I editorially supported Grace. But she had come into the race too late. Had she been elected leader I have no doubt that she would have kept the Social Credit Party intact. She probably wouldn't have won the provincial election in the fall of 1991—though she might have—but she would have done well enough to ensure that the Socreds remained the right-wing alternative to the NDP.

When the Socreds lost the subsequent provincial election and Rita Johnston resigned the leadership, I privately urged Grace to seek the leadership, which she did, and she won, but for a lot of reasons it just didn't work: in a by-election held in a solid Socred constituency, Grace lost to a Liberal. In hindsight, her time had passed. She was unfairly seen by the party's right wing as the person who had brought Bill Vander Zalm down and then tried to torpedo his successor, Rita Johnston. Maybe, as I look back on it, the Socreds turning to Grace McCarthy in 1994, instead of earlier, was like the Vancouver Canucks spending untold millions to get Mark Messier in 1997. The right person, but too late.

Even as I was hammering out a political career throughout the second half of the 1970s, I was also reeling from a devastating personal tragedy and its after-effects. On October 16, 1976, our lovely second daughter, Shawn, was killed in a car accident. Both Eve and I were shattered, but she was able to cope much better than I could. This is not to say that her grief was any the less, of course—she was simply able to handle things with much greater maturity.

Calamities like this often exacerbate the problems in a marriage. While Eve and I had been married for over twenty years, we had begun to drift apart in our interests. Just as she was getting ready to settle down to ranch life—she and the girls loved horseback riding—I was a late bloomer now ready to spread my wings. To make a long story short, I cried on the nearest shoulder available, Eve and I were divorced eighteen months later and Patti Ballard (my secretary, who had separated from her husband) and I were married. She and I stayed together until 1993 when, with neither party being "at fault," we amicably separated and divorced. In August 1993 I met my wonderful wife, Wendy, and we've been together ever since.

As long as I live, my conscience will rightly bother me for the way I treated Eve, who bore the burden of losing her daughter, her mother and father, and her marriage, all in one year. She is a very fine person and deserved a hell of a lot better.

PART TWO

The View from the Trenches

CHAPTER FOUR

Environmental Issues

I was an environmentalist long before that term was in constant use. I've not always been as good at it as I now am, and I've a long way to go before I'm perfect. But I am an environmentalist. One of my heroes is Paul Watson of the Sea Shepherd Conservation Society.

I started fishing as a very small child, trolling for salmon from my parents' cottage at Granthams Landing, on what we now call the "Sunshine Coast." Actually it was more a shack than a cottage, and I especially remember the calcimined walls and the outdoor privy. As a very small boy I fished for shiners, then perch off the wharf, graduating to the bigger wharf perch, and what we Lotuslanders call ling cod and rock cod. Neither of them are a true cod, but they abound—or they did before we allowed them to be fished out.

As the years passed, I became a fly fisherman. Like so many, I came to catch-and-release rather recently. I'm ashamed to admit that as late as the 1970s I would return from a day fishing proudly bearing a sackful of fish, well beyond what I could use. (My life as a fisherman has been recorded in my book *The Last Cast*, published in 1994 by Hancock House.)

In 1978, while minister of consumer and corporate affairs in Bill Bennett's government, I became very vocal about what was happening to the estuary of the Cowichan River near Duncan on Vancouver Island. A local sawmill boomed its logs in the estuary, which, for complicated scientific reasons, interfered with the cutthroat trout. The issue was laden with politics: the owner of the mill, Herb Doman, was a close friend of Russ Bennett, Bill's brother. While Bill Bennett himself certainly put no pressure on his cabinet, the party's right-wingers, led by Don Phillips, were determined to support Doman. In a classic malapropism, Phillips shouted, "Mr. Premier, I'm just as against the environment as anyone else!" (Don was famous for such mis-wordings. Once in the legislature he shouted, "The NDP are just like leopards—they'll never change their stripes!")

In general, Bill Bennett's cabinet was divided—as most cabinets are—on the issue of environmental responsibility versus industrial development. I was the leading, if not only, environmentalist, while Phillips led the capitalists. Don Phillips was a great colleague of whom I was very fond—I just didn't much agree with him.

I'd done a bit of fishing for sea run cutthroat trout (now classified as a Pacific salmon, to the annoyance and bewilderment of most sports fishermen) with some of the guys in the Fish and Wildlife Branch of the Ministry of Environment, and they had filled me in on the effect Doman's sawmill was having. Since the current environment minister, Jim Nielsen (great guy but no environmentalist) was proving ineffectual in dealing with the situation, I raised such a stink that the next thing I knew *I* was minister of environment.

Being minister of environment is a tough role for an environmentalist, because you're supposed to be even-handed. I had much more fun—and I think I was much more effective—as a thorn in the previous minister's side. I do not look upon this ministry as a particularly great chapter of my career, though I did accomplish a couple of things and I'm very proud of the role I played in saving the Skagit River valley from flooding below the border by Seattle Light and Power, who had the contractual right to do so.

The Skagit River rises in the Coast Range and passes through southwestern B.C. about 160 kilometres east of Vancouver, then through the state of Washington to the sea. At one time the British Columbia Skagit was full of Pacific salmon, steelhead—being sea run rainbow trout and cutthroat trout, now both reclassified as Pacific salmon—and dolly varden char (also known as bull trout).

Many years ago the Seattle Light and Power Company built the Ross Dam just below the border, ending all fish migrations above the dam but leaving a resident population of rainbows, cutthroat and dolly varden. In the early 1940s the B.C. government made a deal with Seattle Light and Power permitting them to raise the Ross Dam, which would have flooded the Skagit Valley north of the border. This deal was reconfirmed by the W.A.C. Bennett government in the 1960s.

It's very easy to be critical now, but in those days there always seemed to be another valley to log or flood or both. Only fly fishermen and canoeists (not an especially important lobby group in those days) did any complaining.

By the 1960s environmentalism was coming into vogue, however, and many people, contemplating a huge lake where there had once been a marvelous trout stream, were raising hell. The problem was that the W.A.C. Bennett government, which had built dams like there was no tomorrow, was not interested in preventing the creation of power. For them, the more dams, and the more electric power, the merrier.

In the early 1970s, a group called ROSS (Run Out Skagit Spoilers) was formed. ROSS was a broad coalition of political activists dedicated to stopping Seattle Light and Power from doing what they were contractually entitled to do. This group was highly focused and, like the ram in the Frank Sinatra song "High Hopes," was prepared to keep right on butting against the dam, no matter how long it took.

In 1972 the provincial NDP government of Dave Barrett came to power and there were indeed high hopes that they would settle the matter in favour of preserving the Skagit Valley. This didn't happen, though in fairness, had the NDP been re-elected in 1975 it might have. At any rate, the issue was still unresolved by 1979, when I was environment minister, and the hour of truth was drawing near as Seattle Light and Power made noises that the building of the dam was about to commence.

I took up the cudgels for ROSS in 1978, when I first became really aware of the implications. By the time I was made minister of environment, Bill Bennett knew that by my very appointment, the Ross Dam was not going to be raised—at least not during my watch.

B.C. Hydro became alarmed because they knew that the only settlement Seattle Light and Power would accept for not raising the dam would be equivalent power. Money wouldn't do the trick. This meant that any concession of power would be permanent and B.C. Hydro, ever trying to perpetuate its existence by wildly overestimating our future power needs, were not interested in lessening what power resources they had. They were adamant that no deal should be made.

At a Social Credit caucus meeting in the fall of 1978, B.C. Hydro tried a pre-emptive strike. They came to the caucus meeting with a presentation designed to stop any support for saving the Skagit and, as part of that presentation, showed a valley that looked like a moonscape and implied that this was what the Skagit Valley looked like, so why bother saving it?

Not for the first time, B.C. Hydro overplayed its hand. It was brought to my attention (I had not seen the Skagit Valley since I was a boy) that the pictures were of Ross Lake (which had been *formed* by the existing dam) at low water and on the American side of the border! Instead of gaining support for raising Ross Dam, Hydro gained converts to the notion of settlement.

In April 1979, unbeknownst to me, Bill Bennett was planning a snap election. There were a number of serious environmental issues on the provincial table, including uranium mining and the Skagit. Moreover, the B.C. Wildlife Federation was flat broke. What did the environment minister intend to do about these matters?

Bennett picked the right man because (and this is a fault more often than a virtue) I have always wanted to face and settle every problem now. Even when all good common sense dictated letting a bit of time pass, Rafe Mair could always be relied upon to let impetuosity clearly overrule patience.

I did a number of things.

This was at the very beginning of lottery money coming to the province, so I suggested that we bail out the B.C. Wildlife Federation with a lottery grant of $50,000, which was a hell of a lot of money for them in 1979. I also took the Federation's president, Bill Otway, with me to Sweden, with senior ministry staff, to look at how they handled some of their wildlife problems. (There was an amusing moment on the trip. Bill is a rough and tumble sort of guy and not overly endowed with the royal jelly. Salt of the earth, but you probably wouldn't have him to dinner if the Queen was the guest of honour. We flew first class and Bill and I were seatmates. Needless to say, the odd dram of golden nectar passed our lips as we flew from Vancouver to London. Just as we were landing at Heathrow, with all the delicacy of a bull moose in rut, Bill barfed. His false teeth landed in his lap! Her Majesty would not have been amused.)

I next suggested a moratorium on all mining exploration until Dr. David Bates, sitting as a one-man Royal Commission, looked into the entire question. There was some self-service in this suggestion as I had, through a big mouth and little tact, got the town of Clearwater (in my riding) most upset; I hadn't listened to their concerns about a proposed uranium mine in their backyard. In fact, I had to go to Clearwater, eat a lot of humble pie and apologize to the local doctor, Bob Woollard—who was leading the opposition to uranium mining—for calling him names.

Since there was a lot of uranium mining around the province, including in the premier's constituency, and considering that mining companies supported the Social Credit Party, the moratorium was a gutsy call for Bill Bennett to permit me to make.

I also suggested that it would not be remiss to end the issue of the Ross Dam.

Bill Bennett had been concerned about the Skagit for some time, not only for political reasons. Unlike his father, Bill cared a great deal about environmental matters, though, like his father, when he decided they were not important, he could be brutal. (A classic example was the new Coquihalla Highway in 1986. Environmentalists opposed this development because of possible harmful effects on the Coquihalla River; indeed, that river's wonderful steelhead fishery is now virtually dead.)

Bennett had been in touch with the governor of Washington about making a deal on the Ross Dam issue, but the matter was bogged down in protocol. The governor protested that it was out of his hands because Seattle Light and Power was under the authority of the very popular Seattle mayor, Charles Royer. Bennett suggested that Royer deal with the minister of environment but the mayor refused, saying that the mayor of Washington's largest city was not going to deal with a mere cabinet minister in the B.C. government. Bennett maintained that premiers deal with governors, cabinet ministers deal with mayors.

At Premier Bennett's request, I called Mayor Royer. He refused to take my call but he had his executive assistant, who happened to be his brother Bob, call me instead.

"How about the two of us discussing it?" Bob asked me.

"But will you have authority to make a deal?" was my natural question.

He convinced me that this would be no problem, so in late April of 1979, I flew to Seattle with my deputy minister, a delightful Scot named Ben Marr.

Ben had already determined what the proper price in power should be and what form the negotiations would likely take. He thought we were mad.

Ben is an engineer. As I told him, he would dam a horse peeing if he thought he could thereby get a watt of energy. But Ben, being the good public servant he was, knew I was going to settle this matter and gamely went along.

I arrived at City Hall and was ushered into a small boardroom where I met Bob Royer and one or two officials from Seattle Light and Power. The boardroom was connected to the mayor's office and throughout the discussions, Mayor Royer sat in the next room and listened!

From time to time a note would come to Bob from the mayor and an earnest discussion, or perhaps a caucus, would take place. Then negotiations would continue. By noon we had settled—largely, I admit, on Seattle's terms, though happily for us our case had been buttressed by American environmentalists who had shown solidarity with their Canadian brethren, a group Mayor Royer could not afford to alienate. Moreover, the mayor was a Democrat and keenly sensitive to the voting potential of environmentalists.

The mayor, his brother, Ben and I repaired to the famous Rossellini's Seafood restaurant for wine and lunch. We'd paid a high price for the folly of our predecessors but it was worth it. We'd saved a beautiful valley.

I was back in time for the latter part of the afternoon sitting of the House, but when I got back there was a message to see the premier as soon as possible. I went to Bennett's office and told him we had made, subject to cabinet approval, a deal. The final deal was made after I had left the ministry, but I'm still delighted that I brought this matter to an acceptable conclusion. The premier seemed both agitated and relieved.

That afternoon the mood in the legislature was electric. There was an election in the air, though I couldn't for the life of me understand why we were going to the polls without any discernible major issue, and just three years and five months into our mandate. That very evening Bill Bennett went to the lieutenant-governor, who dissolved the legislature and issued a writ for an election in the middle of May.

I can honestly say that I don't know whether or not my handy work in the Ministry of the Environment had any bearing on Bennett's decision, but I must assume that it did. Bennett had a sense that the economy was going to go badly by fall, which it did, and felt the time was ripe. He was probably right in his call.

In any event, the B.C. Wildlife Federation, never known as rabid Socred supporters, ran an editorial in their newsletter praising the government and the minister. It was published, by happy coincidence, on the eve of the surprise election.

I spent most of the election campaign stumping the province on behalf of colleagues, or what we hoped would be colleagues. I had felt very safe in Kamloops, confident I'd done a good job as MLA and had acquitted myself well in high-profile cabinet posts.

I returned to Kamloops about five days before the election and immediately sensed that something was wrong. Very wrong. Campaign workers, who had had to answer for me in my absence, were just a little less friendly than I thought they should be. When I walked down the main streets or through shopping malls I sensed that people were looking the other way or even outright avoiding me.

I called Bud Smith, again my campaign manager, in Victoria. I said, "Bud, I think we're in trouble." He flew in and we campaigned like no one has ever campaigned before! I was everywhere — in malls, on radio and TV, knocking on doors and simply being in as many places as I could.

It was a very close election. We won by four seats. I won my seat fairly handsomely, but I'm damned glad the poll wasn't held the night I returned.

My environmentalism continued after I got into radio (more on that career change later) and I consistently editorialized on the subject, especially when it concerned fish. The main event was the controversy over the Alcan company's Kemano Completion Project (KCP).

My first brush with this immense project in northern British Columbia came when, as a youth, I first saw the movies of the development in stage one. I wish I could say that I was then converted into an environmentalist, but in truth I was like almost everyone else—everyone except the Natives who were cruelly flooded out of their homes, that is—and thought this was a thrilling development. Wow! Huge industry, new employment, new cities, all that energy—which had previously just been wasted, flowing aimlessly into the ocean. There would be a huge new aluminum smelter, a new town of Kitimat, rivers turned backward, huge lakes built. In those days when there was always another valley just over the hill, it seemed exhilarating. I was a captive to the "Business is moving to B.C." slogan that then prevailed.

The deal started with an act of the legislature called the Industrial Development Act of 1948, which gave rise to a formal agreement between

Alcan (an aluminum-refining company) and the Province of British Columbia. The development was to take place in two parts, Kemano I and Kemano II.

Though I was in the government at the time Alcan began preparing for Kemano II, I can honestly say that I don't remember it being discussed. This is no doubt because it was seen by the government and the minister responsible as a foregone conclusion, and a legitimate one at that. Considerable doubt has now been cast upon the legality of Alcan's commencement of Kemano II, but in the 1970s, when preparations were being made and new deals consummated, its legitimacy wasn't questioned.

In fact, only a few members of the mainstream media were really raising any questions: in Vancouver, only Mark Hume and his brother Stephen for the *Vancouver Sun*, John Massey, a freelancer who often wrote for the *Sun*, and on occasion one or two others.

I remember talking about the matter with Bill Otway, president of the B.C. Wildlife Federation, in 1986. He assured me that Alcan had "done their homework" and that the project would have a benign effect on the environment. If there was damage, he said, there would be mitigation. My first radio editorial on the subject followed; it didn't deal with Alcan *per se* but with the word "mitigation," which I still think is a weasel word. There could be no such thing as meaningful mitigation, as was dramatically revealed to me as events unfolded.

In June 1993 I took my show to Terrace for a day. During the show I interviewed Bill Rich, vice president of Alcan and the point man for the project. I received, in advance of the interview, all sorts of promotional material, bumph, including a video of happy little salmon frolicking in the Nechako River, which was going to lose nearly ninety percent of its water when the deal was finished.

I have been criticized throughout my broadcasting career for being too skeptical of what I hear. I'm told that I should rejoice at good news instead of trying to see the dark side, that I should be better mannered and more respectful. I can tell you that every time I have listened to that advice I have been sorry. This was no exception.

I lobbed one slow pitch after another at Bill, and he neatly batted every one of them out of the park. It was—and this covers a lot of territory, I can tell you—the worst interview of my career.

I thought no more about the issue until the following October, when I received a call from an old friend from my Kamloops days, Ben Meisner. Amongst other things, he was doing a talk show at CKPG in Prince George.

Now it's important to know that Prince George and Vanderhoof are on the east side of the mountains, where the Nechako River flows into the Fraser and where the damage would be done, while Kitimat, Kemano and Terrace are on the west side, where all the real construction work was going to go. Ben had the viewpoint of a man who lived on the east side and in fact had a home on the Nechako.

Ben is a gruff no-nonsense guy with journalistic experience going back to earlier days as a member of the Ottawa press gallery. He was and is also a businessman—a capitalist through and through. Ben was nothing if not blunt.

"Rafe, have you any idea what the fuck these guys at Alcan are planning to do to the Nechako? Have you read a goddamn thing about it?" was gentle Ben's opening thrust.

I had to admit that I had heard Alcan's side and had listened to Bill Otway years before, but had no more to go on than that.

"I'll send you an article," replied Ben. "Read the goddamn thing and see what you think."

Frankly, I was underwhelmed at the notion of looking into this matter. In a day or so the article that changed my mind arrived on my desk. It was a slam dunk on Alcan and Kemano II by John Goddard in *Harrowsmith* magazine. This article was devastating. If it was correct, at the end of the day the Nechako River would be left at about thirteen percent of its original flow, with catastrophic effects on salmon stocks.

I invited Ben Meisner and Bill Rich into my studio to do battle. They did. I hope my friend Meisner will not mind if I say that Rich got the better of the argument, while Meisner won on passion. Bill was as smooth as margarine and had facts coming out of everywhere. Like a good lawyer, he threw so much at Ben that Ben hardly knew where to begin to rebut.

But Ben won on sincerity. Listeners and host alike knew that Ben wasn't bullshitting—that there were real problems here. And his answers and jabbing questions threw Rich off stride on several occasions.

I began a long, long learning curve, but it started with one key fact: Bill Rich had talked incessantly about a chinook run of about three thousand fish, while clearly the real danger, unaddressed (understandably) by Alcan, was the huge sockeye run that passed through the Nechako into the Stuart system.

The Nechako is a very big (though with Kemano I much diminished) tributary of the Fraser, and meets the Fraser at Prince George. The chinook (also called springs and sometimes tyee) are the largest of the Pacific salmon, but nowhere near the most important commercially. The sockeye, a smaller but highly desirable salmon, runs in the millions through the Nechako into the Stuart River system. It's critical that these sockeye have enough water at the right temperature to pass through the Nechako at spawning time. Because they don't themselves spawn in the Nechako, the river Alcan was messing with, Bill Rich had very successfully diverted attention from this run to the chinook, which do. This fact is critical to the entire story from here on.

Bill Rich told us, in essence, that the chinook were not at risk. Alternatively, if they were at risk, a cold-water release mechanism at the Kenney Dam (which dams the Nechako upstream) would see the fish through. In the further alternative, if that didn't work, they would supplement the stock with a hatchery on the river. In the last alternative, if all else failed, they would remove some of the brood stock and plant them in another river.

This sounded too much like lawyer talk: alternatives here, alternatives there. Though no fish biologist, I knew that you just couldn't, with a wave of the hand, transplant one stock into another river. Each river leaves its own fingerprint on its anadromous fish and transplanting is not simple. Besides, what would that do to the salmon already using the substitute river? Bill Rich's argument was just too smooth.

I started to raise questions, following (much later, I'm bound to say) the efforts of Stephen and Mark Hume and John Massey in *The Vancouver Sun*. But the real pioneers in the fight against Kemano were the Cheslatta Native band, which had been cruelly flooded out when the Kenney dam was built. The Cheslatta had received some government money and had hired some researchers at very low wages who did heroic work—which punctually found its way into my hands. I spent many hours on the phone and in the studio with them. They're the unsung heroes of this story.

Not that the government and Alcan didn't have the right to flood all this land, even including Native graveyards. They had the consents of the various chiefs—all duly forged! Even the "X"s of those who could not write English were all signed by the same government agent. All neat and tidy!

Once I started speaking out against the Kemano project, the information poured in. Our office looked like a small law office in the midst of a huge lawsuit. More and more people offered help and if I don't name them all, they will forgive me knowing that they did the job and I was only a some-time spokesman.

David Austin, probably the best-informed lawyer on energy matters in B.C., and counsel to the town of Vanderhoof, spent hours with me explaining the technical issues. Gordon Hartman, Harold Mundie, Bill Schoeuwenberg, Don Alderdice and others, all dubbed the "dissident scientists" in a cruel jibe from Alcan, were unstinting in their assistance. (The "dissident scientists" came to wear that title with a great deal of pride as the story slowly but steadily unfolded.)

There was the Rivers Defence League and Pat Moss, the United Fishermen and Allied Workers and their indomitable fighter, Mae Burrows. And Jim Fulton, former MP and now head of the David Suzuki Foundation. And there were many many others.

Let me now, and I confess that this may be a simplification, review what had happened.

In 1984 the Department of Fisheries and Oceans (DFO) had done a study on the Nechako and the likely effects of the project. This was com-piled much later and only released by way of a "brown envelope" into my hands in early 1994, eight years after the deal received approval from the Mulroney government—which was extremely cosy with Alcan.

In the early 1980s the DFO, very concerned that the flows of the Nechako would damage salmon runs, especially the sockeye runs that Alcan kept con-veniently overlooking, went to court and obtained an interim mandatory injunction obliging Alcan to maintain certain minimum levels of water flow. By 1986, Alcan, frustrated by the inability to do as they wished, were pre-pared to go to court.

On the eve of the trial, Minister of Fisheries Tom Siddon, a hopelessly weak minister who was the last person we needed in that portfolio at that time, did a *volte face*. Instead of simply letting the trial proceed, he instruct-ed the DFO to look at settlement.

The settlement was reached in a typically weasely way, by two weasely governments and one weasely huge corporation.

A committee of seven scientists was cobbled together—three from the Department of Fisheries and Oceans, three from Alcan's group of pet poodles, and one poor blighter along for the ride from the B.C. Fish and Wildlife Branch. The DFO scientists all, incidentally, had no hands-on experience on the project. The so-called "dissident scientists" were deliberately left off. Alcan's scientists were the ones trying to convince people that sockeye could virtually walk up a dry stream bed. They were hired by Alcan and under contract to Alcan.

The chairman was Dr. David Strangway, an Ontarian who had come to B.C. as president of the University of British Columbia and who couldn't have distinguished a sockeye from a squawfish.

The terms of reference were, get this, to find ways to do what Alcan wanted!

The deliberations were to be held and completed over a single weekend and, needless to say, all expenses were paid by Alcan. In fact this "independent" commission was launched by a pep talk from none other than Bill Rich.

Federal Minister of Fisheries and Oceans Tom Siddon utterly abdicated his responsibility and either engineered, or permitted to be engineered, a settlement that was virtually all Alcan wanted. In a list of mostly undistinguished fisheries ministers, Tom Siddon is clearly at the bottom. Instead of acting to save the fish, which was his job, he acted like an industrial development minister.

The project should have, by law, been thoroughly examined by the Environmental Review Assessment Process of the federal government, but the Mulroney government nixed that by order-in-council. That decision was taken to court and upheld there on technical grounds. On its merits, it was roundly criticized by an all-party committee of Parliament, some of the more vocal critics being Tory MPs.

Throughout the entire period leading up to the Strangway Committee deal in August 1986, Alcan had on the one hand protested that the project was environmentally benign—while at the same time it ferociously resisted any effort to have the project independently examined.

There are many sources of information to which the technically minded can turn for that sort of information. I will content myself with a general overview, content in the knowledge that the "dissident scientists," so thoroughly vindicated, support what I have to say.

The key question—though there were many others—was whether or not the flows and temperature of water through the Nechako would be sufficient to allow the huge Stuart River runs to pass safely. By the time that I entered into the debate, the chinook runs had already been all but wiped out.

Alcan's position was that with judicious use of the "cold-water release" system planned for the Kenney Dam, the sockeye would be safe. The one-word answer, supported by the findings of the "dissident scientists," is "bullshit." The *maximum* flows proposed by Alcan in 1986 (and pleaded thereafter throughout the controversy) were lower than the *minimum* flows proposed by the DFO scientists in the Task Force report.

The telling point—which I confess I made *ad nauseam* during the year-long fight—is this: The KCP clearly imposed a risk to the sockeye runs. Even Alcan and their apparent ally Tom Siddon admitted that much. They said, however, that the risk was acceptable. That assertion was grossly illogical and wouldn't have stood the scrutiny of a reasonably bright grade-eight student. If you impose a risk, and do not confine it within any time limit—in other words, if you create an ongoing risk forever—it is only a matter of time before that risk becomes a reality. Such a risk is no risk at all but an absolute inevitability, the only question being when it materializes.

The "when" would not likely be long in coming. Down to thirteen percent of its original flows, the Nechako was a time bomb waiting to explode in the midst of our precious sockeye. How long would it take for a year of low runoff to coincide with a period of low water from Alcan just when the sockeye arrived?

The stakes were enormous, but there was a hidden problem that no one would speak of, though all felt it in their bones. Back in the 1940s it was proposed by Ottawa that the Fraser be dammed above Lytton by what was to be called the Moran Dam. This would have done in all Fraser River salmon runs that spawn above that point, just as Grand Coulee Dam finished off the salmon runs to the Upper Columbia. These plans had never gone away and there is an industrial mindset in B.C. that slavers at the notion of power, power, power!

As long as there are salmon in the Fraser, the demands for a dam will be muted. But what would happen if KCP went ahead and in consequence the sockeye runs were eliminated? A run of a couple of hundred chinooks—for that's all that's left of that run—would never have deterred the would-be dam-builders from their plans for the Fraser.

However, throughout the exercise, I never really considered Alcan the enemy. They were simply doing what any large company does—taking every advantage they could get out of the governments they had to deal with.

One enemy was the government of B.C., although the NDP government of Mike Harcourt (who served as premier from 1991 to 1995) had nothing whatever to do with any of it. They just happened to be holding the bag when the cats got antsy.

The principal villain, though, was the federal government. It got us into all the ultimate trouble by agreeing to the sham Strangway deal. In 1994, when it became obvious that this was a catastrophic undertaking, the feds simply wouldn't respond to the problem. They threw it back onto the province's lap, saying that if they didn't like the deal, they could cancel the water licences and take the heat. This was pretty tough for Premier Harcourt, who by nature didn't like confrontations big or small—and this was a big one.

Premier Harcourt had, in 1992, asked Professor Murray Rankin of the University of Victoria Law School to do a report on the project. Professor Rankin examined the law and decided that the deal had to proceed. It was a shallowly researched report, probably because the terms of reference provided neither the authority nor the money to go into details. This was enough for Premier Harcourt to state that he wouldn't interfere.

When the forces against Alcan finally jelled in 1994, the obstacles should have been insurmountable. Alcan had a court-sanctioned deal. The federal government wouldn't touch the matter with a barge pole. And the provincial government had washed its hands of the matter. Under those circumstances, what the hell could we do?

Well, we could keep on fighting and raising public awareness, and that we did. I came under terrific fire (not from my station, CKNW, I'm glad to say) to lay off. Mark Hume, for no apparent reason, stopped writing about the matter in *The Vancouver Sun* and when he was permitted an article, it was found on the sports page. John Massey suddenly got no more commissions from the *Sun* for his work, work they had gladly accepted in the past. The *Sun* and the *Province* gave little or no ink to the issue. BCTV, the leading news outlet in the province, seemed to be saying, If Rafe Mair is on about it, let him do the talking.

But the fight continued. I began to get leaked documents, including the Task Force Report compiled by "dissident" Bill Schouwenberg. I had enormous assistance from the "dissidents" and from legal beagle David Austin. The case just got stronger and stronger.

By October 1994 I felt able to invite political leaders to look at my files and judge for themselves. To his eternal credit, B.C. Liberal leader Gordon Campbell (the Liberals were the provincial government's Official Opposition at the time), quickly did just that. He and his aides spent hours going over a volume of badly organized papers. Soon afterward, the NDP did the same thing, and Premier Harcourt finally acted. He referred the matter to the British Columbia Utilities Commission for review.

That might have been a sham itself, because the Commission was given very limited terms of reference. For example, they were not permitted to look into the potential impact on the flows of the Fraser, of which the much-reduced Nechako was a principal tributary.

However, the Commission held hearings all around the province, and no limitation of the inquiry's terms of reference could keep out the evidence that this project meant certain destruction of the Stuart system sockeye.

The report did not recommend that the project be tubed. What it did, however, was just as important: it raised very serious doubts as to the project's environmental safety. That was enough for the Harcourt government to act. In January 1995 they cancelled the project.

It was a fantastic victory. I daresay there were tears in the eyes of thousands of British Columbians. Many rightly saw this as Canada's biggest environmental victory of all time, probably bigger than James Bay.

Following this decision, there were plenty of side issues and bits of byplay, but one argument should have put paid to the entire project, and to the notion that the province owed Alcan anything after the project was stopped. A reading of the very short and concise Industrial Development Act of 1948, and the subsequent deal between the government and Alcan, leaves considerable doubt as to whether or not Alcan was permitted, from the outset, to proceed.

Alcan came to B.C. as a refiner of aluminum, not a power company. But refining aluminum takes a lot of electrical energy, so the location with all that hydro potential was ideal.

Under the Act, Alcan's permit to take and divert water for hydroelectric energy was confined to the "works and the vicinity." In other words, Alcan could only produce energy for Kitimat and "vicinity," presumably meaning the settlements that would grow up around the industry. If this is the correct legal position, Alcan had no business proceeding with KCP unless it was for its plant or "vicinity," which no doubt explains why Alcan tried so hard to pretend that it was producing the KCP power for "industrial purposes."

It was, of course, doing no such thing. Bill Rich candidly and publicly admitted to me that they were in the power game, and indeed, as far back as 1978 had made a power deal with B.C. Hydro.

But the government of B.C. did not pursue this argument and made a settlement with Alcan, which compensated the company for not having done something it may not have been entitled to do in the first place, and even paid damages for lost revenues. It's a mark of NDP acumen that they did this even though on three occasions Alcan went to premiers of the province, begging cup in hand, saying that if the government didn't bail them out they would have to stop the project because it was a money loser!

In 1995 CKNW and my program were up for a Michener Award, the most prestigious award in Canada for journalism. We were there because of Kemano. Alcan tried to stop us from getting the award. We won anyway, which shows that at least some elements of the establishment are not over-run by Alcan's "green ooze." It was a marvelous moment when, vacationing in a small town in Wales, Wendy and I got word of the award.

In what is, I suppose, the "dubious distinction" department, I was also the target of the City Council of Terrace, who declared their city a "Rafe Mair free zone"! You'll remember that Terrace is on the west side of the mountains, and looked to the project as a terrific source of construction work. I sympathize with their annoyance, but those construction jobs would have been at the expense of their brothers in the United Fishermen and Allied Workers Union, who would have lost a huge sockeye run.

I cannot leave this chapter without remarking on the station from which I broadcast, CKNW in Vancouver. This was a tough case and the management was under tremendous pressure from the business community to shut me up. However, they never faltered for a moment.

When Tom Siddon first threatened his lawsuit in late 1995, I received a call from CKNW manager Rod Gunn, who said, "Rafe, I've never told you what to say or what not to say but I've got to tell you that I would be very upset to hear you utter the words, 'I apologize.'"

CKNW has built its reputation on standing behind its hosts. They were put under terrific pressure during the Vander Zalm years, during the Charlottetown Accord referendum and throughout the KCP matter. They stood behind me the whole way. I don't know of any other journalist in recent times who has been so far out on so many limbs with the hundred-percent support of ownership.

CHAPTER FIVE

The Health-Care System

In November 1979, following a stint as the minister unofficially responsible for constitutional affairs, I became minister of health for British Columbia, with a budget that was, in those days, a huge sum of money.

Bill Bennett had decided to create a new Ministry of Intergovernmental Affairs, and appointed Garde Gardom (who had been serving as attorney general) to the post. In the resulting cabinet shuffle I went to health and, though still an advisor to the premier on constitutional matters, was no longer in charge of them. My disappointment was keen, though I believe there were two reasons for the shuffle, one of which I was clearly responsible for myself.

First off, Bill Bennett may have wanted someone a tad more diplomatic than I was. Gardom is hale and bluff, and just the man to jolly people past the tough parts rather than dig the heels in, if that was what you wanted.

The second reason is a bit more complicated.

While serving as minister of environment, I chaired the Environment and Land Use Committee (ELUC) which, amongst other things, heard appeals from people who had been refused permission to take their land out of the Agriculture Land Reserve. This committee was a huge minefield for Socreds, for it seemed that each piece of land under appeal had had a Socred sign on it at election time. Later, getting land out of the reserve would prove just as big a problem for the NDP.

I happened to agree with the land freeze, but many of my colleagues did not—especially Don Phillips, who had led opposition to it when the NDP brought it in, and Jim Nielsen, who was my predecessor in the portfolio.

Early in 1979 I convinced Premier Bennett that we should find a better appeal system and he agreed. I seconded a very bright lawyer from the attorney general's department to help me work out a plan. Developing such a system was not as easy as it looked—as I soon found out.

In June of 1979 I presented my appeal model to cabinet, where the right-wingers dumped all over it with the argument that every citizen had a right to go to cabinet if dissatisfied with a land decision. I could not get them to explain why every citizen didn't therefore have a right to bring speeding tickets to cabinet. In the final analysis Bennett referred the decision to a weekend caucus retreat set for early November. I knew that my proposal would be a tough sell, especially with right-wingers who hated the land freeze with a passion, taking it to be a first large step toward communism.

In late October I went to the Far East and arrived back the day of the caucus meeting, which was held in a hotel in Delta. The caucus sat at a large round table and I was two seats to the right of Bill Bennett. To my right were Grace McCarthy and Brian Smith, later attorney general.

My proposed appeal process came to the table and then it happened. One after another, the right-wingers of the caucus went on the offensive, and the attacks seemed personal as much as philosophical. I was dog tired and badly jetlagged and I just didn't need this. I lost my cool—badly.

I leaned across Grace McCarthy and said to Brian Smith, in a loud voice, "You're a lawyer. Is there any fucking law in this country which requires me to take this shit?" Smith, who was not yet in cabinet but had high hopes, was stunned.

I said, "The answer is no, and I'm getting the hell out of here." Which I did, going back to my room. Over the next hour, five or more of my colleagues came to my door to ask me to cool off and come back to the meeting. To each of them I said, "Fuck off and mind your own goddamn business."

That evening, I was sure I was about to be fired from cabinet and couldn't have cared less. I went out to dinner with one of my constituency executives. When I got back there was a note under my door that said "Would the member for Kamloops [meaning me] consider having breakfast with the member for South Okanagan [Bill Bennett] tomorrow morning?"

The next morning I went up to the premier's room, fully expecting the sack yet curiously unrepentant. I felt that the far right wing of the party had been causing us a lot of difficulty, and if I was to go, I would make it clear why that happened—though I'm bound to say that at no time did I feel the slightest animosity toward Bennett himself.

The premier chuckled as we started breakfast and said something very close to this: "Rafe, you've really done it this time. I am creating a post of intergovernmental affairs and wanted you as the first minister. I can't do that now because most of your colleagues are so damned mad at you that, for the time being anyway, they wouldn't give you the cooperation you'd need. I am going to make a major cabinet overhaul and there will be a senior place for you. If Allan [Williams] doesn't want attorney general, it's yours. Your other options are health, finance or staying where you are." Allan Williams was one of the three Liberals who had defected to the Socred party in 1975; he had been serving as Bill Bennett's labour minister. He was in anticipation, and later in fact, a truly great attorney general.

I'd tripped and landed on my own sword insofar as constitutional affairs were concerned. The cabinet shuffle came about a week later, and I was to be in Premier Bennett's office at 5:30 P.M. to learn my fate. I arrived at about 5:15 (I am an annoyingly punctual person) and was greeted outside the door by *Province* reporter Malcolm Turnbull, evidently a bit the worse for wear, who asked me what post I was going to get. I told him that was up to the premier but that I sincerely hoped that in any event I would be present at Government House the following day for the swearing-in of the new cabinet.

I entered the premier's outer office and was surprised to see two of my colleagues there too. They were the premier's five o'clock and five-fifteen appointments, and we were later joined by a couple more. Grace McCarthy was with the premier at this time and, as we later learned, was kicking up a hell of a fuss about losing her deputy premiership and becoming minister of human resources.

It was long after six o'clock when I was ushered into the premier's private office. Bennett got up and asked, "Rafe, have you thought over your options?"

"Has Allan [who had preceded me into the premier's office] taken attorney general?"

"Yes," was the reply, whereupon I said I would very much like the health portfolio if it was available. Bennett smiled, walked around the table and shook my hand. "Congratulations, Mr. Minister of Health." It was all over in two minutes or less.

When I left, Turnbull again accosted me and asked what I had received. I told him to be at Government House the next day to find out. The next morning, before the swearing-in ceremony, there was a headline story in the *Province*, under Turnbull's byline, that Rafe Mair had had a big row with Premier Bennett the previous evening because he had been given the health ministry! I could not believe my eyes.

I then went to Government House. My wife Patti's father had just died in hospital (it had been expected) and she asked if I would leave right after the ceremony and take her to her mother's place. Of course I would. After the ceremony I excused myself from the champagne toasts and took my wife over to her mom's place, then went to my office to meet my new staff.

I received a message that *Sun* reporter Marjorie Nichols (still then in her legendary drinking days) was writing an article following up on Turnbull's of that morning. I went up to the press gallery and spoke to Marjorie, telling her that far from being mad at Bennett, I had received the ministry I wanted. Marjorie would have none of it. "You stormed out of Government House without taking the ceremonial glass of champagne which, as far as I'm concerned, confirms Turnbull's story." I told Marjorie about my father-in-law, but she had written her story and that was that.

Thirteen months later, when I was leaving the government to go into radio, I got a call from *Province* reporter Dave Todd, who I played squash with and had always regarded as a square shooter. "I just want to confirm a story I heard," he said. "I'm told that when you went back to your office after announcing your resignation you were so damned mad that you ripped your MINISTER OF HEALTH sign off the door."

"Dave," I said, "nothing could be further from the truth. When I went back to my office it was a very sad and even teary event. I asked my secretary, Leslie Tait, to get my sign for me as a souvenir, and already it is up on my wall with the door signs from my other three ministries."

I was horrified the next day to see in print that I had angrily ripped my nameplate off my door. Now I was angry, and I phoned the *Province*'s publisher, Paddy Sherman, and told him the story. For my pains I got a column from him the next day saying that he had checked Todd's story and accepted it. Had either Sherman or Todd called Leslie Tait, she would have told them what had happened.

The myth still persists that I hated the health ministry. I am often asked why I dislike the *Vancouver Sun* and *Province* so much—that is one of the reasons.

My initiation into the Ministry of Health was interesting, to say the least. A day or two after the swearing-in I officially opened a new wing at Lions Gate Hospital in North Vancouver (where, incidentally, I now live).

I couldn't help but chuckle. Here I had had nothing whatever to do with the opening, but I got my mug in the papers and on TV. I had to remind myself that later, my successor would be snipping *my* ribbons.

The highlight came when my official guide came to me in great distress. It turned out that the brand-new morgue had no customers at the moment, so they would be unable to show me the new instruments they had for slicing flesh off during autopsies. It was, of course, a bitter disappointment to me, but I managed to somehow contain my grief.

For four years I had watched my very able predecessor guide the health ministry into a very new era. Bob McClelland took his job very seriously indeed. He quit drinking—not that he had a problem, but because it seemed to be an appropriate gesture—and lost a cagillion pounds. He looked and acted like a health minister.

As I watched Bob work, what fascinated me was the high degree of politics in the system. Some of that was party politics—one would expect that, given the polarization in this province—but much of it was raw small-p politics, which permeated the entire health system. Of course it was in all the hospitals, large and small, but it was also in the medical profession, the nursing profession and, indeed, every faction of the system that was on the public teat, as well as all of those that *wanted* to be there—which is to say, everyone.

I learned something of the history of health care watching Bob. Leaving aside the development of Medicare (which had part of its roots in British Columbia, when W.A.C. Bennett, in 1954, increased the sales tax from three to five percent to pay hospital insurance out of the public purse), more recent history was at the root of many of our difficulties.

After the Second World War the entire country got caught up in an acute-care hospital building spree encouraged by Ottawa, which put up fifty cents of every dollar spent on construction. Sounded good, looked good and made superb politics. But just like the Terry Fox case, which I'll discuss in a bit, this had serious unintended consequences.

First off, this made people judge the efficacy of the system by the number of acute-care beds in their community. This was the litmus test for every budding politician: Will you or won't you promise us an extra five, ten, fifty or whatever number of hospital beds the administrator, egged on by the medical community, is demanding?

Second, it created an acute-care mentality where doctors and nurses turned up their noses at work in "lesser" facilities, because of the loss of prestige. The more prominent citizens wanted to be on the general hospital board, not the board of some crummy long-term-care facility.

Third, and perhaps most importantly, it siphoned off funds that should have gone elsewhere. More acute-care hospital beds makes sense in young communities, which have lots of kids, lots of skiing accidents and lots of people cutting off their toes with rotary lawn mowers. But with an aging population—which is what we have everywhere in Canada, but especially in B.C., where many Canadians come to retire—a lot of money must go into extended care (EC) and long-term care (LTC). We had to do a lot of catch-up. This was the dilemma Bob McClelland faced. Insofar as anyone could be successful at such a task, he was.

Before I go further, let me make it clear that acute care is the cornerstone of the system. But someday, hopefully, that will change and preventive medicine will be given the role and funding it deserves. There is a hell of a lot more to the system than acute care—for one thing, preventing people from needing acute care in the first place is pretty important.

What had happened by the mid-1970s was that older people who needed care, but not *acute* care, were still put into acute-care beds, because there was nowhere else to put them. This situation prevails to this day, despite the efforts of governments of all stripes. The catch-up required had just become too much—but more than that, every effort to improve LTC and EC was resisted by those who saw the influence of the acute-care hospital, and those who worked there, diminishing.

The emotions fanned by changes were incredible. The politics were brutal. When this issue first began to boil, I was MLA for Kamloops, which has a fair-sized general hospital, Royal Inland. It was the focal point for all health care. When I was on Kamloops City Council in 1973–74, I heard nothing about mental health, the Ponderosa Lodge long-term-care facility or preventive health care. Whenever the subject of health came up, as it often did, Royal Inland got all the attention.

When I became health minister, a new acute-care hospital called Eagle Ridge was being opened to serve, in part, the area then serviced by Royal Columbian Hospital in New Westminster. The new hospital had been built after exhaustive studies showed that the population of the area was generally getting older and that Eagle Ridge, in the new suburbs, would bring acute care closer to new bedroom communities. This meant that something had to give: if we were to shift responsibilities, we had to do something with the facilities that had hitherto borne them.

Part of the plan was to convert St. Mary's, an old Catholic hospital in New Westminster, from acute care to extended care, to look after the older community. Well, when this was announced it hit the fan in a very big way. When I was sworn in as health minister, I had rather wondered why Bob had such a look of relief as he moved to a new portfolio. I was soon to learn.

Enormous petitions appeared everywhere I moved. I'm sure that more people signed these petitions than have ever lived in British Columbia since Sir Francis Drake discovered it. I was picketed wherever I went. Priests railed at me from the pulpit, to the point that I felt obliged to phone Archbishop Jim Carney and ask him to call them off. And have you ever had a mother superior as your sworn enemy? It's no fun, I can tell you.

Why all this fuss?

It was purely and simply emotional. Mothers screamed at me that their babies had been born in St. Mary's, that they themselves had been born in St. Mary's, and that their mother and grandmother had been born in St Mary's. Angry citizens brought my cabinet colleague Bill Vander Zalm, a Roman Catholic, into the fray and to his credit, he told all who would listen that the health minister was not anti-Catholic but was simply implementing government policy.

Around the world, governments were reducing acute-care beds and building LTC and EC facilities—but in B.C., entire governments were at risk if they removed so much as one acute-care bed, much less a hospital.

Shortly after being sworn in as health minister, I was off to the briefing books. I was staggered by the size and reach of the ministry. While departments had been shuffled in the past—hospitals to a separate ministry and then back, various programs and people to human resources, and so on— the ministry was, and remains, huge. It's too big for one minister, yet is so intertwined that it can't logically seem to be split up. Two or more ministries would lead to more rivalries for shares of the budget, and there are plenty of those already. Two ministers would simply cause bloody sibling rivalry in cabinet. It's an administrative nightmare.

Within the ministry are a number of warring factions caused by the most basic of conflicts of interest—that of the doctors. They are the principal personal payees of the ministry, yet they get to say who does or does not qualify to also be paid by the ministry.

It's understandable and appropriate that they certify medical practitioners, but it goes far further than that. For decades, to give one example, chiropractors were considered quacks. Even after belated and grudging recognition by the legislature, they were not permitted to call themselves "doctors" even though they had received doctors' degrees from accredited schools of chiropractic medicine. This was so as not to confuse the public, although it didn't seem to matter that veterinarians could use the term "doctor." To this day, chiropractors, as well as such other health practitioners as naturopaths and physiotherapists, are not able to participate fully in Medicare, but are subject to "user pay" surcharges.

How illogical can you be? You start by recognizing people as healers, not quacks. In so doing, you acknowledge that some health skills very much include containing pain and making life more enjoyable. Yet you say that one form of healer—the medical doctor—will be paid in full, while the rest will get partial payment.

The issue of medical payments has haunted every health ministry since Medicare came in, because Medicare created an indissoluble mix of socialism and free enterprise. A socialist ideal is the availability of health care to everyone equally. A free-enterprise ideal is the right to be paid for whatever you do, and to do as much work as you please. Socialism spreads the services around the province, while free enterprise gives the doctors the right to practise wherever they please.

The result has brought near-, if not actual, chaos. Rural British Columbia is ill served by doctors while the more salubrious climes of Vancouver, Victoria and the Okanagan have too many doctors. Too many doctors means that patients will be over-referred (though doctors deny this), while two few means that patients must fly at their own expense to Vancouver or other urban centres. It also means that the province must give rural doctors extra money.

The day will come when doctors are put on salary. It's inevitable and to some degree they've asked for it. They have been most reluctant to deal with the question of the urban–rural imbalance, except to have conferences to discuss it. And in a key move, in the mid-1980s B.C. doctors accepted pension contributions from the government, an act that started them on the slippery slope to becoming civil servants.

When a salary system is instituted, B.C. will recall Britain of the 1940s and Saskatchewan of the 1960s, when doctors threatened to leave *en masse.* But they won't, and the world will go on. As a free enterpriser I should be unhappy at this possibility, but I don't see any alternative to keeping health costs within the means of the taxpayer.

My first big task as health minister was to undo the Heroin Treatment Program brought in by my predecessor. The enabling legislation, the Heroin Treatment Act, permitted the state to seize heroin addicts and keep them away from drugs long enough to cure them—the cure was cold turkey and involuntary.

It sounds awful in today's context, but then it seemed a responsible thing to do. I spoke in favour of the bill in the House, and looking back I can't imagine why. I yielded to three factors: our system's need for party unanimity, the inherent nannyism that takes over when politicians reach high office, and plain ignorance. When I was appointed health minister, Premier Bill Bennett made it clear that he wanted us out of this program with the least possible embarrassment to the government or the past minister. Since as health minister I was now in the mess personally, I was not interested in any embarrassment either.

The government had decided to pass legislation implementing the Heroin Treatment Program after recommendations from the Alcohol and Drug Commission. A condition of getting rid of the program, then, was the neutering—or even dismissal—of the Commission. This had to be dealt with before anything could be done.

Dealing with the Alcohol and Drug Commission was challenging, to say the least. It was composed of three men, very conservative, who were getting on a bit and simply couldn't understand any pussyfooting where drugs were concerned. (Of course, it was different if the drug was Scotch whisky or tobacco. Good men, but not terribly up to date.)

Two of the commissioners went easily. One quickly retired when the writing was clearly on the wall and another, a retired provincial court judge seconded from health by the attorney general, was simply transferred back whence he came. That left a retired army officer named Bert Hoskin—a very fine gentleman who had served his province and his country well in peace and war, but who had the misfortune to be on the other side of a politician very determined to have his way.

I was lucky. At the time there was a case in which the Heroin Treatment Program had been involved that raised constitutional and Charter of Rights arguments before the Court of Appeal. I told the press that I thought the government would lose. (I was wrong, as it turned out.) I also opined that the government might well have to seriously review this policy.

Mr. Hoskin wrote me a letter that stated, in effect, that if he and the program did not have the confidence of the health minister, he *might* feel constrained to resign. I promptly answered and, after appropriately thanking him for all his services, accepted his resignation. I then made the letter available to the media.

Not the high-water mark of my career. I should have done it more tactfully. In my own defence I can only say that not only did I want to tube the program, I didn't want anyone around who could oppose its passing in any official capacity.

Around the same time I visited Brannan Lake Facility—which was once a reform school and looked like it—and saw clearly that confining (mostly) young men to jail and forcibly keeping them away from drugs was no way to cure the drug problem in the province.

I also visited Britain because, it was said, they had a super program of free heroin for addicts. This British experiment was bruited about in the mainstream Canadian press as being marvelously modern and an almost perfect way to permit heroin addicts to be good citizens. I met with the director of the program in London and he chuckled at my questions—he'd heard them all before, but no one had truthfully reported his answers.

The program, if not a catastrophe, was certainly a failure. Addicts became more and more dependent on more and more heroin, and if the doctor—who, after all, had to pay attention to his patient's general health—refused to increase the dose, the addict went back to the street. Worse than this, the psychological effect of the government approving the use of heroin—which was the only inference young people could draw—was disastrous. Use of heroin and other "hard" drugs amongst the young increased dramatically, so that instead of the addict population diminishing in size, it was getting a dramatic boost from the very program that was supposed to solve the problem.

B.C.'s Heroin Treatment Program went out with barely a whimper. There was no argument from the NDP opposition, who had quite rightly opposed the idea in the first place. The Socreds, down even to the most right-wing backbencher, were glad to see the end of it. I had, if I do say so myself, carried out the premier's mandate brilliantly.

Probably the most interesting (and annoying) part of being health minister is dealing with the federal government and the federal health minister. In my time it was Monique Begin, who, during the 1980 federal election, typified Ottawa's superiority complex by accusing B.C. of using federal transfer payments (funds earmarked for use in the province's health-care system) to build highways. This was a blatant lie, but one we faced for months thereafter from senior federal health officials.

Constitutionally, the federal government's role in health care is minimal and confined to status Indians, the armed forces and the Territories. Through the power of the purse, however, they have enormous influence, and a great deal of our time and effort in British Columbia was spent fighting off the feds.

The theory behind Ottawa's involvement is that all Canadians, no matter where they live, must have the same or nearly the same health care. It's rather like the National Building Code, which takes into account cold weather (which is unknown in much of B.C.) while overlooking wet weather (which many parts of this province have in abundance). To Ottawa, every region is cold in the winter, speaks French in great numbers and needs precisely the same health care. Well, let me tell you of two areas in which that theory very quickly breaks down.

British Columbia has an old population, which is swelled daily by people coming here to retire. This means that there must be special consideration for extended care and long-term care in this province. This cut no ice with Ottawa, whose one-size-fits-all approach to every province except Quebec and, in election years, Ontario, just doesn't work.

The other area is Native health care. It is here that the federal government's assertion that they know best is blown to the moon. Health care on Native reserves has traditionally been appalling, to the point that as health minister I was asked to extend provincial health programs to several reserves. I offered to do just that, but was huffily refused by the feds. They didn't want to be shown up and they didn't want to give up control.

I served in the health ministry for thirteen months—not, I quite agree, enough time to get a complete grasp of health-care issues. But let me say this in defence of my constant role since as critic. No one involved in a system is sufficiently detached to give anything near an unbiased opinion. Those deeply involved in the system—doctors, nurses, administrators, related civil servants—are biased as hell, no matter how hard they try to be impartial. And there is nothing wrong with this: I offer no criticism of motives, because we all tend to see issues as they affect us personally, no matter how much we may bleat about the problems of others.

Those who *want* to get into the system, or more deeply into the system— such as alternative health-care providers, chiropractors, naturopaths, physiotherapists, herbalists, acupuncturists and the like—are also biased in their own favour. Even professional commentators, university professors, and health consultants have an axe to grind, for their value on the conference circuit—very rewarding—will depend not nearly so much on what they say, but rather how they say it.

What has developed in Canada is a huge health "turf," which depends almost entirely for its nourishment on the government sprinkler. Those getting their regular dousings know that if the turf is expanded, they will get less. Governments, on the theory that the devil you know is better than the one you don't, are also very leery about expanding the turf, for fear that they will have to raise taxes. The health-care system is an ongoing Battle of the Bulge that will never end.

The trouble is that *everything* makes sense—but there is not enough money to implement everything, at least not without concessions from those whose noses are already firmly in the trough.

When the doctors say that they alone have the training to give you a new heart, of course they're right. When the nurses say that they can expand their role, and save doctors' fees, of course they're right. When chiropractors say that they make people better (which is, after all, supposed to be the object of any health-related exercise), of course they're right. When herbalists point to the tremendous public support they get, which suggests that people benefit from their age-old medicines, of course they're right. When practitioners of Eastern medicine challenge the monopoly on wisdom claimed by Western medicine, of course they're right—as are practitioners of Western medicine when they say that by their standards of proof, Eastern medicine hasn't proven itself. And on and on it goes. Everyone is right. And wrong.

But the key to untangling this horrendous briar patch, which every day becomes more tangled, lies in one simple proposition: governments, and ministers of finance especially, must learn how to put money into programs that will have huge—but *unquantifiable*—benefits. The operative word is unquantifiable. Currently, treasury boards simply will not put money into projects unless they are proven to be cost-effective—unless, of course, they are highly political projects that involve an important ethnic community, and so on and so on.

We all claim, rightly, that we have a sickness, not a wellness, system. We're mechanics in the old-style garage waiting for the breakdowns to come in. It's not in our interest to prevent breakdowns, though ethically we'll always do our best. Incentive is a very strong prod. That's why we work: it brings in money. If our goal is defined as repairing broken things, no matter how ethical we are, our efforts will be concentrated on fixing, not preventing.

Let me tell you a story to illustrate this point—a story that had a lot to do with me leaving government. As health minister, I became very concerned about the huge number of unwanted pregnancies in my province and their cost in monetary terms, to say nothing of their enormous psychological and social toll. I had heard of a sex-education program in Minneapolis–St. Paul, so I went and had a look at it.

We all remember what school counselling was all about. No one wanted anyone to know that they had a serious question about sex, pregnancy and birth control. Peer stigma was a substantial disincentive to getting timely advice. Counselling programs just weren't working, as the number of young pregnant women demonstrated.

The Minneapolis–St. Paul program, in contrast, was simple and effective. They would send teams of counsellors into schools, each member of the team having a specialty. There would be a consumer expert, an employment strategist and so on, including an expert on sexual concerns of young people. This meant that young people would not attract any stigma by seeing this group of counsellors. Thirteen-year-old Mary might be getting advice on what educational path she should follow, or on how to buy something, or on how to deal with her raging hormones. No one would know except the individual counsellor Mary spoke with. It seemed like a hell of a good idea to me.

I have no idea whether or not the program still exists, or how it all worked out. But at the time I felt that with the number of abortions we were paying for, surely we should look at it.

I put a proposal to the Treasury Board for two pilot projects, one urban, one rural, to test what I had seen on British Columbia youngsters. The cost would be, for a year, about $220,000 out of a $2-billion budget. I was refused by the minister of finance and Treasury Board, because I couldn't prove the benefits! How many unwanted pregnancies would you have to eliminate to save $220,000?

Governments, like the entire system, are unable and, I submit, quite unwilling to break out of the quantifiable-benefits mold. It's a different world out there from that in which most of the decision makers grew up. People want to keep their health in the first place, not be cured. There is a reason there are diet books offering advice ranging from "eat no meat" to "eat nothing else but meat." People are not satisfied with the advice they're getting, and since most dietitian services are not covered by Medicare, people opt for do-it-yourself.

It sure wasn't the medical profession that interested people in fitness. Doctors who know how to fix the engine seem to know almost nothing about the fuel that is best for the engine, or about how to keep it running well.

There are, of course, prominent exceptions. Dr. Doug Clement of Vancouver, an Olympic athlete of yesteryear, has made enormous contributions in this field, as has his wife, a health-food restaurant owner. But if you go into the average doctor's office, you'll see a life-insurance poster telling you how much you should weigh (no one ever does weigh what they're supposed to), some preachy pamphlets about smoking, and a petition for you to sign complaining about the government's treatment of doctors.

(Lest you think this is just an exercise in doctor bashing, it's not. When I discuss mental health, I'll tell you how I owe my life to my doctor—who, contrary to medical custom, knew something about depression.)

You'd think that the wishes of the people would force governments to change their minds, but they haven't. The system is entrenched and change brings flak from that system, leading to possible electoral grief. Pogo was right: "We have met the enemy and he is us." We the consumers have not translated our private actions into public demands. We love the idea of preventive medicine, but we permit politicians to merely pay solemn lip service to it while continuing the old approach.

The health-care system has become politicized to the point where slogans easily make up for reasoned debate. When some acute-care beds are closed and doctors, nurses and administrators raise spectres of death in the streets, and we sign their petitions. We are so easily seduced by any story that we've become moral cowards.

Let me give you another example.

Terry Fox, who did that magnificent run across Canada that only ended in Thunder Bay because of recurrence of his cancer, is a genuine Canadian hero. Quite rightly, we honour his name and memory at every turn. He was a courageous class act who stands as an everlasting example to all, but to the young especially, of what one can do with courage.

However, there were unintended consequences of Terry's fantastic effort. This is hard to say, because the last thing I want to do is offend any of Terry's friends or family. But since his awareness-boosting run, a disproportionate amount of money and effort has gone into cancer research and treatment— to the detriment of other equally worthy areas, especially mental health. You may remember that after Terry's death, the TV networks did a huge marathon that raised some $20–25 million. A superb effort. But do we really want *all* that money to go to cancer research? Are our priorities such that virtually all attention must be turned to cancer?

Of course! many say. That's precisely the scourge we must concentrate all our efforts on, and research is the key.

I respectfully disagree.

Of course, we must do as much cancer research as is reasonable, bearing in mind all our priorities. But analyze the problem a bit. When you look at the number of cancers we treat in this country, how many of them might be curable if we find a cure, how many are preventable and, I hate to say it, how many simply finish off a very old person?

Looking at the preventable cancers, we immediately turn to smoking, don't we? This is a huge chunk of the problem and it is completely preventable. No cure needed. And what about skin cancers, many of which are preventable by the excellent sunblocks on the market? And how about the stomach cancers, preventable by better diet?

Much current research says that breast cancer amongst women would be reduced to levels similar to cases amongst men—if women would stop wearing brassieres. How much heartache and death the elimination of this terrible scourge would bring—and just by a change in style. No medical funds required!

None of this means that we shouldn't make all reasonable effort to find a cure for cancer, but how can we justify putting hundreds of millions of dollars into research for a cancer cure and at the same time denying a doctor a proper fee for taking the time to diagnose mental illness, which not only affects the patient but all those around him? As you will see, I know something about the impact of mental health problems, and about the number of mentally ill people who remain undiagnosed because they are afraid to see a doctor—a doctor who may well know nothing about mental health, and who is discouraged from learning by the absence of proper fees for this service.

If we as a public think the present health-care system ought to be not only changed but possibly even discarded in favour of a better one; if we feel that the government's priorities are out of whack; if we truly want a *wellness* not a *sickness* system—we must tell our politicians that. But we must do more than just that. We must also tell them that it is not necessary for our tax dollars go to provable cures only—that we are prepared to pay, within reason, for any reasonable effort to reduce sickness.

Otherwise we will simply improve our ability to cure, at the expense of preventing the need for cures in the first place.

One of the enduring hangovers from the acute-care bed binge of the 1950s, 1960s and 1970s was a shortage of facilities for "elective" surgery. You might think that lots of acute-care beds would mean lots of operating capability, but the reverse happened. Because so many beds were occupied by non-acute-care patients who had nowhere else to go, the system failed. Nurses and other support staff needed for operating rooms were tied up with the elderly and other extended-care patients. We had the irony of money going into acute-care hospitals not being used for acute-care purposes, thus clogging the system. While ministries of health busted their asses to take care of burgeoning waiting lists for "elective" surgery, the situation just got worse. (I should point out that there is nothing "elective" about an operation to a lung-cancer patient, but as often as not he's on a waiting list anyway.)

Ministers threw money at the problem, but it was never enough. The problem was that an aging population needing LTC and EC grew so fast that it was all one could do to keep the dike from bursting.

There will always be waiting lists. There's not enough money in taxpayers' pockets to get rid of them. But there is a way to alleviate them, pronto: Permit surgeons to do some private surgery.

Gawdamighty, does *that* get left-wing hackles a-twitching! The politics of envy smothers all other considerations, and the bogeymen are trotted out one by one. The poor will get lousy surgeons while the rich will get all the good ones! The taxpayer won't pay nearly so much attention to public medicine because the rich will corner the market on resources! (This is indeed a concern, but only if we let it be.) And look what has happened in Britain!

Well, it might be instructive to see what indeed has happened in the U.K., and to do so it's necessary to look at history. Britain didn't have the widespread private insurance schemes we had in the 1940s and 1950s. They were coming out of a brutal war, which required hundreds of thousands of homes to be built in a time of not just restraint, but austerity. Building and upgrading hospitals was second to fixing bombed-out houses and providing dwellings for returning servicemen. British hospitals had become, by 1950, obsolete by *First* World War standards.

Britain launched its National Health Service in poverty, not affluence as we launched Medicare here. Not only that, they got off on the wrong foot by making it more attractive to visit the doctor than take an Aspirin, and they had a far wider range of services (free drugs and eyeglasses, for example) than we do.

I've examined the British system and its two-tiered aspect, and by and large it works well. Surgeons can, if they wish, do nothing but private work—but if they do, they collect nothing from NHS. If they do a majority of work on NHS, they can do a minority of private work, for which they charge the patients directly and privately.

What has happened is that private health insurance has made a comeback. Margaret Thatcher was on private insurance. So was John Major. So is Tony Blair and most of his cabinet and backbench. So are most union members and many white-collar workers. This is because they want to avoid lineups by paying privately, and they are are indemnified against those private fees. The result is that elective surgery lists are greatly shortened.

The complaint that this reduces the flow of money into the public system and thus brings back the lineups has enough validity to cause concern. However, it's not the theory or philosophy of a private parallel scheme that is the problem. It's the lack of a *cohesive* scheme, in which the government ensures that the public system is properly funded. Implementing that cohesion takes discipline and I would be the first to concede that if the will isn't there, a two-tiered system will simply soak the rich and provide a poorer service to the less fortunate.

But our health-care system is under terrific attack. Surely it's not beyond the ability of the voters, hence the government, to decide to keep the present budgets but lessen the patient load by permitting private operations—thus providing better service to both those who can pay privately *and* those who can't.

There already is a private system. You don't for a moment think that doctors line up for "elective" or any other kind of surgery, do you? Or politicians? (In Ottawa, doctors and senior bureaucrats have their own system, complete with their own publicly financed hospital!) Or influential members of the community? Or talk-show hosts, for that matter?

Moreover, thousands of people and millions of dollars go "below the line" (that is, into the U.S.) every year. There are clinics in Bellingham, Washington, that cater almost exclusively to B.C. residents who want to avoid waiting lists. I've no doubt that this situation exists across the length of the Canada–U.S. border.

A two-tiered system may be a lousy idea but we'll only know that when we truly examine it in all its aspects. Instead of doing so, we get tied up in political squabbles.

Let me close with some thoughts about mental health.

Humans have never been able to come to grips with mental illness. In earlier times we treated the mentally ill as devils or witches to be burned at the stake or hanged. Latterly we have, always way behind what scientists now know, treated them as "crazy": "half a brick short of a load," candidates for the "funny farm."

We don't call the disabled "cripples" any more (thank God), we don't mock people with MS or Parkinson's disease, and we don't send cancer patients to the lump remover. Yet we constantly make jokes at the expense of mentally ill people. A disc jockey on my station, not long ago, told a joke asserting that his school was so small that the debating team was one schizophrenic. Ha, ha, ha! No matter that schizophrenia does not cause a "split personality." Forget that it is a very serious and widespread mental condition that strikes the homes of thousands of Canadian families. The joke was a great one-liner and great fun, and that's all that counts.

We simply cannot accept that mental illness is just that, an illness. We're afraid. Centuries of inbred fears of "lunatics" attacking us and our loved ones are hard to eradicate.

I was diagnosed with mental illness over ten years ago. I used to be a mental patient; now I've been updated by modern jargon to a "consumer." I'm clinically depressed. And the story of my diagnosis is both humorous and serious.

Like everyone, I've had my share of grief along with my incredible good luck. A daughter killed. A marriage failed through my own fault, leaving a devastated spouse and a devastated conscience. Unofficial bankruptcy, with the stresses of paying back enormous sums. A very stressful profession. You name it.

In early 1988 I detected a pain in my right side. I panicked because my dad had died of liver failure and I concluded, helped by the *Columbia Medical Encyclopedia*, that I was dying of liver cancer. There could be no doubt.

I called my doctor, Mel Bruchet of North Vancouver, and insisted that I see him that day—that I would, if necessary, picket his office until he saw me. It's hard to understand why a particularly prompt visit would be of much help if I was truly dying of liver cancer, but I demanded immediate attention.

Mel examined me immediately—and said I had gallstones. I accused him of lying to me as part of a medical conspiracy to keep the truth from patients. (I didn't know him all that well then. I would get to know him much better in the next ten years.)

He sent me to ultrasound, a sort of tub where a technician runs a microphone-like device over you. You can see your innards on a screen.

Every time the technician ran this instrument over my right side, she frowned.

"I've got it, right?" I cried. "It's liver cancer, isn't it?"

She called the specialist over. He looked at the pictures of my right side and frowned too. "Tell me, doctor," I said, "I can take it. It's liver cancer, right?"

The doctor asked me to lie on my left side, gave me a karate chop at the point in question and looked back up on the screen. "Once more," he said. *Whomp!*

He looked on the screen then told me that I had had a gallstone lodged in the entrance to the gall bladder, and that he had just dislodged it. The pain should disappear.

"You mean," I said, "that all I really needed was a fucking chiropractor?"

It wasn't really funny. I went back to Mel and when he told me that my gallstones did not yet need an operation, I again accused him of lying to me. I had liver cancer and that was that.

Mel looked at me and said, "Rafe, tell me about your daughter's death."

"What the hell has that to do with liver cancer?"

"Please, Rafe, just answer my questions."

We soon got to my divorce, monetary problems and the like, and within five minutes I was in floods of tears that I'd never previously experienced. At least, not since my daughter Shawn had died.

Mel put his arm on my shoulder and let me cry.

Then he told me that he would normally ask about ten questions in this sort of situation but that he'd heard enough. He would reschedule me for another visit and some more questions, but he was satisfied that I was clinically depressed. A visit a few days later confirmed his diagnosis.

What the hell is all this about? I thought. I remembered my childhood and my British-style upbringing. Stick your chin out. Show no fear or hurt. Read some Sir Henry Newbolt or Rudyard Kipling. Remember your forefathers. Take a cold shower. Perhaps listen to a few bars of "Land of Hope and Glory." Show character.

I asked Mel, with great trepidation, what this all meant.

This was 1988 and research on the question of chemical imbalance being at the root of many depressions was only in its infancy. Mel explained to me about serotonin and how this chemical, produced by the body naturally, works on receptors in the brain. If the body stops producing the required amounts, that can lead directly to depression. The everyday issues we have stored up and coped with then become, often quite suddenly, insurmountable problems. Mel assured me that this was not a character flaw and that hundreds of thousands, if not millions, of Canadians suffered from undiagnosed depression.

He told me about the medicine (not drugs, damn it!) that supplemented or replaced the serotonin. And, he said, we will have to experiment until we find what is right.

I was lucky. The first medicine did the trick, and within three weeks of seeing Mel I was right as rain. I hadn't felt so good in years.

After the first visit with Mel, I took my wife Patti to dinner and told her what it was all about, that I would be taking medicine and was going to get well. Her reply was, "You pop your pills, I'll drink my wine."

This is not an atypical attitude, unfortunately. Such are our prejudices toward mental problems that often a mate will say, "I get depressed too, and I don't run off to my doctor and take 'drugs'!" Lack of encouragement by loved ones and friends is often the biggest problem the depressed must deal with. It takes a lot to go to your doctor and say, "I think I'm mentally ill," especially if those fears are compounded by a mate who, far from being sympathetic, is yielding to deep-seated prejudices and fear of being embarrassed by having a "loony" spouse.

Of course, we're all depressed when we're bereaved, or at times of great stress. And not all depression by any means is a result of chemical imbalance. But a lot of it is.

Clinical depression is deep and ongoing. It takes many forms. It's disabling and utterly irrational. People naturally tell you that the overpowering anxiety you have (if, as in my case, depression manifests itself in severe anxiety) is irrational. And it is. The trouble is that irrationality is part of depression. You simply cannot separate the pepper from the fly shit. Common sense, evidence and logic mean nothing. Serious depression is not rational.

The young and the old often will listen but won't hear. Two examples.

I was interviewed a few years ago by a journalism student from Ryerson in Toronto, because I had attained some notoriety over my stand on the Charlottetown Accord. During interviews with others about me she had been told that I was "hooked on Prozac." (I have never made a secret of my illness.) She asked me if that was true. I explained to her that I wasn't hooked on anything and that my medicine, while similar to Prozac, was actually called Elavil.

She wrote the story reporting that she had been told I was "hooked on Prozac." She was right in that she had been told this, and I don't quarrel with her reporting it. What is so troubling is that this sort of statement is so common.

Not that long ago I spoke to a dear friend, who alas I don't see too often because he lives in another country. He was concerned about my health, so I took him aside and carefully explained what clinical depression was and that, because I was being properly treated, I was fine. He showed a very lively interest in the matter and was clearly much better informed and extremely understanding.

A couple of days later he bade me farewell at the airport and said, "Look after your health, and I hope you can get off those tranquilizers."

I don't criticize the young journalist or my old friend. Until 1988 that's exactly how I viewed the matter. But the fact is that I'm not "on" tranquilizers or any sort of drug. I'm now taking a medicine called Serzone, which does for my mental health precisely what Glucophage does for my blood sugar (I'm also diabetic). It makes up for something my body no longer produces in sufficient quantity.

Some years ago I decided, quite spontaneously, to make my illness public to 150,000 of my radio listeners. My guest that day was a wonderful lady named Dr. Teresa Hogarth. She is a general practitioner who has a special interest in depression and has two life goals: to get depressed people to seek help and to get family doctors to understand what depression is all about.

We took calls to Dr. Hogarth and the board lit up like a Christmas tree. There was pleading in the voices on the phone lines, and shame coupled with fear of exposure. You couldn't help but be deeply touched and I found myself telling the audience that I was clinically depressed and had been under treatment for many years.

Dr. Hogarth and I do shows together frequently and we did a truly memorable one in December 1997. My station, knowing of my condition, has been very understanding and supportive throughout. The program director suggested that for this program the station would make available a bank of eight phone lines with the object of hearing people out and directing them, if appropriate, to help. These calls were off-air and anonymous.

During the two hours the lines were open—and bear in mind that every call took time, as people explained their symptoms—they took 241 calls! Whenever a call was finished a new call light came on immediately. We could easily have gone on all day.

It was an eye-opener to all. Even the caregivers who always knew that the problem was widespread were flabbergasted. The problem is *immense.* Virtually none of the callers had had any encouragement from loved ones and friends (in fact, usually quite the opposite) and they were frightened silly to expose themselves as "crazy."

It's all so illogical. Why should I be unashamed and quite public about taking an insulin substitute because I'm diabetic and my pancreas doesn't produce the stuff—yet ashamed to take a serotonin substitute because my body doesn't produce enough of that chemical?

In November 1997 I had quite a lesson. I had become quite complacent about my depression because the Elavil (my first medication) I took worked. I'd really quite forgotten that I was constantly under treatment.

Then Mel Bruchet and I talked of changing medicines to a new-generation model, mainly because in a side effect of Elavil I was plagued by terrible dreams most nights. I had interviewed a doctor about a new product and sought Mel's advice.

He explained that we would be taking a chance—maybe the new stuff, Serzone, wouldn't work. Moreover, he told me, I would have to go right off Elavil for two weeks before I could, very slowly, start the new medicine.

I decided to make the change. It was a good time to do so because my new wife Wendy and I were off to London and Paris for three weeks so I would be under no special pressures.

When we arrived in London I had been off medication for about a week. It was very warm for November, about eighteen degrees Celsius. But I couldn't stop shivering, even though I had on a heavy jacket. On our way to Covent Garden for the Sunday concert I stopped in at a Tie Rack and bought a scarf. I still shivered. After the concert I went into an Irish-sweater shop and bought a heavy sweater. I still couldn't stop shivering.

When we got back to our room I took off my clothes. All of them, including the sweater, were soaking wet from perspiration. Still I couldn't stop shivering.

As the days passed, it got worse. Then I started breaking into crying jags over nothing. Little things that would normally be no more irritating than provoking a *damn it!* brought me into near hysterics. I especially remember one time in Paris, when it took Wendy an hour to stop me crying, over what I don't know.

The Serzone did work well, as it turned out; I'm now well again and I sleep well. But the gap, during which I was taking no medication, took me back nearly ten years. If I needed reminding of the horrors of clinical depression, I'll not need it again. I can truly say that I don't know what I might have done without my darling Wendy, who, in addition to being my loving mate, is the most caring person I've ever met.

I met Wendy in the summer of 1993. Patti and I had not yet officially separated, but we had come to the end. She had met a ship's doctor on a cruise, and went to Prince Edward Island to "find herself"—and, of course, the ship's doctor. There was no bitterness on my part, just the gut-wrenching fear that I would become a lonely old man. Patti was fifteen years younger than I was, and I knew that she could easily be "distracted" again.

I have often led tours as the "personality" host, and had a three-week jaunt to England and Ireland scheduled for late August. Because of scheduling conflicts with CKNW that would force me to return from the tour early, I ended up taking my stepson, Steve, to northwest Scotland *before* the tour, where we fished for trout and I thought a great deal about my domestic predicament.

As Steve and I prepared to meet up with the tour in London, I told him that I'd decided to end my marriage to Patti. I was sixty-two, and it would be best, I reasoned, to get used to being alone then, rather than wait until I was sixty-five or seventy. Steve was understanding. The very last thing on my mind at that point was any involvement of the heart, however minor.

In the group of tour clients I met at Heathrow Airport was a tall, beautiful lady of fifty. Wendy was a nurse from Abbotsford, B.C. By the time the bus reached the hotel, I knew that there was "trouble" ahead. By the end of that first day, Wendy and I had shared with each other the stories of our respective crumbled marriages.

This story could go on forever, but suffice it to say that before the tour was out I had asked Wendy to marry me, and she had accepted. I returned to B.C. before the tour was out, and while she was still in the U.K. we spoke on the phone several times a day, running up a long-distance bill of over $300.

We had agreed to meet at a restaurant near Abbotsford on the evening she returned. I greeted her with two bottles of champagne and eleven red roses. One had somehow broken—that sort of thing happens to me all the time—and we now celebrate the anniversary of the wonderful day with champagne and, yes, eleven red roses! Though I had convinced myself that by the time she arrived she would have changed her mind, she hadn't and we were married the following July 29. Wendy is the most wonderful thing to ever happen to me.

I have very little use for awards in my business. Most of the time you get them when a jury of people who already know that they themselves won't get it decide it's your turn. However I'm very proud of two awards I received in 1997.

I was named media personality of the year by both the Canadian Mental Health Association (I won jointly with Pamela Wallin) and the B.C. Branch of the Canadian Mental Health Association.

All efforts on behalf of any who need help, for whatever reason, are most praiseworthy indeed. But the Canadian Mental Health Association spends its entire existence farting against thunder. It hasn't the cachet of heart and stroke diseases, or cancer, or even diabetes. It's a disease that no one wants to talk about.

Mental health generally and depression particularly are huge medical problems, and the only thing that pisses me off more than the general prevailing attitude of so many Canadians is that it took *me* so long to understand. The light went on only after I was *forced* to understand by my own condition.

The health care system in Canada?

A noble experiment going wrong. Badly wrong.

Wrong priorities, combined with ossified thinking, overlaid with raw emotion and charged politics. It's a system that has never even defined what the "health care" is that we've decided to pay for out of the public purse.

It's a system fraught with absurdities. Have a blemish that might conceivably, one time in ten thousand, be cancerous? Off it comes, fully paid for. Got a child with an unsightly facial birthmark that is virtually guaranteed to have psychological and social side effects? You're on your own.

The good in the system is that it is and always has been based upon human charity in the proper meaning of that word. It is philosophically pure. The bad is that the occupiers of turf, not the consumers, run the show, so that costs have escalated perhaps beyond redemption. The system pretends to be market-driven, but it is really an organization of monopolies, whether of pharmaceutical products or medical services.

We've sort of muddled our way through for the past fifty years. Economics combined with consumer anger must force that to change—or the system will perish.

CHAPTER SIX

Radio Free Rafe

Isn't it amazing how many things happen by the sheerest of chance?

I have always wondered whether or not there is a hidden hand guiding us and I've especially wondered this after two events—meeting my wife Wendy, and going into radio.

In August 1980, Premier Bennett asked all members of his caucus to let him know if they would be seeking re-election in the next campaign. Though we had just been returned to office in May 1979, it was with a slim majority of four seats and, as the premier said, "We're only a heart attack or two away from an election and I want us to be ready."

In the fall I told the premier that I would not be seeking re-election. I'd had some super portfolios and I knew that I would be staying in health, scaling down the administration after the campaign. (This was successfully and courageously undertaken by my successor, Jim Nielsen.) But what next? I was ambitious for only one other job and that was premier. And although I had repaired some fences, I was still out of sorts with many of my colleagues. Anyway, Bill Bennett was three months younger than I, so that mildly held ambition was pretty remote.

I did not want to stay in politics just to be in politics, and I knew that I would soon tire of simply running a ministry. I'd done a lot of things, including many reforms in consumer and corporate affairs. I liked what I had done and enjoyed most of what I was currently doing, but as I approached fifty it was time to fill up the money pot, which had been drastically reduced by divorce. Furthermore, federal politics was not, for me, an option.

Bill Bennett expressed sorrow at my decision not to run again and asked me to make it known, quietly, to my constituency organization, so they could canvass for my successor.

In mid-December, the next turning point in a life that had already had its share of turns occurred when I appeared on the Jack Webster morning TV show. Webster, a Glaswegian who came out to Vancouver as a journalist after the Second World War, had gained local fame in the fifties, during hearings about alleged corruption in the Vancouver Police Department. Recording the events was a no-no—but Jack knew shorthand. He would, at suitable breaks, rush to the phone and broadcast, as verbatim as he wished, exactly what had happened in the last hour or so. He later became a radio talk-show host of deserved repute: tough but fair, Jack became king of the airwaves.

I had known Jack for a long time and admired him enormously. I first met him in 1963 when, as a lawyer, I represented a man whose car had been seized by the attorney general. My client's teenage son had borrowed the car and picked up a friend; they were stopped by the police, and a search uncovered a "mickey" of vodka on the passenger. Under the Liquor Act of the day, the car was impounded: since the passenger was a minor in possession of liquor, the car was forfeit to Her Majesty! I had managed to get the car back after two months of correspondence, but while it had been impounded we'd had a cold snap, and the block had cracked. I tried in vain for compensation, and the story caught the ear of Jack Webster—who had a lot to say on the matter!

Over my five years in government I was a frequent guest of Jack's, first on radio and then on TV. He was the best of his time and you can't do better than that.

As a minister I loved going on talk shows in general. When I visited small towns I would often suggest to a radio reporter that he do an *ad hoc* talk show with me as guest. I went on talk shows all around the province and was pretty good at it because, frankly, I didn't bullshit as much as many politicians do. Oh, I had my patter too, but I usually said what was on my mind. Also, I guess, I'm a born ham.

When I was in government, Jack Webster hosted the province's prime talk show on BCTV, while Gary Bannerman had the big morning radio audience on CKNW, trailed by Pat Burns. (Burns lagged because of the weakness of his station, CJOR, not through any fault of his own.) They were backed up by a couple of solid afternoon talk shows on CKNW and CJOR.

When I would get into trouble I would get my secretary to arrange to get me on Webster, Bannerman or Burns—the three major talk shows—as fast as possible on the theory (a good one) that it was better to get the grilling over with than have them pull the bandage off one millimetre at a time.

I have no special memory of what Jack Webster asked me when I appeared on his show in December 1980, but we did decide to go to lunch after the show at the Hotel Vancouver's Timber Club. I had nothing else scheduled for the day, so it was a fairly liquid lunch and as it got moister, Jack and I started to talk about my future.

Jack ventured the opinion that I was not happy to stay in politics. Gaining from him his word that our conversation would go no further, I confessed that I was indeed quietly looking for something to do next.

"Have you ever thought about going into radio?" he asked. I hadn't. He then went on to say that I handled myself very well in front of a mike and should do well in the talk-radio business. Moreover, he thought that there might be an interesting situation around, and he would let me know.

That evening, when I got home to Victoria, there was a message to call Jack Webster. He asked me to get in touch with Mel Cooper, the owner of CFAX, the leading Victoria station. "Jack," I said, "the last thing I want to do is go to work in Victoria."

"No, you silly bugger," he said, "it isn't about a job in Victoria, it's something else. Just be a good lad and do what you're told."

The next day I called Mel, whom I knew, and arranged to meet him at the Union Club. It was not Mel who had the opening. He was very close to Jimmy Pattison, B.C.'s own homegrown billionaire, who did. Would I go to Vancouver and talk with Jimmy?

Of course I would and within a couple of days I met Jimmy for the first time. He owned CJOR, an old and respected station in Vancouver that was getting its ass regularly whipped by CKNW in the talk show wars. 'OR was ready for a change in its morning talk show, hosted by the legendary Pat Burns.

In his day, Patrick Burns (not to be confused with the former Habs, Leafs, and present Boston Bruins coach) had no peer. In the seventies he spent time in Montreal, where his broadcasts would regularly cause near-riots. The station, fondly called the "upholstered sewer," was located in the basement of the old Grosvenor Hotel. In the CJOR studio, as I was to find out, there was an escape passage where Pat could crawl into safety in the back alley and avoid the crowds at the front of the building. (When I was a kid, my dad used to take me to get my hair cut at Blaker's Barber Shop, right beside the CJOR station.)

The thought of replacing Burns was awesome, but for some reason all my defences were down. I was mesmerized by the prospect of this adventure and at no time really thought it through. I knew all the major players, but I had no real idea of how ratings worked or indeed who was leading whom.

After a few minutes, Jimmy asked me what salary I wanted to leave government and take over his morning show. I asked for $100,000, a very large sum in 1980. It's a pretty good sum today. Jimmy then called in his manager and program director, and we chatted it up for about an hour and agreed to meet again.

The next meeting was in the Vancouver Club, because I had long ago learned that negotiations are best conducted on your home turf. They had an offer to make. It was for three years at $75,000 per year, but the salary could go higher if my ratings reached certain levels.

I turned them down and said I would only consider $100,000 on a one-year basis. This sounds arrogant but it was only common sense. If I failed, they would find a way to get rid of me, no matter what the contract said. If I succeeded, I wanted to be able to renegotiate. As to the hundred grand, I needed a cushion against failure; if I blew it as a talk-show host, I would have to live for a while without any revenue.

Negotiations broke off just before Christmas. In between Christmas and New Year's, I got a call from Jimmy. "What happened?" he asked. (As if he didn't know!) I told him we couldn't reach an understanding. Soon thereafter, I got a call from Frank Callaghan, CJOR's program director, agreeing to my terms.

I then had to find Premier Bennett, and I got him at home the day before New Year's. He was most agitated that I would resign my seat and cause a by-election, which might get the opposition too close in numbers for comfort. I assured him that I would not. I would go back on my word a couple of weeks later, when I realized, as he did, that I couldn't be a journalist and a politician at the same time. After the press conference the following week, at which I announced my decision, Allan Garr, a sometime squash partner (and now sometime colleague at CKNW), rightly convinced me that I simply could not sit in the legislature, on the government side, and still try to be a political commentator in the media. For one thing, the House sat on Friday mornings, which meant that I would miss one session every week.

After about two weeks of further thought (the legislature was not sitting at the time) I wrote a long letter to Bill Bennett explaining the situation. Bill was not satisfied and the next thing I knew I had a call from his senior advisor, the late Hugh Harris, who was a wonderful guy and a good friend to me. Could he come to my house and talk? He would bring the Scotch.

Of course he could.

He arrived about 7:00 P.M. and we ate and drank until about 3:00 A.M. Finally I couldn't stay awake and after showing Hugh to the guest room, I retired. I was up early the next morning and expected to find Hugh ready to continue the debate, if not the Scotch. He had left. I found a note on the kitchen table that simply said that he had thought it over, that I was right, that he would so inform the premier and the best of luck. A class act, Hugh Harris was to die six months later of a sudden embolism. I lost a good friend.

I duly resigned my seat. I felt awful about doing it but was helped immensely from an unexpected quarter—Phil Gaglardi, who had never been high on my popularity list nor I on his. He was quoted as saying that everyone has the right to better themselves, that Rafe Mair was no exception and that I had served my constituency well. I was also delighted to read a wonderful editorial in the *Kamloops Sentinel* (now sadly defunct), which was very complimentary of my service to my constituency.

I'm happy to relate that I've never had an unkind word back from my riding. I had wonderful constituents and a superb constituency organization. I have never really been able to thank them and hope that perhaps one or two of them will read this book and know how much I appreciated their loyalty and hard work.

So there I was—out of cabinet, out of the legislature and into a new job I knew nothing about.

Actually, that's not quite true. During my days as a Kamloops alderman I had spelled off my friend Ben Meisner (now with CKPG in Prince George—our professional paths would cross again during the Kemano controversy) when he was with CFJC with a one hour "talk back" show. I did it for five days and suffered a few glitches—I never took the station breaks on time and even ran over the ten o'clock CBC time check that was so important to so many. My stint was quite forgettable indeed.

My first day on the air at CJOR, in February 1981—I will not likely forget a second of it—had, to my mind, Pat Burns as the hero. Burns found out that I was to replace him by listening to his own station's newscast on the day I resigned from government. I should have known from that that CJOR wasn't much of a class act. But class act Burns was. Just before I was to go on-air for my first show, Burns phoned me and gave me the old show-biz advice, "Break a leg, kid." Pat Burns, always controversial but always the gentleman.

My first morning on-air was a nightmare. For some reason I had not worried a particle about my first show. I was supremely confident and calm—until the nine o'clock news came on and I knew that I was five minutes from the start.

When the red light went on at 9:05 I was struck by panic. I would have fled but in my way were three or four TV cameras to record the moment. In fact, the small studio was packed with media to watch this painful start. I had had no training, which, for a while, I resented. As I thought it through, however, I realized that there was nothing anyone could do. I would either make it or I wouldn't. It was just that simple.

My first guest was Jack Nichol (then president of the United Fishermen and Allied Workers Union) and you couldn't have asked for anyone better. He obviously knew that I was nervous and carried me. It helped that I knew a bit about the subject of fishing. Jack and I had never agreed on anything political but he's a gentleman and that day he became a guy I was deeply in debt to. Thanks to Jack's tender mercies, all the more remarkable since we had been political enemies, I got through the first hour.

Joe Clark, then leader of the federal Official Opposition, was my second guest, this time over the telephone. After Nichol's gentleness, I was feeling pretty cocky as I moved into my second hour. About five minutes into the interview, though, every light in the station went out. We'd had a power failure, meaning that the station's auxiliary power kicked in, but the lights didn't. I had to broadcast in pitch darkness. I'm happy to say that I made it through this crisis and hour two was behind me. I always suspected that CKNW had something to do with this; they didn't, of course—at least, I don't think they did!

My guest in hour three was an alderman from one of the Vancouver suburbs (he would later serve as a Socred MLA), John Parks, who also went out of his way to make things easy for me. Then it was over and I was out of there. The three hours had seemed like a week. Come to think of it, more like a year. I went upstairs to my temporary digs in the Grosvenor Hotel, and slept like a baby until late afternoon.

Everyone (except, of course, the president of CKNW, our big rival) was positive. 'NW's Ted Smith, who would hire me for his own station three and a half years later, huffed that all I could talk about was politics and fishing. He may have been right.

Our first ratings came out in May and they were outstanding. I had pulled us within hailing distance of Gary Bannerman on CKNW, and the station was ecstatic. So much so that we both made the very serious error of re-negotiating my contract. I was raised to $135,000 per year over a three-year contract, plus $10,000 to buy a car (that amount still got the job done in those days), plus a guaranteed number of endorsements, which would each bring $300–500 each month.

Why was it an error? Because I wasn't worth it. Not by a long shot. The ratings really reflected a curiosity factor, not a change in listenership. It was not long before they fell dramatically.

Moreover, two factors combined to make our show pale compared to Gary Bannerman's. First was the overall strength of CKNW. In radio it's "the numbers you leave" that are important—in other words, the person following me should have a large audience to start with. Bannerman came on after Frosty Forst, then still in his prime, who was the leading breakfast man in town by a long shot. Moreover, CKNW had superb features, including an outstanding news department whose reporters, like George Garrett, were household names.

Gary himself, though ponderous and tending to the dull, had a brilliant mind and when things were going right was a formidable broadcaster. This changed with the years, which is how I eventually wound up with CKNW's morning show, but that came later.

The second blow came from the Clifford Olson case. This beast terrorized the community as he killed at least eleven teenage girls and boys, after brutally assaulting them sexually. It was CKNW, and George Garrett in particular, to whom people turned when they wanted news of this terrible case. George, with whom I was later privileged to work on many interesting files, was well known in police circles as a man who could be trusted. He had news on each and every one of the scores of developments in the Olson case before anyone else did. It was not unusual for George to break two or three Olson stories a day. It killed us in the ratings.

There was another reason the new and rewarding contract was a mistake: the recession of 1981 hit. It was the time when Jimmy Pattison sent his famous memo telling senior executives, "Gentlemen, park your Cadillacs."

Jimmy is a very good businessman, which is not to say he has anything of a humanitarian streak when things go badly. I am not badmouthing Jimmy—far from it. At the end of our relationship, when I had a serious complaint about how I was treated by CJOR and sued him, he settled in full out of court. But in the fall of 1981 it really hit the fan. People were fired all over the place and CJOR was reduced by more than fifty percent.

In the spring of 1982 I went in to see the station's manager, Ron Vandenberg, a very tough nut who had been hired to replace the gentle Alan Anaka. "Ron," I said, "we are going down in ratings. CKNW is pulling out all the stops. What do you suggest we do?"

Ron, never known for his gentleness of approach, said, "I don't give a fuck what you do as long as it doesn't cost any money."

It was very tough to do much under these circumstances. If we wanted to capture some of 'NW's listeners, we had to do some special things and we had to advertise. It wasn't going to happen. Ratings fell even further.

Over the next couple of years, leading up to the spring of 1984, ratings improved, as did my broadcasting skills. I learned to do a hell of a lot more than just "politics and fishing" and indeed had to become a pretty good "tap dancer," meaning I could fill the airwaves with something (anything!) when there was nothing else to do, such as when no one phoned in on the open line. However, I was never strong in a technical sense. I believe that a person who has no scientific bent whatsoever shouldn't pretend otherwise. Technical things are for technical people.

I had, however, refined the art of the editorial. I started doing them in early 1982, but at that stage they were uncut, ponderous, portentous monologues. They often ran over station breaks. I learned to edit, something that stood me in good stead when I began to write a lot. By 1984 my editorials were, if I do say so myself, pretty good and widely listened to.

I had learned a lot and I wish I could tell you that someone at CJOR had been my good and faithful teacher. In fact I learned by the "sink or swim" method, the only way you can really do it. Apart from following simple rules like staying close to the microphone, style is an individual thing.

Just before I went on the air for the first time, Jack Webster took me to lunch. "Be yerself," he said in his delightful brogue. "Don't try to imitate Burns or me. Be yerself. And by the way, after we finish lunch, we're enemies and I'm not speaking to you any more." Jack was true to his word—as long as he was regularly broadcasting on BCTV, I did no TV work for them. Not only do I understand and respect his attitude, I agree with it. In this crazy business you don't look up the ladder at who's ahead of you, you stomp the fingers on the guy right below you as hard as you can. I like, admire and respect Jack Webster, and am deeply in his debt.

In late 1983 Ron Vandenberg was replaced by Harvey Gold from Ottawa. When Gold came to town, with his wife to follow, he had no friends here, so Patti and I made him welcome at our house, inviting him to our small Christmas Eve gathering of close friends. We dined and lunched together.

Harvey would often call me in to share gossip—great fun in my business—or the latest joke. He had a keen sense of humour and we laughed a lot together. He had nothing but praise for my work, especially the editorials. His arrival looked like the beginning of a good relationship, both in terms of the business and personally.

But thanks to Harvey Gold I learned a lesson I will never forget: There are no friends in broadcasting. Whatever you get, you get because of results and how hard you fight. You can constantly tell the station to shove it and as long as you are producing "numbers" you're safe. By the same token, it doesn't do a damn bit of good to kiss ass or be the president's pal. You are judged on performance.

Toward the end of 1983 I reminded Harvey that my contract came up on June 30 of the following year. "Would it not make sense for us to talk about it now, not at the last minute?"

Harvey agreed.

After New Year's I reminded him on a number of occasions of his promise and was always assured that a new contract would be offered to me shortly.

One Sunday morning in March, I read Denny Boyd, the superb *Vancouver Province* columnist (but best known in the *Vancouver Sun*, for which he had previously written and to which he would shortly return). In it he suggested that Dave Barrett, former NDP premier and then leader of the province's Official Opposition, was in line for my job. I phoned Harvey and asked if I could come over to his house. When there I laid the Boyd column before him.

"There is no way I would ever hire Dave Barrett," he told me. "You're my man and I'm just waiting for a private ratings survey to confirm that we're doing much better. Then I'll have a contract for you."

"But," I replied, "despite their difference in politics, Jimmy Pattison and Dave are great buddies. How do I know that Boyd is not right, that Jimmy has promised the job to Dave?"

"Rafe," he replied, "Jimmy has given me a complete free hand in this and Dave Barrett is not going to be on my station."

I was reassured, as well I needed to be because unbeknownst to anyone else, I was in a pile of financial trouble. Patti and I had spent far too much, by a wide margin. She was, and presumably still is, improvident (to put it mildly) and I probably wasn't much better. We bought our house at the very top of the terrific "bull market" in March 1981, added a new Cadillac, and compounded our stupidity with government-approved tax shelters. Patti, who handled the books, dealt with finances by borrowing from many Peters to pay Paul—and then forgot to pay Paul. I hated unpleasantness so I went into a permanent state of denial. As a result, we owed Revenue Canada a huge sum, were deeply in debt to two banks and had run every credit card to points beyond our means.

About a week before Easter, Harvey informed me that he would have a contract for me on Easter Monday (which I worked) and that we could put it all to bed then.

On Good Friday, to my considerable surprise, Jimmy Pattison dropped in to see me during my show. We chatted during the commercial breaks and the newscasts and he complimented me on the work I was doing. He said that while he knew that contract negotiations were coming up, he was sure that they would go well. If not, I was to remember that we were friends and that I could always call upon him.

On Easter Monday, Patti (who was producing the show) and I went into the boardroom for lunch and contract negotiations. Little did I know that *I* was for lunch.

Harvey started by opening a bottle of wine, which puzzled me because I wasn't drinking any alcohol at that time. He then laid before me terms that called for an enormous drop in pay, a lessening of time off, a commitment to pay a producer out of my income, and a commitment in writing to do editorials every morning without any further compensation.

After expressing my shock, I asked if I could make some requests and Harvey agreed.

After every request I made, such as, "Could I take the same vacation time as my equivalent broadcaster at CKNW?" he would answer, "Request denied."

I asked for some time to think the offer over. "After all," I said, "we're not in ratings and I am on vacation." I had received a U.S. State Department grant to study American government, and was due to leave in about ten days' time for Washington, D.C. "I will give you my answer upon my return."

"Request denied," said Harvey, and Patti and I left the meeting utterly stunned.

That evening I wrote Harvey a note saying, in essence, that somehow we had got off the rails and that I would like to see him again as soon as possible. I left this note in his office at 6:30 A.M. so that he would have it first thing in his morning.

I came off the air that morning and Harvey asked to see me. I was relieved because I was certain that the day before had been just a bad dream. I went into his office, where he told me that he was looking elsewhere for a morning broadcaster but that if I said anything on-air about this, he would take me off-air and refuse to honour my contract (which ran until June 30).

I was stunned beyond belief. "Harvey," I asked, "what have I ever done to make you think I would do such a thing?"

"Just don't do it," he replied.

A few days later Rick Ouston, a well known local journalist, was my guest. Knowing that I would need work, badly, in about six weeks' time, I asked him, off-air, if he knew of any openings. His reply stunned me. (I know the word stunned is being overworked here, but it describes the series of blows I was taking.)

"Rafe," he said, "this is a news story and I'll have my BCTV cameras at the studio when you come off-air."

I had blown it. I was naive; it never occurred to me that my firing would be of any interest to anyone else. I begged Rick not to do this but could only wring the concession that he would postpone the photo session until 1:00 P.M. at my house.

It happened that Fanny Kiefer, a very fine broadcaster (and now my colleague again, at CKNW), was doing part of my show that morning, so during that interval I went in to see Frank Callaghan (CJOR's program director) and I told him what had happened. I said "Frank, why don't we take the high road on this. I will simply say that I am leaving CJOR and that I have treasured the experience and CJOR can thank me and wish me luck."

At his request, I wrote out such a statement. When I brought it back to Frank he said it looked okay to him but that he would have to "run it by Harvey." I went home in a daze. I had never seen anything like this in my life. I was utterly unprepared for what was happening.

When I got home I called Harvey, who said that as far as he was concerned my suggestion was not on. He threatened to tell the press that he had made a fair offer to me in the six-figure range and that I had turned it down, and that was that.

I pleaded with him to take the high road with me. He hung up.

The cameras arrived and I told them simply that I had been fired and was now looking for work.

That evening Harvey called my wife and stiffly informed her that CJOR had no further need of the services provided by Rafe Mair and that he would pay out the contract in full as long as the said Rafe Mair did not violate any of the terms of the contract.

The following morning I tuned in my show to hear Harvey tell the world that he had made a very fair offer to me, that I had turned it down, and that that was that.

Almost immediately I received a call from Ted Smith at CKNW, who told me that they had nothing for me but asked if I would take over for Barrie Clark, their afternoon host, for a couple of days, as he was off sick. Here was my chance to strut my stuff for the best station in the business. I wanted to make the most of it. However, the red light went on. "Ted," I said, "you'd better clear that with Harvey Gold."

Ten minutes later Ted phoned me back. "Harvey says that if you appear for one minute on CKNW he will consider you in breach of contract and will refuse to pay you through to June 30."

Nice guy.

There is a humorous epilogue to this tale. About five years later I had an operation to remove a benign tumour (we didn't know it was benign until after the operation) from my parotid nerve, just below the left ear. It was a very long operation and they were having a hell of a time getting me to wake up in the recovery room.

Patti was there, trying to wake me up by getting me interested in a Stanley Cup playoff game on TV. I just couldn't wake up.

Then she said, "Rafe, I just heard this morning that Jimmy Pattison has fired Harvey Gold." Which turned out to be true.

"There is a God," I evidently said as I went back to sleep.

I started at CKNW, B.C.'s most listened-to station, in November 1984, with a new show, called "Nightline B.C.," on network around the province from midnight until 2:00 A.M. Just before I started, I was a guest on Gary Bannerman's show, and I remember telling him that being with CKNW, even as low guy on the totem pole, was still like playing for the Montreal Canadiens. (That was when playing for the Canadiens still meant something.)

The midnight show was great fun. We seldom had guests at that time of night but I quickly discovered that there is a whole new society out there after midnight. I've often been asked if I wasn't plagued by drunks and can honestly say that I've had more problems in the morning with people into the cooking sherry than I had with tipplers at night.

I got calls from all around the province—cowboys around a camp fire, lonely prospectors, cops, taxi drivers and hookers in the big city. It is a wonderful, loving, warm and caring audience that listens after midnight, as anyone who has worked that shift can attest.

It was not long, however, before my big mouth got me into trouble.

James Barber is a delightful chef who has become quite a media star in Vancouver and throughout the country. He was the man with the beard who told us how Moneys Mushrooms make things taste mmmmmarvelous.

Well, James and I were reviewing a cookbook and I opened the phone lines. Somehow, and I'm damned if I can remember how since James is a gourmet cook, the subject of McDonald's came up. In one of my stupider unessential remarks I said, "I had a McDonald's hamburger about eight years ago and to this day, when I burp, I can taste the damn thing." It was supposed to be funny. Evidently it wasn't. But at 1:30 A.M., who gives a damn?

Well, McDonald's evidently listens to midnight shows, and McDonald's *does* give a damn.

And it hit the fan with a mighty wallop.

Now I have a real thing about freedom of speech. If you don't have it in my business, you might as well quit because it's as essential as a monkey wrench is to a plumber. Fortunately, most of the time CKNW feels the same way.

So it was this time. Ted Smith took Patti and me to lunch and explained that while McDonald's had threatened to take their advertising away and had indeed written a letter to Frank Griffiths, the chairman of the WIC Corporation (which owns CKNW) demanding that I be fired, Ted would stand by me. He gave me a copy of the letter and I showed it to my lawyer. Not only did he think it was libelous, but it was also clearly inducing CKNW to breach my contract. Now I was mad too.

The issue simmered for a couple of days with me wondering if I would ever broadcast again and with McDonald's mulling over a threatening letter from my lawyer. Then Ted called me at home. "Did you know Ron Marcoux of McDonald's?" he asked.

"No," I said, "and I don't care if I ever do."

"Fair enough," replied Ted, "I was just hoping you could get him off my back. A phone call would do."

"Fuck 'im," said I gracefully, and hung up.

Then I started to think about it. I thought, "What the hell, Ted has been good to me, why not make a call."

So I called Marcoux. "Mr. Marcoux," I said, "don't think I'm going to apologize to you because I'm not."

"Didn't expect it of you," answered Marcoux, "and you'll get no apology from me either."

Then there was silence. And we both started to laugh. Before I knew it I had invited him on my show to tell the McDonald's story and since then, Ron Marcoux and McDonald's have been very good friends of mine. Actually, I often go to the golden arches, especially when I'm away. When I was in Moscow in 1990, it was coincidentally the time of the opening of the first McDonald's in Russia, and the McDonald's people took us under their wing and were just mmmmmarvelous.

One night on the show we decided to play a game of sexual trivia of my own design. Callers were urged to tell about funny sexual anecdotes in which they had been involved or knew about. I asked listeners to behave themselves—this wasn't the same as daytime radio, but there still were rules.

It was great fun. Everyone caught the spirit. One young man phoned to tell how after his girlfriend's folks had gone to the theatre they went up to the bedroom for a romp. After the main event, the guy blew up a number of condoms as balloons and they began, in their birthday suits, to bat these around the room. Suddenly her folks came home. Evidently the movie wasn't until the next day! Great fun.

I have, on the console, a "kill button" to use when I want to censor something. Since our broadcast is delayed six seconds, this is supposed to be used to eliminate naughty words. But I can never, in the moment of truth, remember whether I hit the button and hold it six seconds, wait six seconds and then hit the button, or what. I usually manage some mixture of the two.

During the sexual trivia game, at about 1:45 A.M. someone said "blow job." *Oh-oh!* I thought, *that's got to go.* So I hit the kill button. The next morning, Doug Rutherford, who was then our program director, phoned me.

"I never stay up until 2:00 A.M. listening to radio, but I just couldn't turn off that sexual trivia—it was great. But what was it that you bleeped out?"

"Why do you ask?" I asked with a sinking feeling.

"Because what came over the air was *bleep, bleep, bleep, bleep,* 'blow job'!" said Doug.

Clearly I was not hired for my technical ability.

I very much enjoyed the midnight show, though truthfully I didn't get a decent night's sleep for the year I did it. After a year, though, Doug Rutherford asked me if I would like to start a new talk show running from 6:00 P.M. until 9:00 P.M., designed more along the lines of a news magazine. Of course I would, so in November 1985 we started the new show.

It was bloody hard work, especially for Patti, who had to singlehandedly put together ten to twelve segments a night. Moreover, we were broadcasting from Expo 86 at our studios at the Plaza of Nations, so we had to fight enormous crowds every day. It was a good show but we were glad to move on—which we very nearly didn't.

In September 1986 I went to England on private business and just got through the door of the flat where I was staying when the phone rang. It was Patti, telling me that Barrie Clark, 'NW's afternoon host, was resigning as of November 1, and that I should get my oar in fast. Doug Rutherford had always said that I would move up when a vacancy occurred, so I wasn't much worried, but I called him anyway. He was very noncommittal and suggested that we get together when I returned.

A couple of weeks after I got back, he phoned me just before I went on-air to ask me to come out to the main station the next morning and "audition" for the afternoon show. He advised that there were about seventy-five applicants, including some very big names.

Now I learned the hard way at CJOR that you get absolutely nowhere kissing ass in this business and to Patti's horror—the afternoon show was easier to produce, and she'd have help doing it—I told Doug that he could go to hell. If he didn't know what I could do by now, he never would, and I wasn't going out to the station to be looked over like some mail-order bride at the steamer wharf.

Doug called me during every news break that evening to try to get me to change my mind, and my answer was always the same: "Go to hell."

At nine o'clock he phoned me again and by this time there was some desperation in his voice. Not for the first time and certainly not for the last, Doug had assured management that I would do something when it turned out that I wouldn't.

"Please come out, Rafe," he whined, "everything will be okay."

"Okay, Doug," I said, "but if I'm asked one question about the show or my ability to do it, I'm outta there."

The next morning I went out to President Ron Bremner's office, and all the usual suspects were there. There was an awkward pause after the opening pleasantries. "Brem" cleared his throat and said, "Gentlemen, I understand that our program director Doug Rutherford wants Rafe to take over from Barrie. Are we all agreed?"

Doug nodded vigorously.

"Agreed," said everyone in unison.

"Rafe, would you like the job?"

"Yes I would," I replied. It all took sixty seconds, max!

Everyone shook hands and that was that. I did the afternoon show, 12:35–3:00 P.M., for nearly two years.

During this time, the longtime morning-show host Gary Bannerman was having some personal problems and to make a long story short, he was either going to have to solve those problems or be replaced. The final straw was the morning after the Queen had been in Vancouver to open the Commonwealth Conference in early 1988; Gary had been at the dinner. He needed more than considerable help the next morning, and had to be replaced by a substitute host. Gary is a good guy and I'm happy to report that he is fine now and doing well in his media consulting business—including, until recently, spelling me off when I take vacations.

On September 1, 1988, I took over the 9:00 A.M. to noon show, where I remain, though the hours have changed to 8:30–11:00 A.M.

Gary did, innocently, lead me into another dustup with the station. About six months after I replaced Gary, Doug Rutherford called a meeting of the talk-show hosts and their producers to announce and "get our consensus" on re-hiring Gary Bannerman to do replacement work.

By this time I had already had two rating "books" with enormous improvements over Gary's numbers, so I had no fear for my job, but I expressed serious reservations about this move. It turned out that the real reason behind it was that Gary was part of a group that was trying to buy CFUN, another radio station—CKNW didn't want him competing against them in the marketplace.

I thought this was a lousy thing for CKNW to do. I knew some of the guys who would be hurt, and I said so. Having been advised that while I was responsible for forty-two weeks a year of programming, CKNW could do as they pleased with the other ten, so mind my own bloody business, I folded my tent.

A couple of days later I was watching the six o'clock news on BCTV, and there was Rutherford explaining why Gary Bannerman was being re-hired and vehemently denying that it had anything whatever to do with the group that was trying to buy CFUN. This was a blatant untruth and I knew it. Moreover, I knew one of the principals of that group, Ron Vandenberg. He had been my boss at CJOR; I considered him a friend, and thought he was getting screwed.

The next morning I stewed from 6:00 A.M., when I got to the studio, until 9:05, when I went on-air. I thought I could leave this alone, but also knew that sure as hell, someone was going to ask me about it on the open line. I knew I couldn't lie about it and that I would answer the question truthfully, so I decided that a pre-emptive strike was in order.

I went to air and said approximately this. "You have heard that Gary Bannerman is coming back to CKNW as a backup host and I think it is a very bad move. The reason for the move has nothing to do with the reasons CKNW has given, but everything to do with them trying to break up a syndicate—with which Gary was involved—that wanted to buy CFUN and go into competition with us, with Gary as one of their hosts. CKNW wants only to remove a possible competitor and keep Gary out of any other radio station. That's the truth of the matter. I will say no more on the subject at any time but I think this action by CKNW is crappy."

I waited for it to hit the fan. It never did. To the great credit of CKNW they knew that for fifty years they had been a major part of the community and that they had to take shots just like everyone else.

During the first seven years I was with 'NW I was having a hell of a time financially. There is no doubt that 'NW took considerable advantage of me in negotiations, knowing that I was in a very weak position. For example, when I was moved to the afternoon show, and again when I went to the morning show, I was promised more money. It didn't happen. Moreover, over my constant but ineffective objections 'NW insisted that Patti and I were a "package," two for the price of one.

I don't blame Doug Rutherford, whom I consider to be a very good friend—he and his bosses were just being smart businessmen. But it rankled, oh how it rankled.

For a number of years I had been fishing regularly with Fin Anthony, a man who has been around radio and the advertising business for forty years. Almost every Wednesday we would fish for sea run cutthroat trout on the beaches of the Sunshine Coast. We would talk a lot about my grievances with 'NW, and one day in the spring of 1992 Fin asked me if I employed an agent.

"No," I replied, and then the light went on. Of course! As the lawyers say, if you act for yourself you have a fool for a client. Would Fin take on the task?

He would and he did.

I showed him my contract and he said, "You are worth a hell of a lot more money than that. You don't know your own worth, nor just how difficult it would be to replace you. You especially don't know how much you could hurt 'NW from another radio station. Let me go to work on it."

Within a few weeks he had a bonus of $40,000 for me! Though I had more than a year to run on my existing contract, he got me a brand-new contract that very much better served my needs. Then in September 1993 he renegotiated again, and got an even better one.

I have no idea if I am paid what I'm worth. That is always difficult to determine. I am paid well, but that's not out of CKNW's sense of generosity. I have been asked in recent years by CKNW management why I don't show them more gratitude for all the money they pay me, and for their many kindnesses. My reply is simple. I owe them nothing for which I do not give full measure. If they didn't make a very handsome profit indeed on my labours, they would not be paying me the money they do. No more complicated than that.

The station's usual magnanimity about free speech did not, evidently, apply where the Vancouver Canucks Hockey Club was involved. In early 1993 I got into a serious scrape.

In the fall of 1992 my producers asked Brian Burke, then a vice president of the Vancouver Canucks—proving again the validity of the "Peter Principle," he later became the vice president of the NHL, and is now back as GM of the Canucks—to come on my show on Thanksgiving to tell people about the next year's team. Thanksgiving, like all holidays, is difficult to program. I expected this to be a "slow pitch" sort of interview, on a traditionally laid-back day. It would give Burke a chance to blow the Canucks' horn.

Just before Thanksgiving the Canucks had banned *Vancouver Province* sportswriter Tony Gallagher, a very good and respected journalist, from the Canucks dressing room for some offence or other. I took Tony's side, and just before Burke was to come on my show he cancelled with a vicious letter condemning me for lack of patriotism toward the team. Burke's letter was outrageous and made it appear that if I didn't have him on my show, my ratings would somehow go all to hell.

In the new year Burke got his knickers in a knot over scalpers selling tickets outside the Pacific Coliseum. I trashed him in an editorial and concluded by saying, "Burke may not be the rudest man in the world but he is close to it and gets into the 'rudeness hall of fame' without the usual waiting period." I went on to say, "At this very moment you can bet he's calling CKNW trying to have me fired."

I got off the air at noon to be put on the phone to my agent, Fin. "Now you've really done it with that Burke bit, the station is considering suspending you."

"Great," I said. "They have no right to do so under the contract and if they breach it they owe me the entire balance of monies due me."

The phone calls between Fin and Doug, then back to me, went on for about half an hour. Rutherford wanted to speak to me at my home. I refused. He demanded I go out to the main station and see him. I refused. He then demanded a meeting at the Expo site studio. I refused. Finally I agreed to meet him there as long as Fin came along as a witness.

In due course Doug arrived. He was black with rage. Did I know of the special relationship between CKNW and the Canucks? (The team was then owned by Frank Griffiths, who also owned CKNW.)

Of course I did.

Would I then apologize to Burke?

No, I said. I went further. There were no circumstances in the world that would make me apologize to that man, and I wasn't even going to modify what I had said.

Now this was an unusual conversation I was having, given that CKNW were vigorous defenders of the rights of their hosts to unrestricted free speech. I demanded to know if Rutherford was interfering with my right to give an opinion.

No, it was just this "special relationship," and did I know what trouble I had got him in?

Was I to take it then that free speech was for all the world except where the Vancouver Canucks were concerned?

Then the light dawned. The station manager, in the style of the station, had taken shit from Burke and passed it on to Rutherford with instructions to "do something about it." Foolishly, Doug had thought he could get me to do an apology. He was wrong. The meeting went on for about an hour, and there were tears of rage in Rutherford's eyes when he left the boardroom.

This story also has an amusing ending. A couple of years later, Doug was, deservedly, promoted to manager of an Edmonton station. We had a bit of a party for him at Me and Ed's Pizza.

Ted Smith made the farewell speech and said approximately this: "Doug, at least you won't have to deal with Rafe Mair any more. And let me tell you a story. One day, Doug came into my office, madder than hell, demanding that the company buy a new briefcase. It turned out that after one meeting with Rafe he punched right through both sides of his briefcase!"

Needless to say, that was the Burke meeting.

It must sound as if every day in radio is a blitzkrieg and in many ways I suppose it is. But it must be understood that the electronic medium is a volatile business. I wouldn't want to leave the impression that Doug and management were always wrong and Rafe always right. Far from it. I am like all performers—moody, self-centred, temperamental, full of self-doubts and with an ego that always needs massaging. I am by no means always easy to work with and I have this lifelong habit of resisting any time I'm told I *must* do things. Many, perhaps even most, of the battles I had with management had as much to do with my orneriness as anything the station did.

When I step back and look at things in perspective, I'm lucky to have been associated so long with CKNW, and I'm very proud of that association. I think I have contributed a lot to the station's success, but then they have stuck by me when I needed it, as I took on Bill Vander Zalm, then Alcan, then Prime Minister Mulroney and the entire establishment during the Charlottetown referendum.

CHAPTER SEVEN

Rafe Mair's Political Axioms

I have been a politician, a broadcaster and now a writer, and as such I've often focused on political issues. In all my years of political activity, I've noticed that certain truths about politics seem to apply pretty broadly. Before getting too deeply into my discussion of Canada's political ails, then, I would like to offer you, after long reflection, some axioms.

Axiom I: "You make a very serious mistake in assuming that people in charge know what the hell they are doing."

The evidence supporting this axiom is, surely, irrefutable. Government—large and small, political and bureaucratic—proves it every minute of every day. So does the church. So does business. So do labour unions.

Axiom II: "In politics, you don't have to be a 10. You can be a 3 if everyone else is a 2."

If I mention Jean Chretien, "Buttermilk" Billy Davis, and the curiously sainted Richard Hatfield, to say nothing of Bill Vander Zalm and Joe Clark, that should be more than ample proof of my proposition.

Richard Hatfield was the darling of the Ottawa media because he was the usual leak amongst first ministers. Whatever he may have done as premier of New Brunswick, on constitutional matters he was little more than a tiresome nuisance who became Trudeau's poodle. Joe Clark, while not as clumsy as the media made him out to be, lost a key vote in the Commons, and thus his right to govern, because he couldn't count noses properly. Bill Vander Zalm and his party won a large majority provincial government in B.C. in 1986, and the government and the Social Credit Party were subsequently wiped out. Vander Zalm only avoided official blame because he'd been forced from office in a scandal a few months earlier.

Axiom III: "When you leave politics they all say they'll never forget you. They will, the moment your ability to hurt them is gone."

When I left the government of B.C. in early 1981, all my colleagues assured me that they would never forget the services I had rendered, blah, blah, blah. My leaving created a vacancy, so a by-election was called, won in a squeaker by Claude Richmond, a fellow Socred, an old political ally and a personal friend. He had taken the Kamloops City Council seat that I vacated in 1974. He had also nominated me as a Socred provincial candidate in March 1975.

Shortly after Claude took the provincial seat in 1981, two important events occurred in Kamloops. The new courthouse was officially opened, as was the new bridge over the North Thompson River at Halston Crossing. Both were major undertakings. Both had come about because of my hard work (and that of many others, of course). Both opening ceremonies were my bows to take. However, I was not invited to either. I'm told that at the opening of the courthouse, the late Nathan Nemetz, chief justice of British Columbia, looked around and in *haute voix* asked, "Where's Rafe Mair?"

Some months later I was asked to sit at the head table at a roast to honour Mike Latta, the three-term mayor of Kamloops. He was a great supporter of mine, and vice versa. When I spoke I said, "Mike, there's one thing you'll never have to worry about. You will never be forgotten by the grateful people you've served. Why, look at my case: When the Halston bridge and the new courthouse open, you can be sure that the government will invite me to take an honoured place in the ceremony. Why, our good friend Claude Richmond will see to that!" Everyone in the audience but Claude Richmond laughed—and even he chuckled a little at the end.

In 1984, when I was out of work and desperate for money, I went to Victoria to see if the government had any work to offer. I saw my old friend Brian Smith, who was now attorney general. He asked how he could help.

I levelled with him. "Brian," I said, "I know it seems chickenshit, but I'm desperate enough to go back to the practice of law. It won't cost you or the taxpayer a nickel, but if you could make me a Queen's counsel it would open a lot of doors. I would have been a QC if I'd stayed in private practice, so I would have earned it anyway."

*Rafe Mair's father, Kenneth F.R. Mair,
at the age of about thirty-six, in 1936.*

*A six-year-old Rafe Mair fishing for
shiners at Granthams Landing, 1938.*

*Rafe Mair at thirteen, Woodlands,
B.C., 1945.*

Rafe Mair's fifteenth birthday, Banff, Alberta. Left to right: Lois Hatfield (aunt, née Mair), Dr. W.H. Hatfield (uncle), Blanche Mair (grandmother), Rafe Mair.

Rafe Mair at the age of nineteen.

The children of Rafe and Eve Mair, Kamloops, B.C., 1975. Left to right: Cindy, Shawn, Karen, Ken.

Premier Bill Bennett with his cabinet minister Rafe Mair.

With Roy Romanow (then attorney general of Saskatchewan) at a constitutional conference in Ottawa, 1979.

Bill Bennett, Mel Smith, and Rafe Mair, at a constitutional conference in Ottawa, 1979.

Rafe Mair with Joe Clark (then leader of the Official Opposition) and Flora Macdonald (then constitutional affairs critic for the Official Opposition), 1979.

Rafe Mair being sworn in by Lieutenant-Governor Henry P. Bell-Irving after the May 1979 election. Grace McCarthy is visible standing along the back wall, to the right of Bell-Irving.

Fishing for steelhead on the Dean River, B.C., 1979.

Rafe Mair at his great-great-grandfather's trading post in Wahapu, Bay of Islands, New Zealand, 1981.

With Wendy Conway-Mair.

Three generations of Kenneth Rafe Mairs, at a Toronto restaurant, 1996.

Working on Canada: Is Anyone Listening?, *London, England, November 1997.*

Brian looked very uncomfortable. Clearly the cabinet colleagues I had left three years earlier, who had told me they would do anything for me, would never permit me to become a Queen's counsel.

I don't blame Claude or Brian—we remain friends. I'd likely have behaved the same way. The point is that there's no more reward for an ex-politician than there is fear for a lion that has lost its claws. When you're hot, you're hot; when you're not, you're not—and when you're shot, you're shot.

Axiom IV: "A sort of magic dust gets into some people's eyes where politics is concerned. Otherwise intelligent people assume that they have sufficient talent and appeal to jump from a career of mediocrity to the top of the political pole."

How else do you explain some of the very strange people who go after leaderships when they've never been so much as a member of the local PTA? Examples abound. There was Harold Stassen, a former governor of Minnesota, who in 1940 started a relentless campaign for the Republican presidential nomination that didn't end until the Nixon era. He never stood a chance, but kept on plugging away until he became a national embarrassment.

Everyone who ever watches a leadership convention—or a constituency nomination, for that matter—sees people who are in way out of their depth. No amount of evidence will demonstrate to them that they're out of their league.

I saw a magnificent example of this at the 1986 Socred leadership convention, convened to choose a replacement for Bill Bennett. There were eleven or twelve candidates—the fact that the winner would become premier, at least until the next election, added more than a little spice—but only four of them had a chance. Bud Smith was the premier's unspoken favourite, Brian Smith had the Tory-leaning faction, Grace McCarthy had the party faithful, and Bill Vander Zalm had the impressionable right and the charismatic Christians (a deadly combination, as it turned out—he won easily).

On the day of the vote, I was on my way to my broadcast studio when I walked past the booth of one of the candidates least likely to win. He was a junior cabinet minister with no power base whatsoever, and scarcely what you would call a gladhander. His only discernible supporters were two—his wife and his girlfriend, a former beauty queen. (Incredible. The person I would least associate with sex appeal had enough for two.)

"Psst!" Biff (I'll call him Biff) whistled at me. I went over and politely asked how it was going.

He grabbed my lapels and spoke, fiery-eyed, right into my face. "Rafe, I'm going to win this thing. The big guns are going to knock themselves off and I'll come flying up the middle."

I was stunned. I smiled, wished him the best of luck and went on my way. What on earth would make Biff act like Whistler's version of Harold Stassen?

Maybe for every person goofy enough to think they can win, there are people goofy enough to support him. When the first ballot was counted, Biff had twenty-eight votes (out of more than twelve hundred cast) and was out.

Our radio show had, during the campaign for delegates, decided to track one of the delegates, an uncommitted businessman from the north coast named Pat. He was bright, thirtyish and just the sort of person who should be a political bellwether. During the campaign we interviewed Pat at regular intervals. At first he seemed to lean toward Bud Smith; it was the youth thing and Bud was bright and very personable one-on-one.

Then Pat soured a bit on Bud, and went into Whistler sort of wavering between Grace McCarthy and Bill Vander Zalm. When the speeches were delivered the night before the vote, there were some dreadful performances. None was worse than the one by the late Bob Wenman. He'd gone into the legislature in 1952 with W.A.C. Bennett, then lost in the snap election of 1953. He then went to Ottawa, where he served for years as perhaps the most undistinguished backbencher of his time. Nice guy, earnest, but deadly dull. Even by his standards, his speech was a catastrophe.

In contrast, all four main candidates gave barnburner speeches and the entire convention was abuzz—which of the four would carry the day? The next day, just before the vote, we had Pat on-air.

"Who are you going to vote for on the first ballot, Pat?"

Well, he said, "I liked Brian Smith's fireworks and Grace McCarthy was great. But you know, I'm going with Bob Wenman!"

Bob Wenman, for God's sake! He got forty votes on the first, and for him the last, ballot.

Go figure.

Politics makes strange bedfellows—and strange ducks out of what are usually quite normal people.

Axiom V: "Any policy *stated* (as distinct from *demonstrated*) to be in Canada's national interest is nothing of the sort—it is in Central Canada's parochial but highly populated interest."

For proof of this maxim, we can look to Sir John A. Macdonald's 1878 National Policy (which was only national in the sense that the West was forced to sell its raw resources to the East, and then pay tariff-protected prices for the finished products), bilingualism and biculturalism, and the Trudeau government's infamous National Energy Program (which used taxing power to effectively control petroleum natural resources in Alberta and B.C.—this was clearly contrary to Section 92 of the BNA Act, and the policy was discontinued very quickly in the first Mulroney government). The proposition is so thoroughly evident that I would be surprised if even honest Liberals (if that's not an oxymoron—which, come to think of it, it is) would quarrel with it.

This axiom has a number of corollaries:

(a) The federal government's ideas of "national interests" are almost certain to be contrary to the interests of "outer Canada" and invariably against those of British Columbia.

(b) While the declared national interest is invariably in the interest of Ontario and Quebec, the converse is likewise true: Ontario and Quebec's interest also quickly becomes the declared national interest.

(c) Whatever is clearly in the interest of "outer Canada" is seldom considered to be in the national interest, even if it demonstrably is.

(d) "National culture," as evidenced by the output of the Canadian Broadcasting Corporation, the Toronto *Globe and Mail,* Toronto *Saturday Night,* and *Maclean's,* is really the culture of Toronto, occasionally supplemented by politically correct, suitably cleansed snippets of Toronto's view of "outer Canada."

Axiom VI: "Canada's leadership has an irresistible urge to trivialize the important and create big problems out of the trivial."

The more those in charge ignore or minimize a problem, the bigger it gets. It follows that the longer a national problem is trivialized, the more serious it becomes—until, in due course, it becomes well nigh insurmountable.

In seeking solutions to trivialized questions, leaders invariably put forth ill-thought-out solutions, marked by over-sensitivity to the voters. And because the seriousness of the issue has been minimized, the voters, of course, will be ill prepared for anything other than mindless platitudes.

This explains why questions of national unity have been dealt with solely as "the Quebec question," rather than as matters of serious concern about how national governance manifests itself in all regions of the country. It explains the bilingualism and biculturalism policy of the 1960s, and Ottawa's consistent knee-bending to Quebec's financial extortions. Meanwhile, the deep concerns of provinces like B.C. are put down to mere "bitching," to be considered "in the fullness of time."

Axiom VII: "As a 'trivial' problem becomes chronic and potentially deadly, politicians tend to assume that any lull in the proceedings means that the problem has gone away."

Polls showing that separatism in Quebec is on the wane have been seized upon as signs that all has miraculously become well. This accounts for the absence of any government long-term unity plans and tells us why the federal government was, for example, so unwilling to join Guy Bertrand's court case to seek a declaration that separation was unconstitutional. Readers will recall that the Chretien government was so loath to challenge Quebec's right to secede in the courts that Bertrand, a former vocal separatist and a Quebec City lawyer, mounted his own challenge. Before long, events forced the government to do what they ought to have done in the first place—stand up for the indivisibility of the country.

Axiom VIII: "Everything a government does has, as its first and perhaps only motivation, the desire to stay in power."

The status quo must be maintained at all costs, and all government actions are geared directly to the government's re-election. This respect for the status quo applies to all components of the establishment. However much the various segments of that establishment might hate each other, a strong bond of self-preservation brings them together any time they perceive their sacred position to be under serious attack. A good example is the campaign leading up to the 1992 referendum on the Charlottetown Accord, which brought the entire establishment onside with Brian Mulroney's effort to preserve the status quo forever.

This axiom demonstrates why there are no long-term unity plans, or at least none that extend beyond the government's self-serving mandate.

Axiom IX: "There's no good, much less perfect, political system—only the hope of a better one. And only the people, not the politicians who owe their election to the current system, can ever change the system for the better."

That this is true is obvious. But we must not let the unlikelihood of achieving even a good system keep us from trying to better the one we have. We must keep trying, even though politicians, afraid that reform will put them out of business, will always do what they can to prevent needed changes, even as they pay lip service to them. The inability of the people to be heard under our system has prevented us from changing that system.

Axiom X may be the most important of all: "Whenever someone in charge tells you something, treat it as bullshit. It won't always be—only about ninety-five percent of the time."

Authoritative pronouncements are almost always "spin doctored" to a faretheewell and are made with an eye to public relations, not accuracy. There are gazillions of examples but if I simply mention the Liberal "Red Book," the Charlottetown Accord, and the name Brian Mulroney, that should suffice to make the point.

CHAPTER EIGHT

A Country Divided

One of Canada's fundamental failings is that our culture shares no universally accepted myths.

This is not the case in, say, Britain. King Richard the Lion-Hearted was a bounder and a glory-seeking wastrel who spent almost no time in Britain; his dereliction to duty inflicted his brother "Bad King John" on his long-suffering countrymen. Oliver Cromwell was a regicide who split the country in two; after a few years in power, he had the English so cross that they begged Charles II to return from exile and pick up where his beheaded father had left off.

Today, outside the British Parliament Buildings in Westminster, you can find statues of Richard the Lion-Hearted and Oliver Cromwell.

The myth is the thing. It can be about "heroes" or "facts"—like Alfred burning the cakes or the very horny Queen Victoria (who chased poor Albert from bedroom to bedroom in Buckingham Palace) being held out as a symbol of prurient behaviour. A country must have its own pantheon of heroes—whether they were really heroic or otherwise is mostly irrelevant.

An even better example of a mythmaking culture is the United States. George Washington did not cut down his dad's cherry tree, nor did he throw a silver dollar across the Potomac—for one thing, the silver dollar hadn't yet been minted at that time. Abraham Lincoln did not set out to free the slaves, and in fact he stated that if he could keep the U.S. together by retaining slavery, he would do so.

Don't get me wrong—both Washington and Lincoln were great men. The point is that Americans have encapsulated their leaders' greatness into easily remembered myths that may or may not be accurate, though they do neatly mask all defects.

Perhaps the greatest of all American myths concerns baseball. The Baseball Hall of Fame is in Cooperstown, New York, because that's where General Abner Doubleday invented baseball. At least, that's the story, and baseball is sticking to it. In reality, however, Doubleday and Cooperstown had absolutely nothing whatsoever to do with baseball. Nothing. Zilch. If there is a "founder" of baseball, it's Alexander Cartwright, whose grand-daughter I once dated in my teens. But I digress.

Yet Doubleday as the founder of baseball is an enshrined American myth. Where are the Canadian heroes of myth?

Sir John A. Macdonald? Not a likely candidate—at least not in Quebec, where he is the man who hanged Louis Riel.

Sir Wilfrid Laurier, who many would say was mainly distinguished for looking distinguished? Many think he was a great Canadian, but you'd be hard-pressed to find a British Columbian who could tell you when Laurier was even prime minister, let alone what he did (besides maintain a mistress, that is).

Mackenzie King? Surely no one would seriously suggest him as the role model for the generations that followed him! Unless, of course, you're interested in spiritual contact between a leader, his mother, and his dog.

John Diefenbaker? He has his following, no question, but is scarcely considered a hero from coast to coast.

More recent prime ministers fare no better. The Far Western provinces' bitter feelings of alienation can be laid directly at the feet of Pierre Trudeau. And would anyone even dare to suggest Brian Mulroney?

This isn't to say that there haven't been great Canadians: Billy Bishop, Dr. Frederick Banting, and Sir William Osler all come to mind. But there is no great hero or single defining moment that binds all Canadians together. The only thing that comes close is Paul Henderson's winning goal in the 1972 hockey series with Russia, which I, like all Canadians, exulted in (even though it was scored by a despicable Maple Leaf, and not by one of the Habs). But surely we all would agree that winning games are only defining moments in Central American dictatorships (in the 1970s, El Salvador and Honduras exchanged military actions over a soccer game).

Many people, including those I just mentioned, qualify as Canadian heroes by any reasonable standards. It's just that *all* Canadians, coast to coast, don't accept them as such.

Until recent times, Canadian historians often tried to cram selected heroes down our throats, while ignoring heroic deeds outside the accepted view of Canada. For the most part these "heroes" were romantics, and the selection always favoured audiences in Ontario and English-speaking Quebec.

Recent writings have broken with tradition. I always thought of George Brown as a temperance freak to be contrasted with the *in*temperance of John A. Macdonald. (There is the wonderful story of an obviously worse-for-wear John A. retorting to an indignant Brown, "The people prefer John A. drunk to George Brown sober.") It now seems, though, that there was a very human side of Brown and that he played a significant role in Confederation. But traditionally we haven't been taught this.

In any case, heroes are hard to come by in Canada. Sitting Bull, the Native leader whose people straddled the border and who led them to victory in the last and greatest battle against the American army (slaughtering the lot of the Yanks), is a great American historical icon. Louis Riel, who fought for recognition and civil liberties for his people, is—for the moment, anyway— an unreconstructed Canadian traitor. As they say—go figure.

Riel, though, is not the only person marginalized by the Ontario–Quebec axis of Canadian history. Ukrainian-Canadians have had a huge effect on all walks of Canadian life, but because they didn't fall within either the French or English version of Canada, as seen by those creating history for the nation's schoolrooms, they have to a large degree been trivialized. Indeed, only Newfoundlanders rival them as the butts of smarmy jokes.

British Columbians have also been shortchanged in the annals of our nation's history: there have been excellent modern biographies of many leading B.C. political and historical figures—Judge Matthew Baillie Begbie (unfairly dubbed the "hanging judge"), Duff Pattullo, Gerry McGeer, and W.A.C. Bennett—but they have largely been unread east of the Rockies.

There have been recent efforts to expand Canada's historical focus, such as the steps toward rehabilitating Louis Riel's reputation, or at least recognizing his importance to Canada's past. But much more needs to be done. For a country to be unified and integrated, people in *all* regions must be encouraged to show pride—for themselves and their own contributions as well as for the nation as a whole. The historical significance of many Canadians is still very much trivialized by the Central Canadian view of history. It must be "untrivialized" so that regions are recognized and feel in their souls that they are an integral part of the whole.

Canadians have other impediments to universal national identity. We did not have an east–west expansion across the plains, as the United States did.

There are no battles of Little Big Horn, shootouts at the O.K. Corral, or wars with Mexico in our history.

Not that the displacement of Natives with slaughter, disease and duplicity is anything to be proud of in actual fact, but "actual fact" has precious little to do with establishing national myths. Had John Wayne, Gary Cooper, Roy Rogers and Gene Autry been Canadians looking to star in film representations of the great Canadian trek across the Prairies, they would have starved—because there was no such trek.

We've never shed blood, in this country, for any particularly noble ideal. Even our history's few violent episodes—the Plains of Abraham battle, the War of 1812—have had more to do with political gains than with lofty notions like free speech or freedom from capricious arrest. Admittedly, the Riel Rebellion may have been based on laudable ideals, but it hardly had the support of Canada's general populace.

I am not, be well assured, recommending bloodshed, but merely asserting a fact. We have had no war of independence to affirm our "inalienable rights." Nor have we had a civil war to settle, once and for all, whether power should be administered centrally or regionally.

In contrast to the U.S., our political culture was inherited from Britain, and did not arise from the likes of a Tom Paine, whose ideas inflamed the Americans, or from the musings and writings of men like Thomas Jefferson, Alexander Hamilton, Benjamin Franklin or James Madison. Any ideals of Tory democracy imported from Britain pale beside the stirring words of the American Declaration of Independence.

While I do suggest that the philosophy of the American system of governance is vastly superior to ours, I by no means suggest that we ape it. I would only live in the United States as a last resort. I simply assert that by reason of circumstance, the United States started from a philosophical base and we did not—that their system, tested in political as well as real fires, has served them (though by no means perfectly) much better than ours has served us.

While our culture may be short on compelling and powerful *national* myths, there are strong regional ones. Unfortunately, the most powerful and wide-reaching of these has had a disastrous effect on national unity. I refer to the pernicious piece of nonsense that states that Canada's culture and history is based upon "two founding nations." This notion was first popularized by Prime Minister Lester Pearson in 1965, in his directive to the Royal Commission on Bilingualism and Biculturalism: the commissioners were to "recommend what steps should be taken to develop the Canadian Confederation on the basis of equal partnership between *two founding races*" [emphasis added]. If the emphasized phrase was merely some harmless bit of historical rubbish, or constitutional chatter with no real impact on actual national affairs, that would be one thing. Unhappily, though, it represents a deadly serious and corrosive theory upon which much of our national discontent is founded.

Canada is not and never has been a duality; in fact, French did not even become an official language until over a hundred years after Confederation. A typical argument for the "two founding nations" theory is that Lord Durham, in his *Report on the Affairs of British North America* in 1839, referred to "two nations warring within a single bosom," and that this observation proves that he recommended a "two founding nations" solution. In fact, he was referring to the conflict *within* Lower Canada. The great ongoing debate there centred on the question of Parliament: Should it be balanced regionally, or elected on the "one man, one vote" principle? The subsequent Act of Union in 1841, affecting both Upper and Lower Canada, was not based upon any notion of duality.

Even if it had been, Confederation in 1867 was a new deal entirely. It did not extend the Province of Canada, as it was then called, but spawned a *new* nation. (A nation, incidentally, that was hardly embraced by all its new citizens in the Maritimes. On July 1, 1867, Halifax merchants hung black crepe outside their establishments in protest.)

With the Confederation agreement, our country was founded by four political entities—Upper Canada or Canada West (which became the province of Ontario), Lower Canada or Canada East (which became the province of Quebec) and the colonies of New Brunswick and Nova Scotia. Prince Edward Island was supposed to join as well, but opted out until 1873, because the deal did not include a plan to buy out absentee landlords (much of P.E.I. was owned by Brits). Newfoundland took part in some of the discussions, but remained aloof from Confederation until 1949.

As for British Columbia, that province contemplated entry in 1867 and joined four years later. The myth that B.C. was a tardy arrival on the scene seems deeply entrenched. I well recall a 1980 meeting of provincial cabinet ministers responsible for constitutional affairs: New Brunswick's attorney general, Rodney Logan (who may have been a tad overserved at lunch) started berating the B.C. ministers, Garde Gardom and myself, arguing that as Confederation Johnnies come lately, we should defer to our elders and betters. There was no convincing Logan—or anyone else, it seemed—that B.C. had been considered in the beginning and admitted four years later, after a freewheeling debate and free vote in the legislature.

I cannot speak for Nova Scotia and New Brunswick, of course, but I can say without fear of contradiction that had B.C. been told in 1871 that it and four other provinces (Manitoba had been created the year before) were to form one half of an equal partnership with Quebec, there would have been no deal. In the terms of Confederation, all the provinces were to be equal before the law.

In fact, the great French Canadian hero of 1867 was Sir George-Etienne Cartier, who said of the political union, "In our Confederation there will be Catholics and Protestants, English, French, Irish and Scotch, and each by its great efforts and success will add to the prosperity of the Dominion, to the glory of the new confederation. We are of different races, not to quarrel, but to work together for the common welfare." Cartier went on to state that out of this mixture we would develop a Canadian nationality. Although he could not have foreseen the country's future Ukrainian, Hutterite, Mennonite, and Doukhobor settlements, the massive Asian immigration, the postwar settlements of Jews, Germans and Italians, or the post-1956 arrival of thousands of Hungarian refugees, presumably those developments have enhanced, not diminished, his argument.

The "two founding nations" theory is nonsense, but nonsense very much believed to be fact by many Quebeckers. Indeed, it has given rise to the notion of "sovereignty-association" propounded by the late Quebec premier Rene Levesque, and is the foundation for the "distinct society" idea, which has formed the starting point for most of Quebec's positions on constitutional matters over the past thirty years.

What does Quebec want?

This is the great Canadian question. It's rather like asking what men want. Or what women want. As a British Columbian, I am about as qualified to answer this question as I am to explain what women want. I can only tell you what I've understood Quebeckers to be saying when they outline what they want. Of course, I'm filtering their viewpoint through a B.C. mindset. So be it. This is what I honestly understand to be what the Quebeckers I've talked to want.

Everyone wants power. If someone else has power, the further away it is exercised, the more it is resented. If the exercise of power is essential to your financial well-being (as in the case of the Atlantic Canada provinces) and you accept that this is the case (unlike Quebec), you learn to live with "benevolent dictatorships" beyond your control. But you come to resent that relationship—and you long for the day you can do something about it.

Quebec's appetite for power has been fed by a number of factors.

1. Tradition. There has been a separatist movement in Quebec since the conquest in 1759, just as in other countries there have been movements for Basques, Kurds and Mayans, just to name a few. *Most* political minorities have a separatist movement, and in most cases they get second prize in their struggle for independence.

    This struggle mustn't be confused with "self-determination," in which colonial peoples throw off the yokes of their masters. Canada is a political union that Quebec contracted freely to enter. The question here is of a minority within an existing state: if every minority were allowed to declare independence, political chaos would result. A compromise must therefore be reached between a desire for greater political power and continued participation in a valid political entity.

2. Perceived political abuse. Northern Ireland is an example of a minority long abused, both politically and economically, by the majority. In contrast, the Canadian government's attentions to Quebec can hardly be characterized as "abusive." The French may have been conquered in 1759, but that has not translated into political abuse in the twentieth century. In England, the Normans conquered the Saxons, but at some point after that, the issue of conquest faded, and both groups came to share the benefits and burdens of their country. Similarly, the Quebec francophones are no more or less a part of Canada than everyone else, and must share both the benefits and the burdens of *our* country.

Quebec has convinced itself that it's being shortchanged in its association with Canada, though the precise opposite is easily demonstrated. Ottawa has an obligation to do more than just turn over money to the provinces—it must maintain things like foreign embassies, the armed forces, and a postal service. The common good is a large part of what a country is all about. Quebec, though, has received very large equalization payments for years and by any yardstick is a net "taker." However, most Quebeckers have been programmed to believe that the province has been treated unfairly—a view that ignores those equalization payments, as well as preferred agricultural arrangements, federal government procurement policies, and international trade agreements that benefit Quebec disproportionately.

3. Promises. The political promises made to the Quebec minority have often fanned the flames of separatism. Often, what might have been obliterated by the passage of time can be revived and given new life by new promises—like the one Brian Mulroney made in 1984, when he pledged that future concessions to Quebec would undo the "betrayal" of the 1982 patriation of the Constitution. Having grown used to special treatment, Quebec City now claims that every federal rejection extends the "humiliation" visited upon French Canada in 1759; Ottawa usually agrees, expressly or tacitly. Therefore it has become a "tradition" that Quebec receive far more than its share of federal government largesse, and every dollar reduced from this "traditional" entitlement becomes another "humiliation." The resulting policy of appeasement was evident in the Bristol Aerospace case of October 1986, when the Mulroney government awarded an aircraft repair contract to Montreal—notwithstanding that the winning bid was from Winnipeg.

What does Quebec want? Quebec wants what she can get, just like everyone else. Unfortunately, she's found a formula of "extortion" (Pierre Trudeau's word, not mine) that works like a charm.

Quebec knows that if she holds her nose until her face turns blue, Ottawa will spring into action and make whatever concessions are necessary to keep peace. All that's needed is an occasional threat of secession.

What Quebec *says* it wants most is protection for its language and culture. However, the federal government that Quebec complains about has been the *reason* these things have been protected and enhanced through the years. Since the Peace of Paris in 1763 (when the long war between Britain and France was settled, leaving Quebec in the hands of the British), through all subsequent political arrangements and new constitutions, these protections have been reaffirmed, and in many cases made immutable. Consider the following:

- French is one of Canada's two official languages. This despite the fact that it is a minority language throughout the country as a whole—over seventy-five percent of the country does *not* speak French—and the world language of commerce is English.
- French Canadians are disproportionately well represented in all levels of the federal government and in organizations the government controls, such as the RCMP and the armed forces.
- Quebec has its own civil code of law, assured by the Constitution, and its right to this has never been questioned. Quebec also permanently holds one third of the Supreme Court of Canada's seats, though it has less than one quarter of the country's population. The argument that the distinctiveness of the Quebec Civil Code makes this necessary is nonsense. Just as civil-law judges have never had trouble deciding common-law cases, so have common-law judges similarly coped. Moreover, with rare exceptions, the Supreme Court of Canada doesn't even hear civil cases any more—just Charter of Rights and Freedoms cases and the occasional criminal matter.
- In the cultural field, about forty percent of the CBC's Radio Canada budget is controlled by French Canada.

One might compare Quebec's situation with that of the francophone Acadians, who were exiled by the British to Louisiana in 1755; no longer a vibrant culture, the Acadians of Louisiana—the "Cajuns"—are now a mere social and linguistic curiosity. One would think that a thoughtful look at their situation would illustrate beyond any doubt just how far Canada has gone to preserve Quebecois culture.

In fact, the language and culture of an independent Quebec would certainly be *worse* off without the protection of a sympathetic larger federal government. It makes no sense (though emotions are admittedly not always sensible) to assume that a lone Quebec would be able to protect its interests if surrounded by (not necessarily friendly) anglophone countries.

What Quebec wants is not the only question. If we are a nation "one, indivisible and indissoluble," as most Canadians want us to be, the entire country should be involved in the country's future. Quebec may one day separate, against the wishes of a majority of Canadians—but until that happens, the federal government and the other provincial leaders must encourage and assert the rights of *all* citizens in *all* regions to assert their views and be listened to.

Our country is made up of ten juridically equal provinces plus a federal government. There can surely be no question of that; it was the basis upon which the country was founded in 1867, and was reaffirmed in 1982. We're not a "compact" from which various segments can, at their whim, withdraw.

Of course, not all provinces have equal clout in Ottawa—that would deny the important principles of majority rule and representation by population. Not all provinces are equal in size, population or wealth.

However, all provinces are equal in terms of provincial jurisdiction over matters within their competence. Admittedly, it could be argued that because they must go to Ottawa with a begging bowl, Manitoba, Saskatchewan and the Atlantic Canada provinces do not have power equal to that of their counterparts. That's true, but they are *juridically* equal, and will be equal in reality when they are no longer so economically bound to Ottawa's purse strings that they must always do as they're told.

Juridical equality of provinces—with special status for none—is an ideal in which a great many Canadians believe. And the number of believers increases as one goes west from the Lakehead. It is in no way weakened by the fact that some provinces on entering Confederation were given bribes, such as the railway to B.C., or special-education wrinkles, as in Quebec and Newfoundland.

A further complication in the issue of Quebec separatism is the question of Ungava, the large part of northern Quebec on Hudson Bay. This region did not enter Confederation as part of Quebec, but as part of Rupertsland, an area including the present Northwest Territories, Yukon and Prairie provinces, given to Canada by Britain as a Confederation gift in 1867. The Ungava region of Rupertsland was given to Quebec through two separate *Canadian* statutes in 1892 and 1912. In his excellent book *Who Gets Ungava?* David Varty argues very ably that for several reasons, that land should revert to Canada if Quebec secedes.

This is not merely some theoretical legal question; it is a very practical concern, since the inhabitants of Ungava have voted, by a margin of over ninety percent, that they wish to stay in Canada in the event of a Quebec separation.

British Columbia has its own "Ungava" situation in the Peace River country, that part of northern B.C. that lies east of the Rockies. This part of Rupertsland was considered part of B.C. upon the province's entry into Confederation in 1871, and that boundary was confirmed in 1905, when Alberta and Saskatchewan were formed from other parts of the Rupertsland area. This area, rich in natural gas, oil, hydroelectric power and farmland, is legally (technically) part of B.C. but geographically part of Alberta, and its inhabitants are quite ambivalent about their status as British Columbians. (As B.C. residents, they pay higher income tax, as well as a sales tax that doesn't exist over the Alberta border a few miles east). Over the years the Peace River area has issued occasional threats of seceding from B.C. How serious this issue may become in the future is open to question, but my guess is that historical and economic considerations will outweigh geography.

Of greater concern to British Columbia—and a greater example of Canada's overall disunity—is the issue of Native land claims, exemplified in the Delgamuukw case.

In British Columbia, unlike other areas of Canada and the U.S., the first meetings of Natives and white settlers spawned almost no treaties; two hundred years later, this has left all of B.C. subject to potential Native land claims. Native leaders have claimed several times that Natives own the entire province of British Columbia, "lock, stock and barrel." On the other hand, others have maintained that all Native claims were extinguished by the British Crown's claim of sovereignty, made in 1846 and reaffirmed in 1871.

It has usually been thought—and I still think this—that all Native matters, including land claims, are the responsibility of the federal government. That's what the Constitution says, and that's what Article 13 of the Act of

Union between Canada and British Columbia says. But while the B.C. government made some (admittedly weak) efforts to get settlement discussions going in the 1970s, the feds would have nothing to do with the matter. Ottawa took the position that Native issues were a federal affair in every imaginable way—*except* when it came to land claims.

The Delgamuukw case involved a huge tract of northern British Columbia—over 23,000 square miles, or about the size of New Brunswick—that was the ancestral homeland of the Gitksan and Wet'suwe'ten Native peoples, who sued for land title and joint jurisdiction. In 1991, after a 374-day trial, Chief Justice McEachern of the B.C. Supreme Court found against the Natives on the question of "title," but did find some "rights of use" in the land accruing to Natives.

However, Mike Harcourt's provincial NDP government, laced with conscience-stricken sentimentalists, made it clear in its first throne speech, in March 1992, that it recognized both Native title and Native self-government. (The former had been rejected in the McEachern decision, and the latter would be emphatically rejected by the public of B.C. in the Charlottetown referendum in the fall of 1992.) This ill-thought-out pronouncement began a nightmare that may never end.

The NDP government fired its lawyers and retained new ones for the appeals process, essentially instructing them to lose on the point of "title." Hard to believe? Well, the province's amended Statement of Defence was so radically altered that the Court of Appeal took the most unusual step of appointing the province's *original* lawyers to appear as *amicus curia* ("friends of the court") to defend the trial judgment!

In spite of their dubious effort, though, the government lawyers won in the provincial Court of Appeal. Like the Supreme Court of B.C., the province's Court of Appeal rejected the use of oral histories presented by Native elders as evidence. And understandably so: this was the rawest of hearsay, at best legend mixed with myth, and backed up by little other cogent evidence.

The Natives then appealed to the Supreme Court of Canada, and in December 1997 British Columbians watched in horror as nine aging lawyers—seven of them with no real association with B.C.—proceeded to find in favour of the appellants, heedless of the disastrous consequences this decision would have on the provincial economy. One could argue that it is the job of Supreme Court judges to uphold the law, regardless of consequences—

except that in this case there was no real Canadian law to go on. Nor did the judges look to Australia or New Zealand, to see how their courts had handled Native land claims; instead, they depended on the writings of dewy-eyed left-wing professors or articles by Antonio Lamer, the Court's own chief justice!

This decision set a mind-boggling precedent. The court, abandoning centuries of evidentiary rules, has opened the door for "oral history"—thus permitting the ramblings of self-interested Native elders to not only be heard, but given special weight!

The question as to whether or not Natives have "title" is now moot—they have, and the only question is where and to what. That question should now proceed to occupy another expensive and gut-wrenching decade, to the immense profit of the "Native industry" (mostly comprising lawyers).

Complementing the Delgamuukw case is the Nisga'a settlement. In the early 1970s, representative chief Frank Calder came within an ace of winning a victory for the Nisga'a that would have been comparable in scope to the Delgamuukw settlement.

Frank Calder became an NDP B.C. MLA in the 1960s, then crossed the floor to join the Socreds in 1975; he and I were caucus mates until 1979, when he lost his seat by one vote. So confident was Frank of winning that election that neither he nor his wife bothered to fly back and vote! (Al Passerell, who won the riding for the NDP, later crossed the floor himself, joining the Socreds in the 1980s.) Frank later married a much younger and very rich Japanese lady, and has lived happily ever after.

Though the Nisga'a lost the Calder case, Pierre Trudeau immediately launched new negotiations, which eventually led to an agreement in principle (AIP) in 1996. There is still no final agreement, but the Nisga'a settlement, and the money and sovereignty it proposes to deliver the Natives, will likely prove a template for future deals. The potential effects are manifold, but I believe two will prove especially significant.

First, the deal will establish a new Native level of government in B.C., co-equal with Ottawa and Victoria, with all three having areas of constitutional authority and some overlap. The Criminal Code and the Charter of Rights and Freedoms will prevail in Native territories.

Second, it will create (in essence) Native homelands similar to the so rightly decried South African homelands. In saying this I will outrage many, and I readily concede that the motivations behind the two cases are very different. In South Africa, the government's intention was to box in a repressed majority and thus facilitate the violation of that majority's civil rights. In British Columbia, the intention is to provide minorities with their own land. In both cases, though, the rights and privileges awarded within the "homeland" are determined by one consideration only—race.

In the Nisga'a AIP, the rights of anyone living in the Nisga'a nation are to be determined by the Nisga'a Council. Even a member of another Native nation cannot claim rights there. If this concept is applied to future Native land claims, B.C. will include large areas in which basic political rights will depend upon race. That is already the case with the Native fishery, established by the Tories, which gives special fishing to Natives only.

How curious and ironic it is that in British Columbia we are trying to dispense with the Indian Act, because it treats people differently if they're Indians—only to replace it with legislation (to be "constitutionalized" in due course) that treats people differently if they are Indians.

The Delgamuukw case has huge ramifications—everyone knows that. The trouble is that we don't know what they will be, or how serious. It came as a shock and surprise even to the Glen Clark government, which had pressed for this result. When the NDP spoke in favour of Native "Aboriginal title," they really didn't believe that it would come to pass. It did. And now this same government, which encouraged the result they said they wanted but hoped would never happen, has to face a sudden and very unpleasant dose of reality, ranging all the way from granting title to huge tracts of land to compensating Natives for trees chopped down, rivers dammed and minerals mined. Perhaps the biggest concern—as if the rest weren't bad enough—is compensating the Musqueam and the Squamish for the city of Vancouver.

Canada's lack of national cohesiveness—exemplified by the dearth of inspiring universal historical mythology, the connecting tissue of any culture—is a problem everywhere in the country. But it is a particular problem in British Columbia. Ignored by Canadian historians, repeatedly asked to approve preferential treatment for another province across the continent, and reeling from the potentially disastrous effects of decisions made in Ottawa, British Columbia has never felt more remote from Canada.

CHAPTER NINE

A Constitution Cast in Stone

In 1976 a number of political events very much changed my life.

First, Rene Levesque and his separatist Parti Quebecois were elected as Quebec's provincial government.

Second, Prime Minister Trudeau asked the provincial premiers to reopen the constitutional file and revisit the notion of patriating Canada's Constitution: after patriation, the Constitution would no longer be a British document administered in Westminster, but a Canadian one administered in Ottawa and the provincial capitals.

Third, at the Western Premiers Conference at Medicine Hat, Alberta, I was appointed chair of the committee assigned to identify and evaluate federal intrusions into provincial areas of jurisdiction—and then shame the federal government into backing off. I would chair that committee for three years.

Fourth, I became chairman of the B.C. Cabinet Committee on Confederation, thus becoming the province's unofficial minister of constitutional affairs. In that capacity, I began a long association and firm friendship with Melvin H. Smith, QC (better known as Mel), one of the foremost constitutional experts in the country and then B.C.'s deputy minister of constitutional affairs. Although Mel reported directly to Premier Bennett, for more than three years he and I worked as a team.

Mel Smith was a fun guy to work with, knowledgable as hell without being even a bit pedantic. We travelled thousands of miles together and became good friends, which we very much remain to this day. We became part of a group that I think it's fair to say has had some influence on constitutional affairs in the province of British Columbia.

Mel was my teacher on a subject that had long interested me; as a British Columbian, I felt that in constitutional matters my province was always getting screwed. Mel also had a visceral feeling that B.C. was always on the short end of the stick, coupled with intellect and immense experience. I think that my hawkishness on the subject rubbed off on Mel (at first I often thought he was too soft in his approach), and soon after our teaming we were both pretty aggressive. I only wish that more of his knowledge and brain power had rubbed off on me.

With Mel doing the real work and me (with my untutored ideas) mostly getting in the way, we put together a set of constitutional papers—centring on the issue of Senate reform—to be presented at the First Ministers Constitutional Conference in 1978. We were much assisted by an academic advisory group made up of faculty from the University of Victoria and the University of British Columbia.

With the support of Premier Bennett, Mel and I laboured long and hard on the research for our Senate-reform file, and I was also carrying other senior portfolios at the same time.

In early 1977 Mel and I visited Europe to see how some of the political federations there worked. We needed some hands-on experience—and we got it. We first spent some time in London, talking to senior officials in charge of the "devolution" of political power, from one central unit to smaller regional units. At that time there was much discussion of creating Scottish and Welsh parliaments, and we examined the notion. This was not terribly helpful, though, because in Canada, of course, power is not "devolved" by Ottawa to the provinces—instead, provincial power is a constitutional right.

We then went to Bonn, West Germany (as it then was) and met with many politicians and bureaucrats. This visit proved very worthwhile indeed. Germany is a true federal state, and its system was of great interest to us. Of particular interest was the *bundesrat* (upper legislative house), and the committees through which both houses worked to pass legislation.

In Mainz, the state capital of the Rhineland-Palatinate, we got wonderful briefings on how the *land* (provincial) government worked, and its relationship to the federal government. We also went to Munich and saw how the *land* of Bavaria, so different from the other German regions in every sense, worked within the federal system.

We then went to Karlsruhe and met with officials of the Constitutional Court. (Germany's highest court has two branches: one for ordinary civil and criminal litigation, and one for constitutional matters.) This was of much interest; it struck us again how incredible it was that in Canada, the prime minister handpicks the judges of the Supreme Court—the court that arbitrates disagreements between the provinces and Ottawa! The Germans were similarly shocked, and we could see why: the appointment of *their* Constitutional Court judges had to pass muster in the *bundesrat*, which was controlled by the *lander* (provinces).

Finally, we visited Switzerland. Here we saw how a multilingual country worked. We saw the federal point of view in the capital, Berne, and the *canton* (provincial) point of view in Lugano, in the Italian region. We also visited Lausanne, a *canton* in the French region, and spent considerable time with both elected officials and bureaucrats. Much of what we saw in Switzerland wasn't really appropriate for Canada, mainly because of the difference in size between the two countries. However, we did notice that this government actually trusted *the people* to make decisions.

Overall, our European jaunt was an important visit, and underscored our views that Senate reform was a high priority.

The completed version of our First Ministers Conference presentation was really Mel's work, and it still makes excellent reading. It has been called by no less an authority than Gordon Gibson (the B.C. Liberal leader at the time, and now a noted author and commentator on unity and Native issues) the "best constitutional presentation of any government, including the federal government." It was magnificently researched and presented—and it was unread. No one in the rest of Canada, from the prime minister on down, gave a damn what B.C. had to say.

The situation was not without its humour. At the First Ministers Conference in November 1978, we presented our proposals—in the form of nine booklets all neatly packaged together—to the premiers, the prime minister, and all the senior federal and provincial bureaucrats. They were received with polite acknowledgment. The following spring we consolidated the nine booklets into *one* volume, and re-presented the proposals at another First Ministers Conference. Everyone was amazed that we had been able to present a *new* set of proposals so soon! No one noticed that they were the same proposals, re-packaged. I wonder why?

Our pivotal argument was for a dramatically changed Senate. We proposed an upper house (Senate) that would equally represent the five regions of Canada, permitting British Columbia (as well as the rest of "outer

Canada") to "plug into" the centre of Canada's political power. For decades, the federal government had misrepresented British Columbia as a province that wanted out (and this continues to this day). In fact, we were trying to opt in.

We were, in hindsight, naive. The most powerful opponent to this notion was Premier Peter Lougheed of Alberta, who at that time opposed any change to the Senate. He pushed for "institutionalizing" the First Ministers Conferences instead (though he was pretty vague on what that actually meant). We tried to reason with Alberta that this was elitist and in no way represented "people power." However, Alberta stood firm and Ontario—under the cool pipe-smoker "Buttermilk Billy" Davis—simply sat back and enjoyed the show.

The reason for Alberta's position was simple: under the B.C. plan, Alberta, Saskatchewan and Manitoba were considered one region for Senate representation purposes. As far as Alberta was concerned, though, if B.C. was to be considered a separate region, so were they. On reflection, I think Peter Lougheed was right. In the context of the times—coming as we were out of a four-region theory developed at an earlier Victoria conference—the five-region plan looked pretty good to B.C. Now, though, I concede that such a plan does injury to the notion of juridical equality of the provinces. Mel Smith has indicated that his thinking is also proceeding in this direction. (Ironically, by the 1990s the biggest proponent of Senate reform was Alberta, led by the very same Peter Lougheed.)

From 1867 until today—and for as far ahead as one can see—Canadian politics has been marked by a long and tortuous search to find a way to change the Constitution. Historically, it was generally assumed that amending the British North America Act, especially those provisions concerning provincial powers, required the unanimous consent of the ten Canadian provinces.

Many were troubled by this notion because it meant that, in a practical sense, the Constitution could never be amended. It's often said, in arguing against the principle of unanimity, that it would be preposterous if tiny Prince Edward Island were able to overturn the will of the majority of Canadians. (In fact, this is a specious argument, for P.E.I. is too reliant on the federal purse to likely veto anything. A veto is much more likely to be used by either Ontario or Quebec, to protect the status quo.)

Constitutional change, then, has centred on a seemingly endless debate about an appropriate "amending formula." However, that term is misleading. What our politicians have really been seeking is a way to parcel out veto power.

Efforts to develop an amending formula have waxed and waned, as constitutional matters will, but in the mid-1960s it looked as if the Fulton–Favreau formula might get the job done. This plan gave four regions—"Atlantic Canada," Quebec, Ontario, and "the West"—veto power over all proposed constitutional change. It was rejected, though, and the next attempt came with the 1971 Victoria Conference, at which the first ministers agreed upon a similar regional veto plan. (Take note: These were "veto" plans, not amending formulae.) For reasons that escape rational thought, Premier Robert Bourassa, then in his first incarnation as Quebec premier, went home, got cold feet and vetoed all that had been agreed to at Victoria—although not because of the amending formula.

Bourassa scrapping the Victoria agreement and its amending formula turned out to be a great (if unintentional) act of Canadian statesmanship—one for which we and our descendants ought to be eternally grateful.

What is so bad about a veto formula? Plenty. Once you hand out vetoes, it doesn't matter that you hand them out to several regions, or even every province. The implicit evil is that a constitutional change desired by the majority can be stopped in its tracks by a minority.

When Pierre Trudeau, in the fall of 1976, began the process of patriating the Constitution, the sticking point was the question of how to amend it once it came to Canada. Without an amending formula, patriation would be very difficult, if not impossible.

I attended every First Ministers Conference from 1977 until September 1980, and watched with considerable amusement as Rene Levesque passionately argued that the Constitution ought to stay at Westminster. Why would a confirmed separatist like Levesque want the Constitution to rest with the *British* Parliament? Simply because, like nearly everyone else, he thought that the existing status quo would effectively ensure Quebec veto power over constitutional change.

I can remember chuckling about this with Claude Morin, Levesque's constitutional minister, over a couple of scotches. I twitted Morin about Quebec working like the devil to keep the Constitution in England. He explained that the Parti Quebecois had no interest in the Canadian Constitution in the first place, since it felt that Quebec should leave Canada no matter what. Better that the Constitution remain in Britain than come to Canada, where new negotiations might endanger what he assumed to be Quebec's traditional right to a veto.

Morin was an interesting case. Unlike some colleagues, he did not take matters personally. A brilliant man, he was also good fun, and enjoyed the friendly banter that came over a drink after sessions had finished for the day.

He was also a superb host. When Mel Smith and I visited Quebec City to meet with him, he treated us to a wonderful tour of that most fascinating of cities. (No one could have been more surprised than I to learn that Claude Morin was, at the time, in the pay of the RCMP, spying on his own Parti Quebecois.)

While Rene Levesque wanted the Constitution to stay in Westminster, Prime Minister Trudeau had other thoughts. Trudeau badly needed an effective amending formula to accomplish his goal: a Canadian Constitution, amendable in Canada, by Canadians.

When Trudeau returned to power in 1980, after the short Tory "interregnum" (Joe Clark had beaten Trudeau in the 1979 federal election, only to be deposed after a non-confidence vote eight months later), he set up the Committee of Cabinet Ministers on the Constitution (CCMC), which brought together two ministers from each province and two from the federal government. The present amending formula, achieved by a compromise before the 1982 patriation, was developed by the CCMC. Jean Chretien, our current prime minister, represented the federal government on the committee—I served on it, too—and the amending formula had his personal approval.

The CCMC's principal task was to do what until then seemed impossible: find an amending formula all could agree to. They did actually agree on a formula: the so-called seven-and-fifty clause. This was erroneously named: actually, its formula for approving a constitutional amendment required the support of two thirds of the provinces with fifty percent of the population, and Ottawa (though as long as there are ten provinces, in fact the approval of seven would be required—thus the term "seven and fifty").

This was truly an ingenious amending formula, insofar as the seven-and-fifty part was concerned. Because the formula addressed provinces as well as populations *within* provinces, it effectively meant that for an amendment to pass, *either* Ontario *or* Quebec (as populations then stood) had to be onside. This could change, though, with population swings; the practical application of the formula was adjustable. This formula was in fact approved in writing by Rene Levesque on April 16, 1981, when the premiers of the so-called "Gang of Eight"—from every province except except Ontario, New Brunswick and Ottawa—signed the "Vancouver Consensus Formula."

By way of comparison, the United States also has an "amending formula" where a constitutional amendment requires the consent of three quarters of the states and two thirds of each congressional house. A tough threshold but, as events have clearly demonstrated, an achievable one.

It's important to note—though hardly discussed—that our amending formula came about through hard work and provincial compromise, and was also an integral part of the patriation deal itself. Pierre Trudeau wanted the Constitution to include a Charter of Rights and Freedoms, and wanted it badly. This was the centrepiece of his package.

However, the Charter was initially rejected by many premiers, including Sterling Lyon of Manitoba and Allan Blakeney of Saskatchewan. Lyon and Blakeney conceded that rights had sometimes been inadequately protected by Parliament, but as Blakeney frequently said, "If I have a problem with my rights, I want to go to my MLA or MP, not some cloistered group of tenured judges in Ottawa." This led to the "Gang of Eight," the Vancouver Consensus Formula and the seven-and-fifty amending plan.

Trudeau then offered the premiers a major compromise: You give me my charter and I will give you your amending formula. Trudeau thus got his Charter of Rights and Freedoms, but with one important concession: a "notwithstanding clause," which permitted governments (federal and provincial) to enact legislation breaching the Charter in circumstances they deemed "special"—if they were prepared to face the accompanying political flak. It was through use of this "notwithstanding clause" that Quebec passed its controversial "sign laws" in 1988, which seriously curtailed the use of the English language on public signs in Quebec.

After the final negotiations, Levesque maintained that Quebec had been betrayed by the agreement that permitted Trudeau to bring home the Constitution. Part of the unhelpful mythology Levesque whined about (which whining was exploited by Mulroney to great advantage in 1984) was that Quebec had been betrayed by the "Night of the Long Knives" at the First Ministers Conference in November 1981. This was an impromptu meeting of bureaucrats that also involved Jean Chretien and Roy Romanow. Levesque, tired after a long day, did not attend.

No doubt Levesque had much to be annoyed at, but betrayed he wasn't. Since then, it has become accepted by separatists and their appeasers alike that this all involved cramming the seven-and-fifty amending formula down Quebec's throat. This was the main rationale behind both the new formulas proposed with the Meech Lake and Charlottetown Accords. That's nonsense of course. It was a myth developed for political purposes, just as Mulroney later invented the the notion that Meech Lake was killed by Clyde Wells (a Liberal) and not by Elijah Harper (a Native).

The exposure of the myth is in writing for all to see—Rene Levesque's signature on, in its full name, the "Canadian Patriation Plan on Amending the Constitution"—the Vancouver Consensus Formula.

Why did Levesque endorse that plan in the first place? I can only speculate that there were three reasons. Any chance to cock a snook at Trudeau (whom he despised from another movie) was welcome. Also, it cost Levesque nothing to agree *then*, because he knew that he would never agree to the *final* package. He also probably didn't think there was any chance that Ontario, New Brunswick and Ottawa would agree to implement the Vancouver Formula anyway.

During the leadup to the conference of November 5, 1981 (Guy Fawkes Day, interestingly), Levesque had indicated that he approved the seven-and-fifty formula if all else met with his approval. Then, on the "Night of the Long Knives," Roy Romanow of Saskatchewan and Jean Chretien, then Trudeau's right-hand man on the Constitution, brokered a deal that all other provinces would agree to with or without Quebec. Levesque, who had never had any intention of making a deal anyway, hollered "betrayal," and whether or not Levesque favoured the new amending formula became moot.

Levesque mounted a challenge in the Quebec Court of Appeal, which was subsequently heard on appeal by the Supreme Court of Canada, complaining that unanimous consent of the provinces should be required to patriate the Constitution and that he, for one, wasn't consenting. Quebec was, argued Levesque, a "distinct society" both in fact and, more importantly, in law.

He got second prize. Every judge in each court, including the Supreme Court of Canada sitting with the full nine judges, found against him. The Constitution came to Canada complete with the new seven-and-fifty amending formula. Quebec was not, in law, a "distinct society."

Let me comment upon the remarks of former chief justice Brian Dickson. Dickson has said, in widely read articles and speeches, that in practice the Supreme Court of Canada was already treating Quebec as a "distinct society." If that's true, Canada is in even more trouble than we thought, because our highest court is no longer bound by the rule of law. If Dickson is correct, the Supreme Court is cocking a snook at the Constitution of Canada, and making things up as it goes along.

In fact, Justice Dickson is mistaken. In two key cases—the 1982 decision affirming the validity of the Constitution's patriation, and the Quebec "language case" of 1988—Canada's highest court found that Quebec had no different rights or powers than those of any other province. The main basis cited for the 1982 decision was the B.N.A. Act's lack of reference to any special status for anyone.

Either Dickson is being mischievous, is badly informed or is irresponsibly using his past position to further a political aim. In any event, he's created legitimate fears that the future of this country won't be decided by the people of Canada through their elected representatives, but by an aging cabal of lawyers appointed to our highest court by the prime minister of the day— and subject to the review of no one, either before their appointment or after.

In any case, Rene Levesque wasn't betrayed at all. During the negotiations, I watched the Quebec delegation at work and met with them socially. They were nothing if not honest throughout the patriation exercise. They made it clear that while they would sit through the entire process to safeguard Quebec's interests, *they would never, under any circumstances, make a deal.*

Thus the patriation process, while controversial, was at the end of the day a matter of consensus—which is not to say unanimity. The Conservative opposition under Joe Clark accepted, after many revisions that they had in large measure instigated, that the admittedly imperfect deal was still supportable and something to build upon. I would argue that even the people of Quebec were prepared to live with the deal, as evidenced by the calm that ensued.

But myths are powerful tools. In the wake of the patriation agreement, Rene Levesque, the Parti Quebecois and others created and then perpetuated the myth that Quebec had been snookered. Regardless of Levesque's spin doctoring, though, the amending formula was a "done deal," forged in the crucible of debate and sanctified by the Queen, a constitutional handshake and a new Constitution Act, passed by the Parliament of Canada and signed by the Queen.

A flexible amending formula is crucial to the constitutional and political health of the country, not because a lot of amendments take place—they don't. However, when change may be difficult but is always possible, as with a flexible amending formula, *constitutional change is constantly under debate.* This is critical to the health of a federal state—indeed, any state. Debate is the staff of life to a constitutional democracy. Without serious discussion, pressures build with no hope that they can even be alleviated, much less solved.

Before 1982, debates, organizations and conferences dealing with the yeast of reform abounded. Nothing was solved, but arguments were advanced, people were educated on issues, and a feeling was always in the air that necessary change could be undertaken, albeit slowly. I attended many of these conferences, and while most of them accomplished nothing firm, thoughts were constantly aired and ideas were exchanged between people from all across Canada. I got to know many fascinating people, including one of my sports heroes, Ken Dryden, who is a deeply thoughtful student of this country. (Pity that he fell in with evil companions and is now general manager of the Toronto Maple Leafs!) There were many others; Peter Russell, Ronald Watts, and Peter Hogg—all learned constitutional professors—come to mind. Politicians from coast to coast attended these meetings, as did nationally known public-affairs commentators and senior journalists.

Opinion-makers are by no means confined to society's "elite"; they are people from all walks of life who, on a given subject, usually have sound opinions that we either agree with or use to test our own beliefs. I, for example, am a devout fisherman and a pretty good one, but there are many people in B.C., ranging from train engineers to pulp workers to lawyers, whose opinions I will seek out on fishing questions.

It may be difficult to quantify the results of these ongoing and passionate exchanges of ideas. However, the United States' thirty-odd constitutional amendments point to the value and practical effect of political discussions and debates—they are an important part of the national ferment.

Now, though, these discussions have virtually ended, because there is no longer any point to them. In December 1995, shortly after separatist forces very nearly won a Quebec referendum on separation, Prime Minister Jean Chretien passed a House of Commons resolution that prevented Parliament from amending the Constitution without unanimous consent from four regions: "Atlantic Canada," Quebec, Ontario and "the West." After all hell broke loose, British Columbia was added as a separate region.

After that addition, there was general rejoicing in B.C. Then the freezing came out; British Columbians realized that their veto power didn't make anything better—that the provinces most likely to press for future change were Alberta and B.C., so vetoes were *still* a bad idea, even if B.C. now had one. It's true enough that either Quebec or Ontario might seek constitutional changes to further entrench the status quo—making a virtue of vetoes in other provinces—but that seems highly unlikely.

The bottom line is that no democratic federation can exist for long when its Constitution cannot, for all practical purposes, be changed without unanimous consent. Under Chretien's veto concoction, which promised that the Commons would veto any proposals opposed by any of five regions, almost any constitutional initiative will likely be vetoed by Chretien. So why even discuss it?

Why discuss *any* changes to the Constitution? Or perhaps even more importantly, why even try to look down the road, and face difficulties with some degree of readiness, if the Constitution is cast in stone?

Why even discuss the structural changes that will be necessary in, say, 2050, when B.C.'s population is bigger than Quebec's? How will we then justify six senators for B.C. when Quebec has twenty-four? That state of affairs is ridiculous now and will grow even more so with time.

Vetoes constipate the body politic, and sooner or later constitutional issues become critical. Sometime in the next century, more likely sooner than later, British Columbia will feel the need to secede. B.C. has never been able to participate in national affairs, and will likely be denied the constitutional changes to which its increased population and importance would entitle it.

Perhaps most of the country will agree that B.C. has long-standing griev-ances that need attending to. But so what? What will be the point of even talking about these grievances when either Ontario or Quebec, intent on maintaining the status quo, will veto any proposed constitutional changes, however fair they may be? (It's argued, of course, that Quebec doesn't *want* the status quo—Quebec wants to leave the country. That's true, but as long as Quebec does remain in Canada—as long as the constitutional and finan-cial concessions keep coming—Quebec will resist every constitutional change, no matter how small. Bet on it. Quebec will *certainly* veto any changes that add influence to other provinces at the expense of its own.)

We have become, and will remain so long as we have a veto formula, a country that can't change its institutions to meet new circumstances—and because of that, can't be bothered to discuss critical matters of governance any more. This state of affairs—and the fact that Jean Chretien had a hand in the original seven-and-fifty formula itself—is what makes Chretien's outrageous "amending formula" of December 1995 so disgraceful.

CHAPTER TEN

The Three Disasters

In 1983 Brian Mulroney became leader of the federal Progressive Conservative Party, and set in motion an ongoing series of Canadian disasters.

In the days immediately following patriation in 1982, things had begun to settle down in Quebec, and it appeared that Canada had put a major problem behind it. Mulroney tells a different story, one of great popular unrest, but adherence to the truth (especially when the alternative is politically helpful) was never his strong suit.

Why shouldn't things have been settling down in Quebec? Quebeckers respect the rule of law—and Parliament, Quebec's own Court of Appeal and the Supreme Court of Canada had all ruled the patriation lawful. Moreover, Canada now had its own Constitution and could amend it in Canada under a formula that, while difficult, was possible. All we needed was a spell of constitutional peace, to allow us to get on with meeting other national and regional challenges.

We were not to get one moment's peace, and even today none is foreseeable.

The First Disaster: Brian Mulroney's Election (1984)

At first, Brian Mulroney supported Trudeau's patriation program. He accepted that Quebec was bound by the 1982 Constitution Act and its amending formula. Mulroney's later notion that Quebec had been betrayed came only after he realized that with this stand he could co-opt a great deal of Quebec's separatist leadership and lead the Tories back to federal power after their humiliating 1980 defeat. Mulroney was nothing if not a political animal, in the worst sense of that term.

After his politically helpful conversion, Mulroney went from supporting the 1982 Constitution to toadying favour with Quebec separatists by condemning it. Then he turned up the rhetoric as only Mulroney could. He declared that Quebec was not bound by the Constitution, because the separatist PQ government had refused to sign on. Mulroney would, he said, "bring Quebec into the constitutional family" and "make Canada whole again." More pernicious phrases it is hard to imagine.

Brian Mulroney had two things on his agenda: he would bring in a free trade agreement with the United States, and he would solidify Quebec as a power base—both for himself personally and for the Progressive Conservative Party. This latter ambition was glossed over lightly by Canada's chattering classes, who wanted to see the back of the Liberals so badly that they weren't going to look too deeply into Mulroney's game plan. To most of English Canada, the 1984 federal election was an opportunity to throw out the Trudeau-associated Liberal regime once and for all, and Mulroney looked like the best opportunity.

Part of the Mulroney plan involved putting his own election before all else, by attracting out-and-out separatists to his cause—including Lucien Bouchard, now the separatist premier of Quebec. And he did it by promising constitutional change. Mulroney and his troops referred to their new separatist allies as "nationalists." The centrepiece of his election plan—though it was played down outside of Quebec—was a Quebec veto over all constitutional change.

In 1982, there was a chance for a lengthy constitutional holiday that would allow old wounds to heal and new opportunities to surface. With the reasonably flexible seven-and-fifty amending formula, this might well have led to the calm consideration of needed changes to our system of governance.

Brian Mulroney destroyed all that.

The Second Disaster: The Meech Lake Accord

In politics, as in life in general, you need luck—and in 1986, Brian Mulroney was presented with a miraculous bit of luck. When the perpetrators of Meech Lake come before the celestial bar of justice to account for their part in breaking up their country, the ten provincial leaders who met at the Edmonton Premiers Conference in August 1986 will have every bit as much to answer for as Brian Mulroney. For at that conference, the ten premiers met for lunch, without their officials, deputies and advisors, and decided to postpone dealing with all constitutional matters until the demands of Quebec had been met.

It was dazzling stupidity, a colossal blunder that poisoned the constitutional chalice well into our future. As I watched what happened I couldn't help but think of some of these premiers' predecessors—Bill Bennett, Allan Blakeney, Sterling Lyon—and think how quickly those brains would have seen the obvious: *If you give Quebec what she wants—including a veto—before other important matters like the Senate are considered, Quebec will then have the power to* prevent *these other important matters from being dealt with.* And surely no one could doubt that Quebec would use the veto she so earnestly sought.

This conference (and later constitutional meetings of premiers) inspired a classic witticism from the late great *Vancouver Sun* journalist Marjorie Nichols, who opined that the group needed B.C. premier Bill Vander Zalm around to explain the tough parts to Alberta premier Don Getty. In fact, it can fairly be said that never has so *much* stupidity gathered in one place and done such lasting harm—the obvious exception being Robert Bourassa, who knew exactly what he was doing.

Because British Columbia was as responsible for this incredible blunder as any other province, now is a good time to take a look at Bill Vander Zalm. I know of no one who dislikes Vander Zalm personally; he is thoroughly likable. He has an outgoing personality and is loaded with charisma. What he *hasn't* is an education, or any philosophical grounding to give responsible shape to his administration once he's been elected.

I served in Bill Bennett's provincial cabinet with Vander Zalm for five years and can never remember him making any serious point on discussions that were outside the concerns of his own portfolio. His ministerial career, to be as charitable as humanly possible, was mediocre at best. As human resources minister in 1975, he promised to give "welfare bums" a shovel if they couldn't find work, and started a much vaunted program to put people to work. At the end of the day, despite much bleating to the contrary, he never found anyone a job.

As education minister, Vander Zalm was known for public pronouncements that contained more grammatical errors per line than one would have thought possible from the dullest student in his system. But it was not just a lack of formal education that badly limited his abilities; unlike Bill Bennett, he had no informal education either. Vander Zalm was a successful tulip-bulb salesman who reached his level of incompetence when he left the mayor's chair in Surrey and moved past issues of garbage, sewers and subdivisions. (He reached his level of incompetence before that, according to many Surrey residents, but since I was never a constituent, I shall avoid comment on that.)

Furthermore, at no time in his public life did Bill Vander Zalm show the slightest interest in constitutional matters—except on two occasions. In 1976, when Rene Levesque and the Parti Quebecois were elected in Quebec, Bill's helpful public observation—blasted across the land, electronically and in print, was that perhaps now we wouldn't have to read French on our Corn Flakes boxes. This brilliant contribution to national unity was, unbelievably, surpassed in 1980, when Vander Zalm composed a song about Rene Levesque and "frogs"—and sang it publicly. This was at the time of a First Ministers Conference, and on day one Bill Bennett was greeted with this most embarrassing bit of doggerel. Again, it played coast to coast, and was mortifying to a province that was trying to combat its sometimes "redneck" image. Needless to say, this did little to enhance the seriousness with which B.C.'s presentations were received.

When Bill Vander Zalm went to Edmonton in 1986 and to Meech Lake in 1987, he was not only a neophyte premier, but one who had consciously disregarded all the great national questions he would be called upon to help decide. Moreover, he had a habit of utterly ignoring expert advice.

The implications of the Edmonton Premiers Conference were staggering. Now Brian Mulroney could proceed with his plans, unhindered by barracking from the cheap seats. Not only had the premiers taken their respective publics out of the game, by failing to consult them, but they had taken *themselves* out as well.

Mulroney went to work and in June 1987 entertained the first ministers at Meech Lake, where they came up with a document that, amongst many things, designated Quebec a "distinct society" and gave the province a veto. In effect, the so-called Meech Lake Accord would have required provincial unanimity for virtually all amendments to the Constitution—thus giving Quebec her cherished veto, under the guise of giving a veto to everyone.

It is not my intention (you'll probably be pleased to hear) to discuss all the conferences, elections and other significant events that followed the Meech Lake agreement. For that I would recommend Joe C. W. Armstrong's *Farewell the Peaceful Kingdom*, published by Stoddart in 1995. The best recommendation I can give this book is that it was dumped on by virtually every establishment critic who had contact with it.

Suffice it to say that by June 1990, the deadline for ratification of the agreement, the political scene had changed—especially in Newfoundland, where Liberal Clyde Wells had taken over from Brian Peckford and had repealed Newfoundland's approval of the deal; in New Brunswick, where the boy wonder, Frank McKenna, tried to inject his own amateurish notions (he proposed a "parallel accord," a notion that died quickly); and in Manitoba, which with days to go had still not passed the Accord, and where resistance to it had grown greatly both inside and outside the legislature.

As for British Columbia, it was with the Meech Lake deal that the province's public cut its teeth on matters constitutional. This exercise would lead, to the astonishment of the establishment, to the massive rejection of the Charlottetown Accord in 1992.

In the beginning, the public seemed ready to accept what their "masters" had concocted at Meech Lake, but there were niggling concerns. What about this "distinct society" bit? Would it mean, for example, that if Quebec wanted to pass a new restrictive language law, it would not have to even bother invoking the "notwithstanding clause" to run roughshod over minority rights? And what about the absence of any reform to the Senate, long a bugaboo in Lotusland? Would we now, because of Quebec's veto, be stuck with the present nonsensical Senate forever more?

The answer to these questions, when people thought about them, was a clear "Yes."

The B.C. legislature, controlled by Bill Vander Zalm and the Socreds, approved Meech Lake promptly, a decision supported by Official Opposition leader Mike Harcourt. Difficult though it may be to believe, Harcourt knew even less about constitutional matters than Bill Vander Zalm. (That would become evident when the Charlottetown agreement was reached in 1992.)

Between June 1987, when the deal was initialed at Meech Lake, and June 1990, when all provinces were due to be officially signed on, people in B.C.

got more and more uneasy. They began to ask the questions that Canada's leadership ought to have been asking.

When Premier Clyde Wells of Newfoundland began, in 1989, to seriously and studiously demand answers, he became a folk hero in B.C. He visited the province several times and was on my show, either in person or by phone, half a dozen times or more. Around the same time, Gordon Wilson (to become in 1997, ironically, a sometime special advisor to the provincial NDP government on constitutional matters) became leader of the B.C. Liberal Party, and established himself very quickly as emphatically opposed to Meech. He began to reach an audience too, and was a frequent and always provocative guest on my show.

(I have no idea what influence I had, if any, on the approximately 150,000 British Columbians around the province who hear my editorial every morning, but I had started editorializing on the subject of Quebec appeasement in the days *before* Meech Lake, when Brian Mulroney first came to power, declaiming that he would make Canada "whole again.")

In all events, Clyde Wells became such a hero to British Columbians that, according to his office, he received more than ten thousand letters, faxes and, yes, flowers from this province. This was before e-mail and, judging by how much my own mail has increased with the Internet, one can only speculate at the volume of e-mail Wells would have received.

In an attempt to rally the flagging forces, Mulroney summoned the premiers to Ottawa in May 1990 for the famous "hothouse" meeting where, as Mulroney smugly told the nation, he "rolled the dice." He took the premiers behind closed doors and pressured them tremendously; even Mr. Cool, the cerebral Clyde Wells, was overwhelmed.

The deal still needed ratification in the Manitoba and Newfoundland legislatures, though, and it missed the deadline when Elijah Harper, a Manitoba MLA, stonewalled the proceedings. This didn't prevent Mulroney and his pet toadies, John Crosbie and Senator Lowell Murray, from laying all the blame on Wells, dumping all over him from a great height and for a very long time. Wells had refused to call the vote on Meech in the Newfoundland legislature, even though the debate had finished; as he told my audience, a vote would have caused deep wounds that were entirely unnecessary, since Manitoba had already tubed the deal. Still, Mulroney could hardly blame a Native, and Wells was, after all, a Liberal.

It's my strong feeling that this tremendous beating is what turned Clyde Wells around to Mulroney's side when the Charlottetown agreement was reached. I believe that Wells was put under immense pressure by Ottawa— pressure that a severely economically disabled province could not resist.

In fairness, I must say that Wells has stoutly denied this to me, both publicly and privately. I am a great admirer of Clyde Wells, but on this point (having spent so much time publicly and privately with him over the Meech Lake issue), I just don't believe him. I don't say he's lying; not at all. I just think Wells was so thoroughly battered in the Meech Lake fight that by the time of the Charlottetown agreement, he simply *knew* that his province would face economic reprisals if he acted on his personal principles. I may be wrong, but I don't think so.

In any case, Meech Lake was a disaster for many reasons, not the least of which was the utter absence of public input. We must surely thank God it failed. But Brian Mulroney wasn't through, and within a year he started the whole process again, with a couple of wrinkles. That leads us to Charlottetown.

The Third Disaster: The Charlottetown Accord

Brian Mulroney learned some lessons from Meech Lake. Not many, but some. For one thing, he learned that he had better personally stay away from the constitutional process. If he had kept to that self-discipline, the Charlottetown referendum might have turned out differently, though I doubt it.

After the demise of Meech Lake, Quebec opted to remain aloof and wait for the rest of the country, super new deal in hand, to apologize for the "humiliation." This time Joe Clark, surely the modern version of Jackie Gleason's "The Poor Soul," was to quarterback the appeasement effort for the feds.

In July 1992, Clark reached a deal with nine premiers, but of course Robert Bourassa of Quebec was having none of it—so in August, at Charlottetown, Bourassa and Brian Mulroney brokered a new deal acceptable to all ten premiers.

In the so-called Charlottetown Accord, there were only two important changes to the amending formula proposed at Meech Lake: the seven-and-fifty rule would now apply to the selection of Supreme Court judges, and Quebec (with its falling population) would be guaranteed a permanent twenty-five percent of the House of Commons. This was unamendable, of course, because Quebec would also get a constitutional veto. This was supposed to compensate Quebec for losing some power in the new Senate, which constitutional expert (and now Liberal MP) Ted McWhinney called a "damp squib." The Senate proposed was only a small part "triple-E" (which was the demand of Alberta and B.C.)—it was elected all right, but scarcely equal and certainly not effective.

Were there no politicians, business leaders, labour leaders or members of the arts community who could see what a fundamental breach of democratic principles this deal involved? Had we come to the point that we would do whatever it took to satisfy Quebec, without regard to principle or consequences?

Luckily, by this time both Quebec and British Columbia had provincial legislation requiring a public referendum before approving any constitutional changes, and there was no safe political way for Mulroney to avoid extending that referendum to include the entire country. And because the amending formula to the Constitution could not be changed except by unanimous consent, the Charlottetown Accord had to be passed by every province. As a result, a country-wide referendum on whether or not to accept the terms of the Charlottetown Accord was set for Monday, October 26, 1992. I can only thank a merciful God for the blessings bestowed on the country by Quebec City and Victoria when they passed their respective referendum laws.

Again, this is not the place for a blow-by-blow rehash of the Charlottetown process (if it can be so dignified). And I am not the person to do it, because I was a very outspoken opponent of the deal from the start. It was difficult for me because, having gotten into the media game late, I knew that others in the business resented my success, and they were quick to point out my many failings as a journalist. But I felt so strongly that this deal would ruin the country that I simply could not do the customary "on the one hand, on the other hand" journalism. I decided that I wasn't, after all, a journalist but an editorialist. Editorialists have opinions and they express them. That was my style and I would stick with it.

Why did I become so persistent that before the Canadian people killed the Charlottetown deal, Brian Mulroney would call me a traitor and John Crosbie would label me "Canada's most dangerous man"? Mainly because it seemed that Canada's entire establishment was going to uncritically support the deal. Business, labour, virtually all politicians, the artsy-fartsy set, and especially the media were going to support this compact without ever asking any questions.

Let me pause here to deal with the question of whether or not there is an "establishment," though I should have thought that matter settled by Peter C. Newman's fine book *The Canadian Establishment*. Admittedly, there is no formal organization that meets in secret to run the affairs of the country. There *is*, however, a network of powerful people with interlocking interests, who can sometimes be counted upon to toe a common line. This group includes not only the senior business community, but organized labour, the professions and the arts. All of these factions may quarrel amongst themselves as to their respective shares of the pie from time to time, but they will huddle together like musk ox if the status quo is seriously challenged. For all his stated hatred of big business, "Buzz" Hargrove, the Canadian Auto Workers Union leader, has a vested interest in seeing the system continue. Similarly, the auto industry needs Hargrove. The artsy-fartsy crowd, which constantly complains that business and government don't do enough for its interests, but doesn't ever want to upset any applecarts, also has a deep interest in maintaining the status quo. And the establishment *certainly* includes the mainstream media.

But never mind my assertions. The very uniformity of the original establishment reaction to the Charlottetown Accord ought to demonstrate to the most dubious jury that an establishment does indeed exist. For at the beck and call of Prime Minister Mulroney, who personally called his network of friends and political contacts, everyone who was anyone in this country rallied to the "Yes" side of the issue. Management and labour alike dropped their swords and waded into the fray. The legal profession jumped in with enthusiasm. The arts crowd jumped aboard too, as did what Vancouver writer Denny Boyd calls the "higher-purpose persons": those people from all walks of life who portray their small-l liberal views as emanating from a higher plateau than those expressed by ordinary mortals. The latter is perhaps best represented by June Callwood: when I heard her oh-so-Toronto voice urging British Columbians to support Charlottetown for the good of the nation, I saw another big boost for B.C.'s "No" vote—not because of the province's legendary dislike for Toronto, but because Callwood was so representative of Toronto's control over this country that most British Columbians would have no doubt about whose good she was really talking. As various other "national" figures began speaking out in favour of Charlottetown, I knew that each such pronouncement was a nail in the accord's coffin. The Ontario-dominated "Yes" committee, though, *didn't* understand this.

Then there was the media. Every single strand of the mainstream media across the land jumped on the "Yes" side. How could that happen in a free country? Surely there would be someone somewhere in the media, especially in the newspaper field, who would at least raise some questions. But no; so far as I know, with the exceptions of myself, Dave Rutherford of Calgary's QR77, Mel Smith in *B.C. Report* and *Alberta Report* magazines, Gordon Gibson and Brian Kieran of the *Vancouver Province*, everyone was clearly onside. In fact, the Maclean Hunter corporation actually registered with the "Yes" committee!

Finally, where were opposition politicians? The Official Opposition and the NDP supported Charlottetown, as did provincial politicians from coast to coast (with the important exception of Gordon Wilson, the B.C. Liberal leader whose party split on the issue).

Brian Mulroney's ability to co-opt such a disparate group into supporting Charlottetown is indeed a testament to his enormous powers of persuasion. People who utterly loathed each other banded together to support this deal. Few of them *thought* about the deal, but they supported it.

For me, though, Mair's *Axiom I* came into play: Why on earth should we assume that these men in charge knew what the hell they were doing? After all, it was the ten premiers of Canada who had decided back in August 1986 to place the pacification of Quebec before all else in the first place. Why on earth should any intelligent Canadian assume that this sort of leadership would now conclude an equitable pact?

My attack on the Charlottetown Accord was launched from my morning show at CKNW. Because I was so vocally against the deal and had the station's largest audience, the station took to giving editorial time to spokespeople for the "Yes" side just before I went on-air, to "balance" the debate — a debate in which everywhere else in the country, the "Yes" side had all the money and all the media onside.

I well remember Jack Munro—head of the B.C. Forestry Alliance, a former labour leader and a man definitely opposed to Mulroney politically—likening Charlottetown to a labour contract. He argued that if our leaders had hammered out what they felt was a good deal, we should accept it. This notion was clearly nonsense, and very dangerous nonsense to boot. While labour and management can renegotiate their deals every two or three years, Charlottetown was, because of the vetoes it awarded to potential future amendments, cast in stone forever. In the end, this distinction was not lost on the public.

Without exception, other community leaders also supported the deal, not because it was a good one (they never dealt with any specific merits) but because it would "save Canada." Ironically, such testimony did a great deal to convince British Columbia that the deal was rotten. All I had to do each morning was ask when someone on the "Yes" side was going to answer the questions that I, Mel Smith and Gordon Gibson were asking. As the wait for those answers lengthened, you could sense support growing for the "No" side.

Even if Charlottetown were the best of deals, which it clearly was not, I strongly felt that it should be fully debated. To have a matter of great importance accepted without any opposition struck me as similar to political procedure in the old Soviet Union. Since I could see so much wrong with the deal—as did people whose judgment I trusted—how could the entire Canadian ruling class see it to be blemish-free? And why did they make Charlottetown's opponents out to be bad Canadians?

The strength of a free society is the testing of every government initiative by opposition. To say that there was nothing in the Charlottetown deal to oppose is a denial of common sense. Constitutional experts like Mel Smith and Professor Ron Cheffens of the University of Victoria were very much opposed. After the campaign, many other students of national affairs—whose help I would have welcomed at the time—made it clear that they had always had serious reservations about the Accord.

The pressure during the pre-referendum campaign was enormous, and I must say that as a lonely, perhaps shrill, voice in the wilderness, I would from time to time ask myself if perhaps I was wrong, and thus doing a great disservice to the country I love.

I comforted myself with two thoughts. First, my voice did not get outside of British Columbia much, although as it became clear, in the campaign's dying days, that B.C. was going "No," that may have helped the "No" cause elsewhere. Second, I thought that if this deal, supported as it was by virtually everyone in Canada who counted, couldn't survive a lonely talk-show host in Vancouver, perhaps it didn't warrant passage for that reason alone.

Happily, I wasn't completely alone. I took considerable comfort from the reasoned, logical arguments Gordon Wilson was making, in speeches in the provincial legislature and around the province. My two major comrades in arms, though, became Melvin H. Smith, QC, and Gordon F. Gibson. We lunched together, spoke on the phone a lot and generally kept in touch, forming a sort of "No" support group.

Mel, a constitutional advisor extraordinaire, was my old colleague during the constitutional wranglings of the late 1970s. We established a firm respect and enduring friendship, and Mel later became one of the staunchest supporters of the seven-and-fifty amending formula he did so much to hammer out. (Though I now recall with some embarrassment that in our B.C. constitutional proposals of 1978, we proposed an amending formula that was, in essence, a five-region veto plan. Our only excuse, I suppose—and it's not on very high moral ground, I grant you—is that had our proposal been accepted, the reforms B.C. wanted would thereby have been in place.)

Because I had been vacationing in Britain when the Charlottetown deal was first reached, an article by Mel in *B.C. Report* magazine was first off the mark opposing Charlottetown. (I like to think that I later made up for lost time.) Throughout the campaign, Mel's articles were magnificent and were reprinted in huge quantities. Without any question at all, the influence of his writings and many speeches had a profound effect on the outcome of the referendum, in British Columbia and elsewhere.

As for Gordon Gibson, he had been the provincial Liberal leader when I was in the legislature. Sired by Gordon Gibson, Sr., the "Bull of the Woods" who broke the Sommers scandal back in the early sixties (in which a Socred forests minister went to jail for accepting bribes), Gordon, Jr., was steeped in British Columbia history, geography, business and politics. During my stint as Bill Bennett's constitutional point man in the 1970s, Gordon was the only member of the Opposition who showed any interest in what we were doing—and he showed a lot. Gordon and I spent time together, and he became an admirer of B.C.'s 1978 constitutional position and the process from which it was derived. He has been a thinker and writer on constitutional matters for many years now, and writes a weekly column from the B.C. perspective in the Toronto *Globe and Mail*, and he is also a senior fellow with the Fraser Institute headquartered in Vancouver.

There was an unreal air about the whole Charlottetown campaign. All the media, especially the Toronto *Globe and Mail*, gave the impression that this one was a no-brainer. It was bound to pass. Yet that's not the way it felt to me. And political prognostication very much depends upon the feeling in the pit of your tummy. My tummy told me that the referendum would go down the tube in British Columbia, and thus the deal would be killed.

Early in the Charlottetown campaign, I appeared on the CBC's TV news program *The Journal*, hosted that night by Bill Cameron. I did my piece from the very cruddy Studio 60 at CBC Vancouver, where, as I have so often done, I sat with a plug in my right ear and stared into the glass eye of a TV camera. It's not easy to do this sort of television, because you have no eye contact with anyone and have no way of judging when to interrupt (something the producers strongly suggest that you do).

The show started with Donna Dasko, a pollster. With an air of absolute confidence, she advised the nation that British Columbians had supported Meech Lake (which was arrant nonsense) and that they would likely come around to the correct view—that is to say, they would vote "Yes"—in the impending Charlottetown referendum. I struggled not to holler "bullshit."

Then Robert Sheppard, at the time a columnist on the op-ed page of the Toronto *Globe and Mail*, smugly said that while support "out in British Columbia" may have been a little soft, as soon as the prime minister and the country's business leaders came to B.C., the citizens would all support this unity initiative. Again I pleaded with myself not to holler "bullshit."

When Bill Cameron asked me for my views, I screamed "rubbish," and then offered a short soliloquy on why the Charlottetown Accord didn't have a prayer of passing in British Columbia. I must in fairness record that shortly afterward, Robert Sheppard wrote in his Toronto *Globe and Mail* column that the questions Rafe Mair was asking had to be answered, or else the deal would not only fail, it would deserve to fail. Unfortunately, the questions never *were* answered.

On September 19, 1992, the *Vancouver Sun* (published by Southam, a firm based in Don Mills, Ontario, and edited accordingly), dubbed me "Dr. No," a name that caught on. This nickname was repeated in news stories about the referendum all around the world—including, would you believe, Vietnam.

I had long since ceased caring what the Don Mills *Sun* and the Don Mills *Province* had to say about me. They hated my guts and for very good reason—the feeling was thoroughly reciprocated. On my radio show, I never said anything good about either paper, for the simple reason that there was nothing good to say. Both papers were totally out of touch with the community they were supposed to serve and represent, and it showed. Every editorial praising the Charlottetown Accord represented, to me, one more step toward victory for the "No" side. After the referendum, *Sun* editor Ian Haysom, a charming and very decent man, asked in his Sunday column how he and his paper could have so badly missed the public mood. He promised that there would be a sea change in the paper's approach to matters constitutional. Unhappily, the only sea change came in the life of Haysom, who was sacked—not that this was in any way reflected by a change, sea or otherwise, in the *Sun's* highly centrist editorial policy.

In the April 1998 issue of *B.C. Business* magazine, Richard Littlemore— the man who wrote the last-minute *Vancouver Sun* editorial, "Is it too late to say yes?"—called that editorial "stupid" and said simply, "Rafe was right." He added, "after which none of us [presumably meaning *Sun* staffers] was very inclined to forgive."

In life you'll be forgiven your errors but will be hated for being right. I can live with that.

There were some fun moments in the campaign. One day I was able to announce that for "No" supporters I had bad news and good news. The bad news was that the government was sending a cabinet minister to all the "No" meetings to tell the good folks how wrongheaded they were and persuade them to change their minds. The good news was that the minister in question was Tom Siddon, easily the dullest politician of any stripe I had ever met.

One of the highlights of the campaign was a two-hour appearance on my show by the then-premier of B.C., Mike Harcourt. I have always liked Mike personally, and I thought he was a thoroughly decent, if often naive, politician. He plunged on his own sword to save his party (successfully) in November 1995, and is an admirable man. (Harcourt was ostensibly brought down because he mishandled a huge scandal involving actions of the party years before. The real reason, I think, was that the power clique led by ministers Glen Clark (now premier) and Dan Miller (now minister of nearly all that matters) recognized the lesson of Charlottetown and knew that a complete turnaround in NDP policy on constitutional matters—and, for that matter referenda—had to come.) However, Harcourt had no knowledge of, or feeling for, matters constitutional—and even worse, he didn't know it. He was full of tiresome phrases like, "The whole is greater than the sum of the parts," or, "Why not recognize Quebec as a distinct society, because it obviously *is* very different?"

On the day in question, Harcourt came into my studio wearing his "Yes" button, utterly convinced that his side would win. In fact, he took my producer aside and said that he was worried about how Rafe would take it when he was publicly humiliated by the referendum result. She replied that Rafe didn't appear to be overly concerned about the prospect.

There is only one way to describe the interview that followed: as a catastrophe for Harcourt and his government, one that probably created a breach in the NDP until Harcourt resigned. First the premier answered *my* questions badly. Then I let *the public* loose on him, and they murdered him. Clearly Harcourt did not realize that the public was beginning to understand the real issues. Callers hit him with everything but the ringpost. It was so bad that during Harcourt's two-hour appearance, my producer received calls from two prominent NDP supporters—Ken Georgetti, president of the British Columbia Federation of Labour, and Jack Munro, former head of the IWA—each of whom screamed, "Get him the fuck off the air!" Very few who heard Harcourt's performance could have thereafter supported the "Yes" side.

Another guest was Moe Sihota, a man who attracts trouble like molasses attracts flies. A bright and articulate lawyer, Sihota was the B.C. constitutional minister at the time of the referendum, and took the time to understand his brief and plead it well. Each time he came on the show it was a barnburner, and was generally critically acclaimed as such. I don't believe that anyone of Sihota's talents could have actually *believed* his arguments, but he was counsel for the government and he argued well, if often disingenuously.

In July, Sihota and I had been in London at the same time, and he had previously gone to great pains to get my number so we could have dinner. I had very much looked forward to it, for I like the man and love jousting with him. He never called.

When Moe came on my show shortly after we returned, I asked him off-air why he had not called me; I got a very convoluted explanation, which both he and I knew was bullshit. We also both knew the real reason for his failure to call. While we were both in London, the Charlottetown agreement had been reached, and Sihota had had a hell of a long-distance row with Mike Harcourt, even threatening resignation.

Whether Moe was *ordered* by Harcourt not to see me in London or whether he simply concluded that sometimes discretion is the better part of valour, I'll probably never know. What I do know is that Sihota was never the same again. He put forward the Charlottetown case as best he could, but his heart was no longer in it. Mulroney and Bourassa had gone far too far, and when Moe appeared on my show it was evident that he could no longer intellectually support Charlottetown. I think this was sensed by the Indo-Canadian community who, despite Sihota's pleading, at the end of the day voted as the rest of B.C. voted.

The most difficult interview I had (and if one can win or lose these things, this one I clearly lost) was with Premier Clyde Wells. The night before Wells's appearance, I went over transcripts of all our Meech Lake interviews, and other pronouncements he had made at that time, and noted all the numerous and serious inconsistencies between his positions of 1990 and 1992. The blatant contradictions amounted to a complete *volte face* by Wells, and I prepared as a cross-examiner might prepare for a big case.

However, rightly or wrongly I felt that Clyde (we were on a first-name basis) had been bullied by Mulroney and his cronies—that this was the only possible explanation for his about-face. I decided that while I would point out all of the many inconsistencies of Clyde's position, I would not in any way be seen to be bullying him. Normally I feel (as I did when I was a politician, being bullied by the likes of Jack Webster), that rough questions go with the territory occupied by politicians, especially premiers. But with the Wells interview I abandoned my usual position and went pretty easy. I got hammered.

There was perhaps some subconscious deviousness in this approach, because I knew how popular Clyde Wells was in B.C. It would not help the "No" cause if I were seen to be overly pressing a man who two years ago had been our hero. But this did not really form part of my thinking; I simply respected Clyde Wells and felt he had changed under severe pressure. I simply wanted both of us to get out of the interview relatively unscathed.

In all events, after it was all over, this was the only interview I would have liked to do again. Given another chance, I would have cross-examined hell out of Premier Wells, though I'm bound to say he might still have hammered me.

Joe Clark also appeared on my show during the campaign, and had an experience similar to Harcourt's. I first met Joe in Edmonton in 1976; our meeting was brief, but later a colleague told me that if the forthcoming P.C. leadership convention became deadlocked, Joe Clark might just come up the middle and win. Despite the power of political mythology, "coming up the middle" at leadership conventions is pretty rare, and when I later recounted what I had heard to Bill Bennett and my cabinet colleagues, I was met with skepticism, to put it mildly. Of course, we all know who won that Tory convention.

Over the years I encountered Joe Clark from time to time, both on my radio show and in Ottawa, where he was usually an observer at constitutional conferences. I liked Joe and, until the time of Charlottetown, admired his approach to matters constitutional. I also admired his guts in fighting off Brian Mulroney, who had plotted to overthrow Clark for years before beating him at the 1983 Tory leadership convention.

When Joe Clark came into my studio in September 1992, I could not believe what I saw. He was bloated and red-faced, and his hands shook uncontrollably. He had borne the entire emotional brunt of the Charlottetown exercise, and after Mulroney and Bourassa had brokered the arrangement of Quebec receiving a permanent one quarter of the House of Commons, Clark must have known that the deal was no longer intellectually or philosophically sustainable. Clark had already started to throw the term "asymmetrical federalism" around—a euphemism for the harsh fact that under Charlottetown, Canada would be a union of *un*equal provinces. The public saw through this, though, as Clark would find out.

On the air, we got into a shouting match. I had argued that if Charlottetown was passed, B.C. could only achieve future constitutional change by taking a leaf from Quebec's book and threatening to secede. "Rafe, you are wrong, wrong, wrong!" Joe shouted, to which I made the brilliant retort, "No, Joe, right, right, right!" This scintillating repartee somehow made the TV news across the nation for a couple of days.

As with Harcourt, though, my callers did most of the damage, and Joe Clark was, I'm sure, mighty glad when the ordeal was over. I felt sorry for him; he is a thoroughly decent man who has had more than his share of political setbacks. However, I could not believe that anyone as smart as Clark could examine the Charlottetown deal carefully—hell, even superficially—and intellectually accept it as being in Canada's interest.

Another pro-"Yes" guest who literally quaked in fear on the air was New Brunswick Premier Frank McKenna, the *wunderkind* of Canadian politics, who came to B.C. without the faintest idea of what he was going to find—yet started preaching from the moment he stepped off the plane. When he appeared on my show, he had just observed, at a Victoria speech, that the servicemen who had died for Canada would roll over in their graves if British Columbians let Canada down by voting "No." To say that this did not go over well would be a gross understatement. When I was a schoolboy it was the habit of masters, when appropriate, to mark a report card, "A most unsatisfactory boy." Frank McKenna was a most unsatisfactory witness on behalf of the "Yes" side.

My last scheduled key guest was Brian Mulroney. Here was the man who had called me a traitor in caucus (I had a spy, the late Chuck Cook, who had courageously broken ranks with his party on this issue) and had fretted about what he was going to do with that loudmouth Mair in Vancouver.

Mulroney's people had reserved my entire show on the Friday prior to the referendum. All week I had been telling my listeners that if they thought that I was wrong, on Friday the prime minister of Canada himself would set me straight in no uncertain terms.

By Wednesday, I was beginning to suggest on-air that Mulroney might not have the guts to face me and my audience. I was right. On Friday, he simply didn't show up. We received no notice of cancellation, just a simple no-show. It wasn't a lack of guts, of course; I would never seriously accuse Brian Mulroney of running away from a fight through cowardice. He simply knew that the jig was up and that it was time for damage control.

On the morning of the vote—Monday, October 26, 1992—I received a call from my good pal Diane Francis, the editor of the *Financial Post*, for which I wrote (and still write) a regular column. I had previously told her that B.C. would vote "No," but she didn't quite believe me. By now, though, the light was dawning, and Diane asked me by what percentage B.C. would reject Charlottetown.

"About sixty-five to thirty-five," was my reply.

Diane was obviously much taken aback. "My God! No vote ever goes sixty-five to thirty-five!"

As it turned out, I was off a bit. The B.C. "No" vote was actually 67.9 percent. *Not one single polling station in the entire province voted "Yes."* The whole exercise was simultaneously wearying, exciting and interesting. The "Yes" forces were beaten from the start, yet they persistently claimed victory on every front. Cabinet ministers were confident. B.C.'s NDP MLAs went into the legislature on voting day wearing "Yes" buttons (in defiance of House rules).

Before I leave this subject and move on to the referendum's after-effects, let me tell you how and why the vote really failed in British Columbia.

Bud and Monica Smith are retired schoolteachers who live in a very ordinary neighbourhood, surrounded by very ordinary neighbours—salt of the earth, all of them. Bud and Monica got angry—real angry. They were convinced that Charlottetown was not only bad for B.C. but bad for the whole country. With about a dozen neighbours, the Smiths formed a group called "Friends of Canada Voting No." Early in the campaign, Bud called my talk show's open line to tell me that a "higher-purpose" group called "Friends of Canada" had gotten very huffy and had sicced a lawyer on "Friends of Canada Voting No." Bud and Monica had also received a letter from Canada's secretary of state instructing them, in no uncertain terms, to cease and desist using the "Friends of Canada" name. (And still some doubt that there is a Canadian establishment!)

Bud Smith (no relation to the former B.C. attorney general of the same name) wasn't complaining; he was mad. I asked him what he was going to do. "Change our name and carry on," was his reply. As "The Loyal Canadians," the Smiths and their neighbours went to work. By the time of the referendum, several hundred volunteers were handing out pamphlets (as well as copies of Mel Smith's articles and my editorials) on the streets, at bus stops, at ferry terminals, and elsewhere. It was a stupendous effort.

When I hear those in authority tell me that British Columbians didn't understand the issues, I think of Bud and Monica, and other people all around the province who, without much money or any centralizing leadership, rallied to defeat this noxious deal.

About a year after the vote, I was invited to pay tribute to John Fraser, an old friend who was retiring from the Speaker's chair, and from Parliament. John and I go back to the mists of childhood, and graduated together from then-very tiny Prince of Wales high school (which also spawned Kim Campbell) in 1949. At a breakfast in Fraser's honour, I was first to address the crowd of about five hundred three-piece-suited businessmen. I was introduced, somewhat uncordially, by Peter C. Newman, the chair of the bun toss. (His lack of enthusiasm arose from a nasty remark in an article I had written about his involvement, as an Order of Canada member, in the "Yes" side of the Charlottetown referendum.)

I opened with this: "As I look about me, I have the feeling that I'm seeing the entire 'Yes' committee for the referendum. Hell, I'm probably looking at the entire 'Yes' vote."

It was a delicious moment and none laughed harder than John Fraser, who had supported the "Yes" side. Indeed, he and I had agreed from the outset that we would simply avoid one another until the whole thing was over; real friendship must be protected from the passions and vagaries of politics.

Amongst many Canadians, though, divisive feelings lingered. During the campaign, Mel Smith, Gordon Gibson and I had all been heaped with plenty of personal abuse. The debate got so heated that at one point Kim Campbell, to her very great credit, admonished all to cool it, pointing out that we all had to live with one another after the vote.

Still, five years later, Jean Chretien appointed Michel Bastarache to the ·

Supreme Court of Canada, purportedly on the strength of Bastarache's patriotism—as proven by the fact that he had co-chaired the "Yes" committee on the Charlottetown referendum! What does this say to non-separatist Quebeckers who voted "No"? What does it say to the people of Nova Scotia, or the Prairie provinces—or especially to British Columbians, who voted "No" by a two-to-one margin?

If one's patriotism—and suitability for high office—is determined by a "Yes" vote in the Charlottetown referendum, it surely follows that those on the "No" side are *un*patriotic, if not outright treasonous. These "traitors," though, include a majority of Canadians and nearly seventy percent of British Columbians. The Central Canadian establishment simply refuses to accept the "No" victory as anything other than proof of our ignorance.

I suppose one could write an entire book on the consequences of the Charlottetown referendum. One of the most dramatic was the shift in policy on the part of the B.C. wing of the NDP. Following the resounding "No" win in B.C., the NDP experienced a conversion second only to that of Saul on the road to Damascus. Off came the "Yes" buttons. Andrew Petter, a constitutional law professor who had supported Charlottetown, became committed to the very opposite of the deal's principles. Glen Clark, the new NDP premier as of 1996, suddenly became "Captain B.C.," and Saskatchewan Premier Roy Romanow, hitherto an NDP hero, became a "nonperson."

To be fair, I believe that the *volte face* was a change of mind as much as a necessary political survival package. I have spoken to both Petter and Clark at length and believe that they sincerely rethought the matter.

The most obvious consequence of Charlottetown, though, was that it empowered the people. Permitting the people to vote on something their masters had already decided on was a most un-Canadian thing to do. In Canada, referenda have traditionally been used by politicians not to confirm their own decisions, but to pass the buck of responsibility to the public at large. The two wartime conscription referenda are good examples of issues in which the heat was just too great for the politicians, so they threw the matter to the voter.

Referenda have also been used by municipalities to avoid responsibility for decisions on things like liquor policy or Sunday shopping.

Charlottetown was different, because the public were called upon to *confirm* a decision already made. This act of pure democracy wasn't Brian Mulroney's idea; it was thrust upon him by the provincial laws of Quebec and B.C. And it certainly wasn't in line with Canadian tradition. The Victoria Charter of 1971, which died because Robert Bourassa later backed out, saw absolutely no involvement of the public. Pierre Trudeau's patriation exercise gave no thought to consulting the people. Meech Lake was a series of backroom political deals, with the only public consultation being sham committees—characterized by preordained recommendations and the testimony of only "safe" intervenors.

So Charlottetown let the genie out of the bottle for all time. Never again can such a major decision be made without the public having a vote.

CHAPTER ELEVEN

Problems with Parliament

If we Canadians think that we live in a democracy, or anything approaching it, we're kidding ourselves. We have an autocracy, which we get to renew, or replace with another, every four years or so, at a time deemed most propitious by the autocrat's advisors.

It's true that we have the trappings of a democracy, free elections being a very important one. But we do not have a system where a vote in one area of the country has the same importance as a vote in any other area. Most important, we invest no real power in our representatives. All power in the country is exercised by one person: the person who has undemocratically been selected to lead the party that has won the most seats in the election. When I say all power, I mean *all* power. In fact, the prime minister is so all-powerful that his (or, in rare cases, her) closest advisors are grey-haired (mostly) men, unelected and unaccountable to any but the prime minister himself.

I can imagine readers shaking their heads and saying, "Maybe Mair has a point here, but surely he's gone too far." Shake your head again: We've given the prime minister the power of a Russian czar. To realize this, one only has to look at our government and determine what real power is, who truly exercises it, and what, if any, are the real brakes on that power.

We've been taught in this country that what we always wanted, and finally achieved in 1867, was "responsible government." This does not necessarily mean that our government will behave responsibly, only that the government—that is to say, the prime minister and his cabinet—is responsible to the elected House of Commons. This also means that our MPs can, if suitably cross, turn on the government and throw it out of office. And this is certainly how it works—*on paper*.

However, it's certainly *not* how it works in practice. In fact, during the entire 130 years of our existence, a majority government has almost never been seriously chastened by Parliament, much less thrown out. Perhaps the only such cases of note are William Vander Zalm of British Columbia (who resigned as premier in 1991 after having been found guilty—by a hand-picked commissioner!—of breaching conflict-of-interest guidelines) and Sir John A. Macdonald (who resigned in 1873 over the Pacific Scandal; a railway had received a letters patent in what seemed an obvious exchange for donations to Macdonald's Tories). The Macdonald case (an excellent account of which can be found in Donald Creighton's marvelous biography *John A. Macdonald*) occurred long before party discipline as we know it had strangled the House of Commons.

A comparison might be made to the old Soviet Union. On paper, it had the most democratic constitution, with the most expansive recitation of citizens' rights, in the world. Yet in reality, there was no democracy and no one had any rights. Great Britain, in contrast, has no written constitution and is one of the freest of countries. (It's interesting to note that British Prime Minister Tony Blair has drawn criticism for becoming "presidential" and ignoring Parliament. Sound familiar?) It's much more important to look at what *actually* happens, not what's *supposed* to happen.

By that standard, Canada maintains the appearance of democracy but nothing more.

How does the prime minister end up with this extraordinary power? Simple. Under our political system the prime minister is guaranteed ironclad discipline.

To start with, the prime minister's caucus members all have a very strong desire to survive, and they know that if the government topples their own jobs are at stake. I can tell you from experience that no member of a legislature wants to test his right to be there any sooner than is absolutely necessary—and this is especially true of those in "swing" ridings (in which no particular party traditionally dominates), which are most likely the first to go when a government topples. You will note a remarkable lack of resignations from government caucuses that have a small majority—mine in 1981 being an exception.

The prime minister appoints his cabinet and parliamentary secretaries entirely of his own initiative (though he will, of course, seek political advice). The parliamentary-secretary positions, often stepping stones for MPs toward a cabinet position, offer more money and prestige.

The prime minister appoints the heads of Commons committees, the first rung up the ladder of power, and decides who sits on what committee. In theory these matters are within the purview of the Commons, but in practice they aren't. The prime minister even gets to say which good little boys or girls amongst his caucus get to go to that utterly useless conference on a warm Caribbean island during an Ottawa February.

The most devastating power the prime minister wields over all MPs is that he must sign the candidate's election form. In other words, if an MP doesn't behave well according to the prime minister's lights, he will be dumped by the party at the next election. This is not some abstract threat: it is always in the back of the backbenchers' minds, and quickly comes to the forefront if they anger the prime minister.

The prime minister has other very persuasive powers as well. It has been said by the late Speaker of the U.S. House of Representatives Thomas (Tip) O'Neill that all politics is local. All candidates for Parliament make promises of local improvements as part of their campaigns. It's often critical to an MP's re-election that these promises be fulfilled. You might think that getting these projects done would depend upon how hard and well the MP lobbies the minister responsible. However, cabinet ministers are themselves responsible to the prime minister.

Here is what often happens (I've seen it happen at the provincial level, which is an almost precise microcosm of Ottawa): The appropriate department approves a project promised by MP Bloggs, whereupon MP Sniffle, who has also made promises to his constituency, screams blue murder to the prime minister. Sniffle points out Bloggs' shortcomings in loyalty, and argues that he himself has been much more supportive of the government, in caucus and elsewhere. Why, then, should Bloggs go to the front of the line?

Maybe the prime minister intercedes on Sniffle's behalf and Bloggs' lack of sufficient obeisance kills his project. On the other hand, it may simply be that Sniffle is on the prime minister's shit list. Or perhaps Sniffle's seat is viewed as a safe one, so why waste money and effort pleasing voters who are unlikely to revolt when you can reward the also-loyal Bloggs? Maybe somebody else's seat—in Toronto, shall we say—needs some political lubrication. In any case, the point is simply this: Any goodies an MP garners for his constituents are always politically motivated to accord with the wishes of the prime minister. Always.

In theory, we elect members of Parliament based on what the candidates have to say and on who we think will do the best job. Unquestionably we consider the party, too. So we expect our elected member to keep, if not all the specific local promises he or she made, at least the national promises that the party made. We do not elect zombies committed to doing what they are told. That, at any rate, is the theory.

The reality is that we *do* elect zombies—at least we do when we elect MPs to the government benches. Our fresh-faced new MP goes back to Ottawa determined to be different. However, he soon learns, in the words of Sam Rayburn, the great Speaker of the U.S. House of Representatives, that "to get along, one must go along."

How well I remember Vancouver Centre MP Hedy Fry assuring me and my audience during the 1993 federal election campaign that if elected, she would always, without fail, put the interests of her constituency and her province ahead of the wishes of her party. Since then, however, no one in the Liberal caucus has been a more faithful toady to the wishes of the prime minister than the Hon. Ms. Fry. She has not uttered a peep of criticism about the government that has made her a junior minister. She is B.C.'s Number One Liberal lickspittle.

It is said, of course, that these MPs, so reticent in public, do make our case behind closed doors. That's largely nonsense. The only ones who do that are those who have already lost all hope for personal advancement, or who have gained such political prominence that they are virtually secure against the sack. These MPs are very few in number. None, I assure you, are from British Columbia.

There is, granted, the occasional exceptional backbencher. We had one in the provincial Socred caucus of the 1970s. Jack Kempf from Omineca was, for reasons unbeknownst to me, high on Bill Bennett's shit list. He bellowed like a bull in caucus but was largely free from repercussion—mainly because, no matter what he did or said, he always voted loyally. In discussions, though, Jack's overpowering desire to make his point overrode his desire for a cabinet posting. Though I was scarcely a follower of his political views, I always admired his courage. (He later did become a rather unsuccessful forests minister in the Vander Zalm government. A maverick himself, Vander Zalm surrounded himself with rebels.)

All others in our caucus behaved themselves, however much they belly-ached privately. As Napoleon said, "Every foot soldier carries a marshall's baton in his knapsack." Similarly, every backbencher is sure he has been unjustly overlooked for advancement by the premier or prime minister, an oversight that can be cured by good behaviour.

A classic example of lacklustre constituency representation on the part of MPs occurred in December 1995, when Jean Chretien instituted his four-region veto formula for constitutional amendments. In the face of outrage from B.C. quarters, Chretien was forced to declare our province a fifth region, with veto rights equal to those of the other four.

The B.C. Liberal MPs were quick to take credit. But according to then-Liberal MP John Nunziata, the six Liberal toadies from B.C. kept their thoughts entirely to themselves, and it was then-Fisheries Minister Brian Tobin, a Newfoundland MP, who passionately made B.C.'s point. He could do so safely, you see, because both he and Chretien knew that he was about to leave Parliament and seek the premiership of Newfoundland. Nunziata was so disgusted that he told my radio audience in the fall of 1996 that British Columbians would be far better represented by an MP from an opposition party—any opposition party—than one from the governing Liberals!

Isn't that something? At least in British Columbia, your most effective MP is not on the government side, where you would think he could exercise some direct influence, but on the opposition benches!

Even more recently, any doubt about ironclad discipline in the government caucus was surely erased in May 1998, during the hepatitis C vote on the question of whether or not to award compensation to those who had been infected before 1986. Prime Minister Chretien interpreted an Official Opposition motion to expand terms of compensation to include those infected before 1986 as a question of confidence, and forced all his MPs to vote for the government. Dozens of government MPs on record as opposed to their party's plan were compelled to vote against the wishes of their constituents, the people of Canada and, I might say, their own consciences.

A good example of how prime ministers shut out independent thinkers was the case of the late Tory MP from North Vancouver, Chuck Cook. Chuck was a lawyer with media experience, and one would have thought that after his long service Brian Mulroney would reward him with at least a parliamentary secretaryship, if not a cabinet post. He got diddley squat. As a senior MP from B.C. he should have been acknowledged, but his position against the

Meech Lake Accord and later the Charlottetown Accord (reflecting the views of his constituents, incidentally) got him firmly on Mulroney's shit list.

Why? Because Chuck spoke for his constituents, especially on constitutional matters, where he (and nearly seventy percent of his constituents) very much disagreed with Brian Mulroney. For this and other "sins" he was permanently in the prime minister's penalty box.

Another maverick was Nova Scotia Tory Patrick Nowlan, who, sick of his party's inability to deal with national unity questions through the people, rather than through the poohbahs, resigned the whip and sat as an independent.

Look also at what happened to The Honourable Warren Allmand, long a cabinet minister in the Trudeau government. Jean Chretien didn't want him in cabinet (fair enough) but because of seniority (Allmand had once been solicitor general) made him chair of the Justice Committee. Then Allmand voted against Finance Minister Paul Martin's second budget; he conscientiously believed that the budget was contrary to what the Liberals stood for, and more particularly, it contradicted what he had personally campaigned on. There was no danger whatsoever that Allmand's vote would affect the outcome; at that time, the Liberals had an enormous majority. This was simply a senior MP expressing his displeasure.

For his pains, Allmand was fired from his chairmanship of the Justice Committee by Chretien. His chances of any advancement in Parliament, *which in theory is controlled by its members,* are currently nonexistent.

And how about John Nunziata, the Toronto MP who was one of the Liberal Party's most effective voices when they were the Official Opposition? He was a member of the famous "Rat Pack" with Don Boudria, Sheila Copps and Brian Tobin, all of whom went on, after the Liberal landslide in 1993, to receive great rewards for their unswerving loyalty. But when the governing Liberals voted on whether or not to maintain the Goods and Services Tax, Nunziata voted against the GST—and against his Liberal colleagues. Why did he do this? Because during the 1993 election he had campaigned against the GST. That was not surprising, because so did all the other Liberals. Opposition to the GST was party policy, as outlined in the Liberal "Red Book."

Before the vote, Nunziata warned the prime minister and the caucus that he felt conscience-bound to honour his firm and uncomplicated promise to his constituents. Nunziata voted against the bill and was promptly thrown out of caucus and the Liberal Party. Despite long service to the party, he was excommunicated and denied support in the next election — and all this for adhering to an official party policy, written for all to see in plain, unadorned English (and French)! Nunziata was re-elected in 1997 as an independent even after the Liberals threw everything but the kitchen sink at him.

In 1996, the same John Nunziata saw a potential problem, especially but by no means exclusively for British Columbians, which could and should have been headed off. Mass child molester and murderer Clifford Robert Olson would, in August 1996, be entitled to a parole hearing under section 745 of the Criminal Code, the so-called "faint-hope clause."

Anyone who lived in greater Vancouver in 1981, especially those with young teenagers, had been scared out of their wits by the almost daily reports of gruesome sexual abuse and sadistic, violent murder. The entire community lived with this fear every minute of every day. As the stepfather of two teenagers, a girl and a boy, I felt this terror keenly as well. When Olson was captured, convicted and put away, after being paid money by the Crown to disclose where he had buried the bodies of his victims, there was enormous collective relief. But there was also a deep emotional scar left on the community.

From the start of his incarceration, Olson has been given special treatment, complete with a computer and the ability to make himself heard outside prison. He has used every waking hour to badger authorities and taunt the families of his victims. Should Olson be given his "faint-hope" hearing, objections to his parole would be provided by victims' families, with the convict having the right to cross-examine—a process Olson would almost certainly use as a platform to do everything he could to upset the families.

After unsuccessfully pleading the case for repealing Section 745 with Justice Minister Allan Rock, Nunziata put forward a private member's bill. The bill came before the Commons for first reading and, in a free vote, was passed. It must be noted, however, that four of the six Liberals from B.C. voted *against* Nunziata's bill, even though it was a "free vote." The four who voted against were all either in cabinet or close to it: Raymond Chan (a junior minister); Herb Dhaliwal (who had been offered a cabinet post and would later get one); Hedy Fry (also a junior minister); and David Anderson (a full minister).

Why did these four Liberal MPs vote against their constituents and against all that was decent? Because Allan Rock told them to. It seems clear to me that this was because Prime Minister Chretien did not want John Nunziata, who had caused him grief over the GST issue, to get any credit for anything. In short, the four B.C. Liberals put the political comfort of the prime minister and his justice minister ahead of doing what was right.

Nunziata's one-section bill, after passing, was sent to the Justice Committee, which, one would have thought, would have reported the bill back to the Speaker without amendment. After all, what was there to amend in a bill that simply repealed one section of the Criminal Code?

Allan Rock ordered the committee not to report the bill back because he was bringing in his own legislation. Which he did. Unfortunately, this most influential of cabinet ministers, with nine months to go before Olson became entitled to his hearing, could not find the time to get the matter before the Commons before Olson's right to a hearing vested. As a result, Olson became entitled to his hearing—and to his "right" to hassle the families of his victims. That's exactly what happened; Olson's parole was denied, and the law that allowed this to happen has since been changed.

The lesson of the Olson case is surely clear. Under our system, an MP will do the unthinkable before he will defy the demands of his superiors—*even when those superiors are not acting in the public interest, but for selfish and personal political aggrandizement.*

Under our system of political appointments, the prime minister himself has many more personal powers, for which he is not, in practice, the slightest bit accountable. In theory, he is accountable at election time. However, because he will make all his outrageously biased political appointments long before the election, any controversy surrounding them will later be subsumed by the larger issues that government spin doctors convince us we really ought to be concerned about.

The prime minister appoints all the senior judges in the country—including, of course, the justices of the Supreme Court of Canada. Amongst other things, the Supreme Court of Canada rules on constitutional disputes between the federal and provincial governments. How would you like it if you were involved in a lawsuit and it turned out that the judge was your opponent's brother? That's essentially what provinces face in the Supreme Court of Canada—the members of that court have been appointed entirely by the other side.

The establishment argues that these men and women take an oath, and by reason of the robes they wear and the bench they occupy, we can count on them to be fair. Of course, that's what your opponent says about his brother, too. It is said that once judges are appointed they become absolutely even-handed, and it is very rude to dispute that contention. Well, I'm not averse to being rude when the occasion demands it. And I think we'd all be better off if more of us citizens were rude from time to time.

The fact is that traditionally the Supreme Court of Canada has been biased toward Ottawa. One of the reasons the Supreme Court replaced the Judicial Committee of the Privy Council (JCPC) in 1949, by Ottawa's insistence, was that the Privy Council (to give its common name) was seen by Ottawa as biased in favour of the provinces. The federal government's point of view was that if there was to be any bias, let it be in *its* favour. Since 1949, the Supreme Court of Canada has been the highest court in the land, its members have been appointed by the prime minister, it's been dominated by centrists—and the decisions have reflected it.

An example is the contentious case of the legality of a Quebec unilateral declaration of independence, now being heard by the Supreme Court of Canada. While I do not believe that any province has the right to secede from Canada, and that this decision should be a no-brainer for the Supreme Court of Canada, look at the appointment of Mr. Justice Michel Bastarache, in 1997, from Quebec's point of view.

However thin your case may be, you have the right to demand that the judges commence their deliberations with an absolutely open mind. Where they have personal prejudices, as do we all, we expect them to put those aside in the interests of fair play.

Bastarache, though, was appointed for a very special and obvious reason. He was a federalist—he was also a patriotic Canadian, it was said, because he had chaired the "Yes" committee for the Charlottetown referendum. With this appointment, Jean Chretien said in clear terms to Quebec's government, "We will do all we can to win this constitutional case, including appointing a judge who we know in advance has already made up his mind on the question of secession." Notwithstanding this, says Chretien, all Quebeckers must, of course, accept decisions of the Supreme Court of Canada as being completely fair and impartial. Yeah, sure.

In fairness to Bastarache, he did not, so far as we know, apply for the job by giving as his qualifications the fact that he defined patriotism as being in favour of the establishment line, or that he was most unlikely to pay any attention to Quebec's arguments on constitutional matters. I have no reason to believe that the judge is anything other than a fine, conscientious man. I make no criticism of *him*, except to point out that he was full of prunes on the Charlottetown issue.

My criticism of the appointment, though, is threefold.

First, the prime minister should never, under even the most compelling of political reasons (including the salvation of the country) appoint someone to the bench in anticipation of a sensitive constitutional case because of the judge's position on that issue, no matter how righteaded that position may seem. If the Supreme Court of Canada can be "loaded" for "good" reasons, it can be loaded for "bad" reasons too. The real objection is that appointment of any judge with any serious bias is wrong, period. *We are either a country of principle or we aren't.*

Second, not a whisper of complaint was heard from any government MP. Even though the impartiality of all courts goes to the very root of what democracy and liberty are all about, there was not a peep from anyone sworn to do their duty by a free society.

Third, and most important by far, there is no process in place for the people's representatives to screen potential Supreme Court judges. Though they often exercise more power than elected governments, there is no need for any potential judge to justify his qualifications for such high office. He may, of course, have to demonstrate that he was a loyal Liberal (or Tory in other times), but he need do nothing to convince the Canadian electorate or its representatives of his essential qualifications for the highest judicial position in the land.

Another very important area of prime ministerial privilege is often overlooked. The prime minister and his cabinet ministers also get to make hundreds of appointments, ranging from international ambassadors to directors of Crown corporations, boards and commissions. Many times these appointments are utterly shameless, such as Prime Minister Chretien appointing his nephew, Raymond Chretien, as Canada's ambassador to the United States, the plum of the diplomatic service.

In most cases, senior government appointees will be either Liberals or people suited to the Liberals—appointments are political payoffs. This doesn't mean that the appointees will necessarily be incompetent. There are, I suppose, competent Liberals. It does mean that the country is run, from stem to gudgeon, out of the prime minister's office.

In my early days of law practice, virtually all such federal judicial appointments were rawly political. For the most part the appointees were long-serving Liberals. Occasionally there was an exception, such as my classmate Tom Berger—whose 1972 appointment to the B.C. Supreme Court, because he was a longtime NDPer and was even once leader of the B.C. NDP, stood out in stark contrast to existing practice (like a drunken cow at a christening).

In recent years things have much changed, the saints be praised. There is now a process that includes the prospective judge quietly declaring his ambition. For appointments below the level of Supreme Court of Canada, there is a vetting system in which the provincial attorneys general and various bar associations are asked their views. It doesn't hurt, of course, if the candidate has belonged to and worked for the party in power, as did the two chief justices in British Columbia (both of whom are extremely competent, I might add, and personal friends of mine). However, for the most part political background plays a much lesser role in the judgemaking game than it once did.

This isn't to say that the public has any real or even indirect say, because it doesn't. Whatever say it may have through others is advisory only. Which is nice, but it isn't power. Power is what the people are supposed to have in a democracy.

The federal government could do worse than to examine the British Columbia system for appointing court judges; it is almost entirely free of political influence. I say "almost" because politics at some level comes into everything from the placement of a stop sign to the appointment of the governor general. But for the past twenty-five years or more, there has been hardly a murmur concerning the appointment of provincial court judges—who, incidentally, do the bulk of judging in any given province.

The appointment process is also an issue in any discussion of the governor general. The highest office in the land, the governor generalship has fallen on very sorry times indeed. It's thought that the governor general is merely a figurehead: a man or woman who stands on the dais at Government House, accepts the obsequious greetings of his loyal subjects, and dispenses utterly banal comments on nothing in particular. Mostly the post is ceremonial, but it's prestigious, costly and it pays well.

However, although this has not happened for sixty years, the governor general can play a key role in the affairs of the country, especially if a minority government loses a key vote in the House of Commons. The classic case involved Mackenzie King and Governor General Lord Byng in 1926. When King, as a minority government prime minister, wished to dissolve Parliament and call an election, Byng refused to issue a writ, preferring to call upon the leader of the Official Opposition, Arthur Meighen, to form a government—which Meighen did. Meighen soon lost the confidence of the Commons, however, and an election was held, which King won in large measure because he stood up to the governor general, over what King saw as an usurpation of power. The trouble is that on paper, the sovereign has enormous power that by long custom has not been exercised—meaning that the ability to say in advance just what the governor general can do is difficult.

A similar situation arose in British Columbia in 1952, when the upstart W.A.C. Bennett won an upset victory in the provincial election, with a minority government of nineteen seats to the CCF's eighteen (with several other seats sprinkled amongst other parties). The CCF leader demanded that the lieutenant-governor (the provincial equivalent of the governor general), Clarence Wallace, ask *him* to form a government, because he had been leader of the Official Opposition and was sure that independent Labour MLA Tom Uphill would support him, giving him nineteen seats too. The lieutenant-governor dithered for weeks, and finally consulted experts in Ottawa who advised him that he should call upon Bennett—who, it turned out, had Tom Uphill's letter of support in his pocket.

The point is that the governor general has great powers on paper only, and has hitherto, with a couple exceptions, behaved appropriately.

Selecting heads of state, as opposed to breeding them, is a tricky business. Unless you elect your figureheads, as do other countries such as Ireland, you must appoint them—which means that the office usually degenerates into a big political payoff.

For Canada's first eighty years the governor general was appointed by the British (and, technically, Canadian) monarch—who, in consultation with Ottawa, usually appointed a chinless aristocrat, often a member of the royal family no one knew what to do with.

In 1952 Vincent Massey, scion of the farm-implement company and a member of Toronto's version of the Canadian aristocracy, became the first Canadian governor general. Though he had impeccable Liberal connections, it was not seen at the time as a particularly political appointment.

We've had one disaster after another since then. With a couple of notable exceptions—General Georges Vanier and Roland Michener come to mind—governors general have virtually all been political hacks to whom the prime minister felt he owed a personal and party debt that should be paid by the Canadian taxpayer. So far this has not caused any legal difficulties—just embarrassment at the politics involved in the appointment, and at some personal behaviour. It's a real concern, however, when another Byng or Bennett issue arises and the governor general is the prime minister's pet poodle.

Why not *elect* the governor general? The problem with electing largely symbolic heads of state is that these elections are seen to confer some sort of power. If they don't, why hold them? For example, the presidency of Ireland is supposed to be ceremonial only, but past president Mary Robinson turned it into an important political weapon. Though she had precious little legal power to wield, she had, because of her enormously popular victory, gained a lot of influence—which she used. Influence used is power exercised.

Most would argue that Mrs. Robinson exercised her power for good: against violence, poverty and the like. That's not the point. Not all ceremonial heads of state are Mary Robinsons.

What, then, to do?

The British Columbia legislature chooses its non-political appointments (auditor general, ombudsman, and conflict-of-interest commissioner) by selecting a committee, which must unanimously recommend a name, which must then be passed by two thirds of the House in a free vote. Why not do something like this for the office of governor general?

It's argued that this would make the appointment a demeaning political one. Really? More politically demeaning than the appointment of a good pal of the prime minister's who's also just lost an election, like Ray Hnatyshyn? Or a decision politically correct as hell, like francophone female Jeanne Sauvé? Give me a break!

Senate appointments, too, are entirely within the prerogative of the prime minister. Let's think about what the Senate's function is, at least on paper: to give sober, second thought to legislation from the House of Commons (though I know of no evidence that senators are any more sober, as a rule, than MPs) and to *represent the regional interest*. Yet these regional representatives are appointed by the prime minister, not the provinces that are to be represented. It is utterly preposterous!

If you were, God forbid, in a pissing match with your spouse, would you want him or her to have the right to select your lawyer for you? This is what the Senate selection system amounts to. B.C.'s "advocates" in the Senate of Canada are appointed by the prime minister—the very man whose potential abuse of power is supposed to be restrained by the institution!

Invariably senators are political hacks or politically correct appointments, like a reasonably pliable Native chief. The Senate has also been used to reward public servants who have served the Liberal Party well (Michael Kirby and former Prime Minister's Office Secretary Michael Pitfield come to mind). Some selections have seemed more than a bit mischievous, such as the selection of Anne Cools, who had been an outspoken student protestor at Sir George Williams, and that of my good friend Ed Lawson from Vancouver, whose main claim to fame is that as head of the Teamsters Union, he was a member of the very capitalistic and ultra-exclusive Capilano Golf and Country Club.

The Senate is a bad constitutional joke, with great powers on paper exercised by an elite group of political creditors of the party in power. Senators have never really represented the provinces they are appointed to represent—unless those provinces happen to be Ontario or Quebec. Some might say that current B.C. Senator Pat Carney is an exception, and she certainly has done a great deal to promote British Columbia's concerns. But when it got down, as the cowboys say, to the nut cutting (in this case, the Charlottetown Accord), she danced with the guy what brung her: good old Brian.

Surely no one can argue that British Columbia is not royally diddled in terms of Senate representation. It is now and always has been a separate region of Canada. It is the third largest province in terms of population, and will be the second largest before the middle of the next century. Quebec, which may be the second largest province in terms of population but is slipping fast, has twenty-four senators. New Brunswick, with about one quarter of B.C.'s population, has eight senators, as does Nova Scotia. Prince Edward Island, smaller than most municipalities in the greater Vancouver area, has four.

British Columbia has six.

Huge changes must be made, but they will not happen—because Quebec, Ontario, and Atlantic Canada (acting together), who all profit from the present gross inequities, will have the power to veto them.

One possible Senate reform would be electing senators, as many propose, but *under the present system* that would be disastrous. Without reforming the composition of the Senate itself, elections will mean that B.C. will still only have six senators, but the Central-Canadian-dominated Senate will see its election as a mandate to *do things*. The only good thing about the present Senate is that in practice it can't do much; like the governor general, the Senate has the theoretical power to do anything the House of Commons does, but an appointed Senate has no mandate to act.

Elected senators, though, would rightly claim that as elected representatives of the people, they had a clear mandate, if not duty, not only to review House of Commons matters but to take initiatives of their own. With Central Canada having or controlling the majority of seats, we would have an infinitely worse system than the one we now endure!

Electing senators may well be the way to go, but not before the entire electoral system has been revamped. Just why Preston Manning and the Reform Party have gone brain-dead on this issue, proposing that we elect senators under the current system, is beyond me.

I have saved the worst for the last. The fundamental evil in the Canadian system of governance is that at the end of the day, fifty percent plus one of the House of Commons has not fifty percent plus one of the nation's political power, but one hundred percent. Consider that. It would be somewhat comforting to know that British Columbia, with thirteen percent of the

Canadian population, had a thirteen-percent share in federal power. However, that is distinctly *not* how it works.

On paper, "rep by pop" is pure democracy. The fact that the majority, however small, has one hundred percent of the power is defended on the basis that this is what the word democracy means. However, even in small, compact countries like the U.K., it has long been recognized that rule by the majority inevitably leads to oppression of the minority. In the U.K., the House of Lords is supposed to protect the aristocracy, which, while hardly a noble (pardon the pun) notion, does show that Britain was always conscious of the need to have some brakes on the House of Commons. Most European countries have some sort of bicameral setup, or, like Switzerland, have decentralized power so much that the *cantons* are for all intents and purposes self-governing.

Before Canada faced this problem, the United States faced the dilemma of balancing the power exerted by straight "rep by pop" with the interests of the various states. The U.S. developed a bicameral Congress, where the lower house, the House of Representatives, was elected purely on the basis of population while the upper house, the Senate, was made up of two seats per state, regardless of population.

Canada's Fathers of Confederation, influenced by Britain's fairly heavy hand, opted for a compromise. Like the committee that started out to develop a horse and ended up with a camel on their hands, Canada ended up with the worst of all worlds. For example, the Senate, nominally representing the 1867 notion of regions, was appointed by the federal government.

While the provinces were given specific powers under the Constitution, these have been substantially invaded by the federal government, usually with use of the public treasury. For example, health and education are provincial jurisdictions, yet by using the "temporary" First World War income tax, Ottawa has invaded these areas in a big way. Doing so is encouraged by the poorer provinces, which naturally put money for universities and hospitals ahead of constitutional principles.

As a result we have provincial governments, who are after all much closer to the people than Ottawa (the importance of the national capital dramatically decreases the further away a province is), essentially spending money on orders from a federal government that controls the purse strings—in areas the provinces are supposed to control. We have a Senate that, far from representing provinces or even regions, is peopled by prime ministerial appointees who will do the PM's bidding.

Thus all meaningful power is exercised by the cabinet of the federal government—which is run by the prime minister. From there it's hardly rocket science to see that the country is run by the provinces that send the government caucus to Ottawa—always Ontario or Quebec, or a combination of the two.

Back to square one: fifty percent plus one of the House of Commons has one hundred percent of the power, which in 1998 means the Ontario Liberal caucus plus the Quebec caucus. (Not because the latter's numbers are necessary, but because the government is scared witless that Quebec will vamoose if not suitably bribed.)

The real problem can perhaps best be illustrated by this example: Suppose it was proposed that Hamilton and Toronto be combined under one civic government, for reasons of economies of scale and all that stuff. That might make sense—until the people of Hamilton discovered that under the new "rep by pop" city they were always outvoted. Even if Toronto really did deserve those new streetlights or whatever, you'd never convince Hamiltonians that they were getting a fair shake under the sacred principle of rep by pop.

The problems of Canada as a whole simply form an extension of this argument. You will never convince British Columbians that they're getting a fair deal under the present system, because they can see with their own eyes that they exercise no power.

In a unitary state where geography is not a large factor, pure representation by population is fair enough. In Britain, for example, the remote regions of Scotland no doubt have legitimate claims of being ignored, but the country is so small that most MPs are familiar with the problems and concerns of all regions. Moreover, because regionalism is a much smaller problem, more often than not an MP does not live in, or even near, the constituency he represents. Winston Churchill, for much of his earlier political life, represented Dundee, Scotland, while living all the while in London.

What the British system means in Canada, however, is that the prime minister need only satisfy the Central Canadian government members in order to retain power.

I do not say, of course, that the Ontario Liberal caucus meets clandestinely in order to give Jean Chretien his marching orders. For one thing, Chretien doesn't have to obey the Ontario Liberal caucus, merely keep them from mutinying. The important point is the reality that MPs from Ontario and Quebec not only have proportionally more power than MPs from "outer Canada," *they effectively have* all *the power.* The prime minister knows that he need not worry about B.C. MPs (in such issues as the Olson case or the five-region veto matter)—because British Columbia, while a vital part of the country, simply doesn't matter politically.

Cabinet posts are a matter, in large measure, of making sure that Quebec and Ontario are not only satisfied with what they get but also with the scraps being scattered elsewhere. If you're an MP from B.C., you don't become a cabinet minister or parliamentary secretary unless you are "safe"—that is, quite satisfied with the way the system works and the status quo. B.C. MPs who may make waves are not given offices; simple as that. It's the same with the senior political appointments to Crown corporations, boards and commissions. Such posts rarely, if ever, go to British Columbians. Certainly the number and importance of such appointments bear no relationship to B.C.'s share of the population, its unique geographical position as Canada's window on the Pacific, or its overall importance. Back in the Trudeau years, it was so bad that British Columbians were not even appointed to boards in which there was a statutory requirement that this be done, such as the Bank of Canada!

Even if an Ottawa government were to have a dramatic and miraculous conversion to a truly representative democracy, it wouldn't bind future governments. There is no legal requirement that power be fairly shared. In fact, the system points those in power in the opposite direction. Even if there is enlightened government today, there will always be another Pierre Trudeau with another National Energy Program, usurping the powers of the provinces over their own natural resources through the strategem of taxation.

It wasn't always that way.

Mackenzie King always felt a mandate to have a national government, and appointed powerful ministers from both the Prairies and British Columbia, like the two Jimmys, Gardiner and Sinclair. While there was a high degree of condescension, if not outright colonialism, in this approach, it was a hell of a lot better than what has happened since. At least in those days there was a sense, albeit only felt only from time to time when the mood arose, that Canada was indeed more than Ontario and Quebec.

Pierre Trudeau spawned the present system. That he is a great man is beyond dispute. He may not have been a great prime minister, though—he may, indeed, have been a lousy one upon whom much of the blame for our present difficulties must rest.

Trudeau, and his political insiders like Jimmy Coutts, discovered that any national election could be won if you did very well in either Ontario or Quebec and moderately well in the other areas of the country. In short, only Central Canada really counted electorally. This had always been true, but Trudeau cynically exploited this reality and treated "outer Canada" accordingly—even, at a train stop in Salmon Arm, B.C., giving some unhappy spectators the finger in 1981, something he wouldn't have dared in Trois Rivières or Guelph. The damage he did with the National Energy Program left such deep and lasting scars in the Far West that the federal Liberals may never really be trusted there again.

Trudeau had no understanding of British Columbia, and perhaps never forgave it for spawning his ex-wife. He saw Canada as defined by the great Upper Canada–Lower Canada debate, with the rest of the country largely irrelevant. This attitude remains and is exploited, if a bit more politely, by Jean Chretien.

I first met Trudeau in 1976, when he came to Victoria to meet with the B.C. premier and some cabinet ministers, including me. He struck me first by his smallness in physical stature. I had always thought of him as a tall man—certainly taller than Joe Clark. In fact, in a physical sense, Clark towered over Trudeau. Intellectually, however, Clark is a pygmy by comparison.

Trudeau seemed very shy and retiring. He was soft-spoken, and clearly not about to discuss anything much more serious than the weather. The lunch passed as no more than a pleasant couple of hours of idle chitchat. I do recall our finance minister, Evan Wolfe, trying to engage the prime minister in some serious discussion about matters fiscal, but Trudeau seemed quite uninterested in such mundane matters.

I then began to see Trudeau at First Ministers Conferences. There seemed to be an awful lot of them, but there were probably only a half-dozen or so. Until the one in September 1980, the prime minister seemed indifferent to the proceedings, content to simply let the clock run out and adjourn. My occasional interventions were greeted by "Yes, Mr. Rafe," which I took as a deliberate yet most amusing putdown. I wasn't the only one—Trudeau constantly called then-Saskatchewan attorney general (now premier) Roy Romanow "Mr. Romanoff"!

Trudeau clearly despised Rene Levesque, and *vice versa.* He usually deferred to Ontario Premier Bill Davis, whom he shamelessly used to put forth his centrist views. These views were of course shared by Davis, who constantly referred to Ontario as the lynchpin of Canada; this was an irrelevant annoyance to others, which annoyance Trudeau clearly delighted in.

For similar reasons, Trudeau was fond of Richard Hatfield, a strange duck if there ever was one. Hatfield could be counted upon to faithfully support Trudeau. Since he sat next to Levesque, who sat immediately to Trudeau's left, he was a useful person to turn to for comment when an already enraged Levesque was to be tormented further. Hatfield was loved by the media, because he always told them what went on in private and confidential meetings. This wasn't cupidity on Hatfield's part; he was simply an incurable gossip.

Hatfield visibly irked Levesque and his constant companions, Jacques Parizeau, Bernard Landry and (to a lesser extent) Claude Morin (who was not easily irritated), because he was pressing to make New Brunswick officially bilingual. (Would that Lucien Bouchard would do the same in Quebec!) Many Canadians thought that this would be seen by Quebec as a peace offering, but it was taken quite differently. Levesque saw the "plight" of Acadians as a distractive irrelevancy. It was always the position of the Parti Quebecois that French-language rights outside Quebec were more a Liberal ploy to satisfy non-separatists in Quebec than an honest effort to confer any advantage upon French-Canadians in other provinces. In this he was no doubt quite right. But it took me a while to understand what the real issue was, and until I saw the contempt the Parti Quebecois had for bilingualism and biculturalism I bought the notion that the Liberals had peddled in British Columbia, that the policy would appease separatist sentiment in *la belle province.* In reality, Levesque and the Parti Quebecois couldn't care less about francophones outside Quebec.

Trudeau's contempt for the premiers was palpable. They could not see the big picture, which was probably true, since they were elected by provinces to represent their interest.

But if the premiers were myopic in their national vision, it by no means followed that Trudeau and his party saw it more clearly. Their view was just as provincial as that of, say, Bill Bennett of British Columbia, the difference being that Trudeau and his government saw the country through the eyes of Central Canada and viewed the issues as a linear extension of the ancient Upper Canada–Lower Canada debate. While no one with any sense of history or geography or demographics would deny the fundamental importance of this debate to Canada as a nation, it is by no means the only important issue. It may not even be the main one, the way things are developing in the Far West.

Trudeau was unwilling, or perhaps unable, to comprehend that other regions of Canada saw the nation and its future through quite a different prism and were not prepared to line up behind Ontario to share Canada in a bigger partnership with Quebec.

Trudeau's contempt for premiers filtered down. Federal cabinet ministers like Marc Lalonde and Otto Lang looked down their noses at their provincial counterparts. Indeed, it was these very two men, the cream of Ottawa arrogance, whom Trudeau appointed as federal representatives to the federal constitutional committee to negotiate with the provinces on the terms of patriation of the Constitution. Lest this be considered overly sensitive, I feel safe in asserting that all of us felt it (though some took it with considerably more good nature than I did).

I suppose, looking back, that a substantial indicator of the Trudeau attitude to provincial concerns came in the spring 1980 First Ministers Conference in the Convention Centre in Ottawa. The late journalist Charles Lynch refused to leave the hall when Trudeau called for the session to go *in camera*. The prime minister, who was quite unused to having his authority challenged, gave in to a journalist! The reason now, if not then, was obvious. In Trudeau's mind, nothing of any lasting importance could come out of a meeting with premiers and their lackeys anyway, so why grant it the dignity of privacy?

The proof of Trudeau's contempt came in September 1980, when by design he scuppered the conference that was supposedly the culmination of all the work of the previous four years. That the fix was in was indicated when, on the eve of the conference, the famous Michael Kirby memo was leaked (almost certainly by design, though I'm not suggesting by Kirby himself) to Rene Levesque, who promptly circulated it to his colleagues. Kirby, a senior bureaucrat advising Trudeau on constitutional matters, had prepared a lengthy memo for him that dealt with every possibility of any or all of the provinces looking good at this conference. Every possible constructive move by any premier was covered off by this memo, which even referred to Machiavelli. In the hands of the various premiers, this memo was bound to fatally sour the conference from the start, which it did.

For those of us who had worked hard and felt that we had reached decisions that would truly allow all first ministers to see themselves as the new Fathers of Confederation, it was a bitter pill to swallow. We watched in horror as the plan outlined in the Kirby memo unfolded, and each premier was put down by the prime minister, on national television. For me it was a combination of anger and depression as I watched Trudeau sum up by castigating his provincial colleagues—vowing that he, as the only man with a truly national vision, would now have to go it alone in bringing the Constitution home.

The fight was far from over. There would be court battles and, insofar as these are possible, debates in Parliament. There were compromises and what was seen by the Parti Quebecois as a betrayal. But at the end of the day Trudeau got his Constitution home, complete with a Charter of Rights and Freedoms.

We have, then, a country that is governed by and for the benefit of the two largest provinces by a government that, because it owes its electoral life to Central Canada, is hell-bent on giving those provinces vetoes by which to prevent any change.

Can anything short of radical surgery be done to restore the integrity and dignity of Parliament?

In his marvelous book *1867*, Christopher Moore opines that the House of Commons can take charge of its own affairs once more, and be like the legislatures were at the time of Confederation, when premiers brought leaders and members of the opposition to Charlottetown and Quebec conferences—because they knew that they would otherwise never get legislative approval for what they did, even if they had a majority in legislatures.

Christopher is right, technically. But it will never happen. The system has been locked in place for too long, and has roots far too deep, to dislodge merely by a resolve to do better.

Many of the parliamentary reforms that have been proposed, especially by Preston Manning, are useless. Take, for example, free votes, where the party whips, on instructions, tell members that they can vote their consciences. Does anyone think for a moment that the prime minister will not still make his views known, and still watch very carefully how his flock votes? Refer back, if you will, to the Clifford Olson case discussed above.

The truth is that you cannot depend upon a prime minister, even if it is Preston Manning (unlikely though that prospect seems), to yield more than a token amount of power. One need only look at the penalties Manning has exacted on those within the Reform caucus who have opposed him to see the how strong the aphrodisiac of power is. Those who have crossed him have been dealt with most severely indeed. Why would Prime Minister Preston Manning be any more indulgent of contrary opinion?

What about changing the voting system to one of proportional representation (PR), where members are elected not by constituency but off a party list? For a full and learned discussion of this subject I recommend Nick Loenen's book *Citizenship and Democracy*, which the former B.C. MLA did as his Master's thesis.

There are several variations on this theme. Under a pure PR system, every party with one percent or more of the vote elects the appropriate number of MPs from a political party's list. This system and any variation on it becomes confused in a federation like ours. Does the list simply mean a pool from which the leaders choose, or must there be a list from each province so that Parliament, while made up of people selected from a party list, will also represent provinces in proportion to their population? The other key question is, how is this list compiled. Will there be conventions, and if so, province by province? As always, the devil is in the details, and all we really have to go on here is the experience of small countries like Israel, New Zealand and Germany, where the regions have significant power right from the upper house.

I by no means reject the notion of PR, full or partial, but only point out that it makes a better abbreviation than it does an explanation.

Some systems, recognizing that there must be regional representation or constituencies, have a mixed system, in which half of the MPs are elected off the list, the other by the "first past the post" method that is currently used in Canadian elections. New Zealand and Germany are examples of this compromise.

I have a great deal of sympathy for PR or some variation of it. But it does not, if New Zealand provides any example, really solve the problem. The great advantage of a PR system is that it requires the prime minister to go back to Parliament and respectfully ask for money instead of getting it from compliant backbenchers under strict discipline. That, at any rate, is the theory.

What often happens, however, is that a deal is made, usually between two party leaders, to form a majority government. Even though these two leaders may be poles apart politically, they now have a common interest: staying in power. With some minor lessening of the autocracy of the prime minister, you're back where you started. If PR were, in practice, to mean that the largest party would form a minority government and thereafter have to treat Parliament with respect, or fall, that would be one thing. But politicians, like capitalists, prefer monopolies and do handsprings to create them.

Even in countries like Israel, where there are dozens of parties, once the prime minister is chosen it's hell on wheels to get rid of him; such is the interest of his coalition in staying in power. The obverse side of the Israel coin is, of course, Italy, where there is pure PR—and where the length of a government is usually measured in days.

There is another very important question to consider. Much of whether or not a system works depends upon the country and its people. Proponents of PR (as I sometimes am) tend to look at the 1993 Canadian election and state that had there been PR, the Tories would have elected a good slug of MPs from every region of Canada, and wouldn't that have been a good thing?

The problem is, we are mixing apples and oranges. If PR had been in place in 1993, the voters' options would have been considerably different, as would have been the results. There would likely have been an anti-abortion party in the race (I'm against abortion, by the way), a number of religious parties, a strong Green Party, more regional parties, and so on. I'm not saying that this would be a bad thing—just that if PR had been in place, the 1993 election would have been a very different exercise. This makes the figures from the last "first past the post" election of dubious value in evaluating the case for PR.

What *is* for sure is that there would be more regional parties. How much electoral strength they would have is speculative, but it's not hard to imagine some regional parties getting, say, five percent of the vote. I don't say that this is a bad thing, merely that we must take it into account. Many regional parties (unless the national election was province by province) would be shut out by failing to get five percent of the entire national vote: this would mean, in effect, that Quebec or Ontario (and perhaps B.C.) could elect regional parties, but not the rest of the country.

There is one more thing. Under PR would we ever get any real change?

In the U.K., where the Liberal–Democrats are pushing for PR (for obvious reasons) there's fear that if it's implemented by Tony Blair's Labour Party, future governments will simply be the latest edition of a "Lib–Lab" pact where the Liberal leader, indistinguishable from his Labour counterpart, will simply replace the latter when the public gets bored with him. The left and the right will become marginalized to the extent that not only can they never attain power again, they will lose all influence.

There is another proposal that doesn't, as far as I can see, do anything to restore the power and dignity of Parliament, but since it is often mentioned in the same breath as PR, I will deal with it very briefly.

The "transferable ballot," which has a number of variations, asks a voter to vote by number rather than by an "x." With, say, five candidates the voter lists his choices one, two, three, four, five, and the votes are counted until one candidate gets a clear majority. This is how most political conventions work, so Canadians are aware of the system.

British Columbia had such a system in 1952, when W.A.C. Bennett and his Socreds won a minority government, and in the 1953 election that gave him a majority. By the 1956 election, Bennett had abolished the transferable ballot and gone back to the traditional "first past the post."

If one is to have a "first past the post" system, the transferable ballot certainly suits those who lose, only because there is a splitting of the vote. The transferable ballot would have defeated the NDP in B.C. in 1996 (and perhaps for that reason alone should be seriously considered). It does not, of course, do anything for minority parties and does nothing to reduce, let alone eliminate, the four-to-five year dictatorship we've been discussing.

I don't want to leave this subject without this observation. Proportional representation, in its many forms, *should* be seriously considered by the citizenry of Canada. It *won't* be, though, because it is in the interests of the major parties that the idea not be discussed. No more complicated than that. As Nick Loenen says in his book, "If you were a turkey, would you vote for an early Thanksgiving?"

The present system of changeable autocracy will continue unless Canadians, with unwonted political vigour, rise as one to demand change.

1867 was not a deal between Upper and Lower Canada alone—it included two other provinces and contemplated two more. It was clearly a national deal, not a provincial settlement. "Two founding nations" and "juridical equality" are simply not compatible philosophies. You cannot have a country that is a partnership, between Quebec on the one hand and the rest of the country on the other, and still have a country based upon equality.

Some reject all other systems because of what they see as serious difficulties therein. I can well remember constitutional expert Dr. Edward McWhinney (now Liberal MP for Vancouver Quadra) publicly pooh-poohing the visit Mel Smith and I took to (then) West Germany in 1978. It was, he thought, an idle exercise.

But Mel and I were looking not for something to copy, but for guidance from a country that had tackled, much more successfully than Canada had, the problems facing a nation with clearly defined regions.

The United States is also rejected as an example, perhaps because of inherent anti-Americanism, but surely also because we don't like the abuses we see in that system. We tend to overlook the facts that no one is ever entitled to expect a perfect system and that Canadians can adapt without aping. We are a different people than the Americans and that should not be forgotten.

Let me put some meat on these bones. In order to survive and prosper as a nation we must empower MPs. Pierre Trudeau once said that a few yards from Parliament Hill, MPs were nobodies. I'm puzzled at the qualification, for they are nobodies even inside the Commons chamber.

Not only must we empower the only people we directly elect, we must ensure that their power is equal, no matter what constituency they represent. I concede that the latter is more a hope than an achievable reality, but it must always be the goal. At present it is only a theory.

How do we do this? Simple—if we have the will and the guts to do it.

What we must do, first and foremost, is divorce the executive and legislative branches of government.

This, of course, runs against all the sacred cows that we have been taught are essential to our democratic way of life. But what is this democratic way of life we preserve by pronouncing "responsible government" in hushed tones of reverence whenever change is proposed? It's changeable fascism, that's what it is. It's one-man power, with that one man accountable, in reality, to no one between elections.

As we have seen earlier, our system has destroyed the independence and power of the MP and has placed it all in the Prime Minister's Office, where it is largely exercised by men who are unknown outside inner circles—and who certainly have not been elected. This is democracy? This is what was meant by "responsible government," the virtues of which are driven into the crania of our schoolkids?

What would a separation of powers accomplish? A whole hell of a lot, that's what.

Yes, it would be a republican style of government, as opposed to a strictly British Parliamentary system. The prime minister would be elected quite separately from the Commons, on a fixed-term basis, and there would be a deputy prime minister elected as well. There would no need to adopt the American system of having both candidates elected from the same party— why not elect the deputy prime minister from a different party, if that's what the people wish?

The prime minister would be able to select his cabinet, or the heads of various administrative departments, from the public at large, with this important proviso: they must each be approved by Parliament. I suggest that, as in the U.S., the prime minister could veto legislation—with a two-thirds majority of Parliament being able to override that veto.

Let me deal here with the argument that this would cause the government to grind to a halt. That's not so in the United States and would not be so here. The Commons would understand, as the American Senate does, that the country must be administered and that their job is to apply, in the name of the voters, a potential safeguard against executive abuse. Indeed, if a new, useful Senate was put in place, this job would ideally suit it.

In this country we have become so used to what we perceive as "efficient" government that we readily overlook the right of the people to *control* who governs them. If we do think about that right, we console ourselves with the thought that, in theory at least, the people can defeat bad cabinet ministers at the next election—which, as we have seen, is about as powerful a democratic tool as was the power of the Soviet Presidium to toss out Josef Stalin.

What's wrong with our elected representatives having at least the power to veto cabinet ministers—and other senior appointments—if in their view the choices are clearly unsuitable? And what on earth about our system's record over the past decades gives us the impression that it is efficient at all, much less more efficient than the system below the border?

The legislative branch should also vet appointments to the Supreme Court of Canada. And senior administrative appointments, including senior diplomatic posts.

But there is a more fundamental reason to divorce the legislative from the executive. *The principal consequence of this reform would be that the executive would have to come to Parliament for funding supply, without any guarantees that it would be granted.*

Why should the prime minister have whatever money he tells his captive MPs he would like, imposing iron discipline on members during budget votes? Why shouldn't he have to get genuine—freely debated and freely voted upon—approval from the people who are supposed to be the guardians of the public purse, the members of the House of Commons?

On paper the House of Commons controls the exchequer, but in practice it does precisely what it is told. This is so clearly and utterly undemocratic that I'm astonished that we have put up with it for 130 years.

Under a republican system, would the Commons behave irresponsibly, and even be guided by party political considerations? Of course it would! It does in the United States—but the reality is that the executive and the legislative must cooperate and govern, or the people will toss them out on their ears.

Under the American system the president and his cabinet spend the money, but Congress must authorize it. This would seem, on the face of it, to set up a Mexican standoff between the executive and the legislative. In fact, what has developed is a consultative process where the president says what he wants and Congress says what it will deliver, followed by meetings to resolve differences.

In practice, of course, the majority of the budget is agreed upon because it is pre-ordained by enormous ongoing expenses from programs long in place which, it seems, cannot even be modified, much less tubed. One need only look at the vast sums spent financing multicultural groups. I stand strongly for the rights of all Canadians to keep in touch with their roots — but at their own expense, not mine. But I digress.

The important point of the American arrangement is that the legislative arm controls the public purse. The system is far from perfect. But it's arguably better and unarguably more democratic.

The choice is how we want monetary decisions to be made. Do we want the budget to continue to be concocted in secret, by faceless bureaucrats and unelected insiders in the Prime Minister's Office? Are we content to have the budget crammed down the throats of those we elect by a prime minister who, because of the virtually absolute power the system gives him, can order up whatever he likes?

Or do we insist that before the executive spends a nickel of our money, it be approved by those we send to Ottawa to protect the public purse?

What about legislation? How do we get laws passed if the executive can't simply demand approval from a compliant parliament? Well, the United States doesn't seem to want for legislation. We would have a similar procedure. The prime minister would present a bill to the Commons, and then convince MPs that it should be passed. Or Parliament could initiate and pass its own legislation, subject to the same sort of prime ministerial veto power that the president of the United States has. The critical point being that legislation not popular with the majority of Canadians (as the Liberal gun-control legislation probably wasn't—though it was fine with me) could not be jammed through a compliant legislature by the prime minister.

The second and extremely important result of this reform would be that Parliament would be free of the ironclad party discipline that is necessary in a system in which governments fall upon losing a vote.

There would still be political parties, as there are in other republican systems, and these parties would exercise some discipline. But it would be limited by the reality that MPs, no longer dependent upon the prime minister for their jobs, could not easily be compelled to toe a party line.

The prime minister would still exert pressure on MPs, just as the president does upon members of Congress. But that pressure would be much ameliorated by the fact that the prime minister could suggest in strong terms, and threaten political consequences, but he could not give orders based upon an ability to terminate an MP's political career. There would be pressure from majority and minority leaders, but you would quickly find, as has happened in the States, that on most controversial bills there would be considerable cross-party voting.

Regions would, for the first time, have real power. While the more populous provinces would still have the most MPs, outside experience teaches us that MPs from Ontario will not necessarily all feel the same about all issues. Moreover, one would find that provinces like Ontario and those in Atlantic Canada would be less reluctant to vote for the Reform Party when they have a direct vote for the prime minister of their choice. Similarly, voters in the Far West could be expected to be less distrustful of Liberals and Tories if they knew that the new breed of MP was accountable not to the prime minister, but to them.

Would this mean that legislation and policy would develop by log rolling and taffy pulling amongst MPs, with compromises and concessions being common? Of course it would. And why not? Why should fifty percent plus one have one hundred percent of the power? Why shouldn't other regions be taken into account, not because of some act of Christian charity by benevolent Central Canadian politicians, but because they *must* be? Why should the national interest be that which best suits Ontario and Quebec? Those two provinces will continue to be very powerful, but in order to have their way, they will have to make concessions to other regions.

Fairer play in senior appointments will also result. Can you imagine British Columbians being deprived of seats on things like the Wheat Board (after all, most Canadian wheat is shipped through B.C. ports), the CBC, the Bank of Canada and the like, if B.C. MPs could make mischief with other appointments if there was not fair play all around?

It must also be remembered that MPs would no longer be forced to put the political survival of the prime minister ahead of their duty to their province and their constituency. No more could an Allan Rock give solace to Clifford Olson because to do otherwise might be politically embarrassing to the prime minister. Never again could an executive decide to dictate a "Commons" constitutional veto, and nor could the prime minister personally invent an amending formula that offended the law and made a mockery of the democratic process. Most importantly, MPs would be able to call the executive into account, rather than skulking like frightened curs at the threat of prime ministerial displeasure.

(When I say "call the executive into account," I am suggesting that it goes without saying that the Commons must have the right, upon a substantial majority—perhaps two thirds—to impeach the prime minister.)

There are less radical solutions to Canada's governmental ails suggested. The Reform Party has long called for more "free votes"—that is, votes where the "whip" is off and MPs can vote as they please. Sounds great. But as pointed out earlier, in fact it means little or nothing. Every MP knows that the prime minister will be watching to see who votes how, and making later judgments accordingly. This point bears repeating because the leader of the Official Opposition, Preston Manning, is holding out "free votes" as a basic reform to our system. They would be no such thing, simply another nice-sounding nostrum to distract Canadians, for a while, from the real governance problems that beset the nation.

There's some talk of giving parliamentary committees more power, but the fact remains that the prime minister *appoints* the committees, so where does that get you?

No, radical surgery is required.

If the changes I propose, or ones like them, are undertaken, it doesn't mean that pension cheques won't arrive, or that law cases won't be heard, or that government business will grind to a halt. From day to day, things will go on as usual.

There will, however, be a new relationship between Canadian voters and the men and women they elect to Parliament. MPs, having a great deal more power, will develop a closeness with their ridings hitherto not even imagined. Legislation will become a matter of consultation, as will the budget. The MP who doesn't consult will not be re-elected.

This strikes fear into those who support the present system. Why, they say, Mair's changes will mean government by survey. MPs will just become ciphers at the mercy of the loudest mouth in their constituency. It will bring inefficiency. How will anything ever get done?

Well, things will get done just fine. The substitution here is the people for the prime minister and his unelected insiders. What I am proposing is that if we like democracy so much, let's try it for a change. As has happened elsewhere, mechanisms will be found to smooth off the rough spots when an executive is divorced from the legislative. One need only look at the liaison techniques developed in the United States and Germany to see how a republican form of government can be just as efficient (or inefficient, if you prefer) as a parliamentary "democracy."

Indeed, from a practical point of view, much of Parliament's business will proceed as usual. Politicians rarely move events—events move politicians. Much of a legislature's business is routine. But under a proper democracy, when it comes to the issues of the day, the public will have a direct say.

Let's look at a graphic example: capital punishment, that euphemism for the death penalty. I oppose the death penalty with all my soul, yet I say that if this is what the people of Canada want, they should have it. But the prime minister is the boss. His views on this most vexatious of issues prevail. Members of Parliament, our representatives, have no real say in the matter. It's true that the last time it was debated there was a free vote, but it would have taken a very brave Liberal indeed (the Liberals are not especially known for their bravery) to have voted "Yes" after Trudeau's impassioned summing-up of the "No" case.

I support gun control, but if the people of Canada don't want it, or want another form of it, that's what should happen.

The "higher-purpose persons" hate this because they believe that they know best—that some things just cannot be left to the people. People who "know what's best" should judge things like gun control, unrestricted abortion and the death penalty. It's horrifying to the elite that the rabble, including their MLAs and MPs, should have any real say. Apparent say, OK, but let's not get carried away and let the people decide anything of consequence. They'll only get it wrong—at least, wrong in the eyes of the elite.

Well, in a free country, the people are entitled to get it wrong. That's the essence of democracy. Moreover, does anyone seriously argue that the "establishment" always gets it right—or even usually does?

We're talking here of developing a new respect for Parliament, which means a new respect for those who make it up. MPs would no longer be nobodies anywhere.

There is another argument, of course. It is said that while MPs come from constituencies within provinces, they must, upon election, look at the national interest—it being implied that under a republican system they would not.

That argument is unsustainable. Is it really suggested that the U.S. Congress, with its lower house elected by "rep by pop" and its upper house by state, does not represent the national interest? Of course it does, and it is helped to do so by the immense prestige accruing to the president, who is elected across the land—a prestige that would also accrue to a prime minister elected at large.

Will there be problems if my suggestions are adopted in whole or in part? Of course there will. Lots of them. No matter what system we adopt, there will be problems. The devil, as they say, is in the details. In putting something new into place, care must be taken to learn from the experiences of others. I'm not seeking a perfect system—just a better one. A much better one that will keep the country together. And one that it is possible to change. No vetoes.

The most important impact of the changes I propose comes in the area of national unity. Because all MPs would be equal—or much closer to equal, at any rate—the "outer" regions of Canada would be much better plugged in to the centre. The people in these regions will feel that they have a real say in what is happening. An energy policy will no longer be adopted despite the rage of one part of the country because it is helpful to a politically more important part.

Let me now deal with some of the other criticisms that are bound to emerge. Somehow there is this feeling that prospective judges should not be subject to any vetting process. Perhaps this is because of what we have sometimes seen happen in the United States, although we quickly forget that some most unsatisfactory candidates have been rejected by the American process.

How we conduct our hearings is up to us. Perhaps it's no more complicated than keeping the TV cameras out so as to avoid what seems to be a circus atmosphere when the appropriate committee questions prospective judges.

The point is this: Why should the only criterion be that the prime minister is satisfied with the selection? He's bound to be—after all, he made it. Why shouldn't a candidate be questioned on how he or she views matters constitutional? Could they, in the opinion of Parliament, fairly and without bias, judge the balance between federal and provincial rights? And what about attitudes toward criminal law? Are we not entitled to know in advance whether a prospective judge will be a "hang 'em high" judge or one who is very "liberal" on such matters—or, more importantly, one who has an open mind?

The argument is that this process preprograms court decisions. To an extent it does, but nowhere near to the extent that the present system does. Prime ministers who serve a couple of terms have the opportunity to put their personal imprint on the Supreme Court of Canada—which lasts long after they're gone. Then their successors use their appointments to counteract the previous ones and put their *own* long-term stamp on the judiciary.

Surely it would be better if the prime minister's choice for the top court in the land were tempered by the influence of members of Parliament, representing all regions and all points of view.

What about superior court judges on provincial benches? I see no reason why their appointments should not be vetted by provincial legislatures. In practice the minister of justice, who formally makes the appointments, will have a very good idea in advance what Parliament on the one hand, and the legislatures on the other, are thinking. The hearings in the U.S. Senate, such as the one for Robert Bork, turned out to be so messy because the president didn't listen in advance to objections that were bound to be raised.

What, then, about the Senate? This should, in a country as large as Canada, be a very important part of Parliament. Our Senate was set up in 1867 as a sort of compromise between the British House of Lords and the American Senate, with all the defects of both and none of their virtues. It was to be representative of the regions, yet was not selected by the regions but by the prime minister. It was to have substantial powers to initiate and pass legislation, but because it wasn't elected it lacked the moral authority to assert itself.

Because the Senate couldn't amend itself, problems were exacerbated, not solved. Senators are, for the most part, political hacks whose usefulness has passed or bank presidents who'll make sure, through the Senate's regular reviews of the Bank Act, that nothing is ever done to curb the powers and wealth of our national banks.

And, of course, the system of representation becomes more and more absurd with every passing day.

The Senate does do good things from time to time, and there have been moments when the Canadian public turned to the upper house for help when a prime minister became especially abusive. This is what makes it important that the Senate change: It *is* powerful, as its role in almost blocking the Mulroney government's Goods and Services Tax (GST) legislation proved (the Liberal-dominated Senate was clearly going to block the GST, so Mulroney created new openings and appointed loyal Tories), but its fatal flaw is that it's not a legitimate democratic organ of a government that, in name at least, is supposed to be democratic.

If the Senate is powerful enough to block key fiscal legislation, and if only six of its number represent British Columbia (the third largest province), and even those by appointment of the prime minister, then surely its reform is critical. The Senate *could* become a valuable part of a national system of governance that *contributes* to, instead of derogating from, national unity.

The first problem is representation. I have never been a fan of the "triple-E" senate proposed by some, because it is ludicrous to give Prince Edward Island the same representation as Ontario. I know that this seems to derogate from my position on provincial equality—except it doesn't really. Equality means that under the Constitution all provinces have equal powers. It does not mean that all provinces have equal shares of *federal* power. This could not, as we have developed, ever work at all, let alone fairly.

While the United States has two senators for each state, irrespective of population, they have developed into *fifty* states, not ten. While it's silly for Rhode Island to have the same number of senators as California, it has happened, more by good luck than good management, that these anachronisms have pretty well balanced out across the nation.

On the other hand, if it is unfair to give a tiny province of 150,000 people the same number of Senate seats as Ontario, it defeats the purpose of a Senate to give seats based upon population. A Senate, after all, is supposed to balance off the tyranny of the "rep by pop" Commons majority with regional influence.

It is not my purpose here to set forth the nuts and bolts of a new Senate, but there are two suggestions that I think merit attention.

One system would have a regional Senate, but with *some* attention paid to population. This is, essentially, the German system—in which the upper house, far from being selected based on "rep by pop," does have a "load" factor, where populous provinces will have more members than less populous ones. This loading will not be in direct relationship to their respective populations, but nevertheless will recognize that where populations are grossly unequal, equal representation to all provinces is inequitable.

The second is a regional Senate such as the one proposed by B.C. back in 1978. This would mean that five regions of Canada—Atlantic Canada, Quebec, Ontario, the Prairies, and British Columbia—would each have the same representation.

This system presents some problems. What about the territories? They must be represented. And what happens if a province, part of a region, becomes itself a region? Newfoundland and Alberta come to mind as provinces that may well outgrow their present relationships with their neighbours and clearly become separate regions. In fact, Newfoundland never really has been part of "the Maritimes," but has remained quite separate and distinct. Who will make such determinations? The existing regions would be most unlikely to want to add power anywhere but to themselves. That's human nature, unfortunately.

But these are problems that can surely be worked out. The trick will be to come up with a Senate that can be changed as the needs arise. *For there is a great danger in locking arrangements that are sensible today into place for all time.* Lebanon provides an excellent example of why you don't do that. When Lebanon got her independence after the Second World War, the population was approximately fifty-fifty between Christians and Muslims, so it was agreed, constitutionally, that the president should alternate between these two groups.

After forty years, much changed, and the population ratios were now approximately two-to-one in favour of Muslims—who showed an understandable disinclination to continue an arrangement no longer warranted by the circumstances.

We know what happened: bloody revolution in which many neighbouring countries, and countries not at all neighbouring, got into the act.

This was the evil of the Charlottetown arrangement, which would have given Quebec twenty-five percent of the House of Commons forever more. It wouldn't have mattered for some years, but when it began to matter, it would have become an ever more serious running sore on the body politic—a sore which, because of Quebec's veto, could never be healed.

What about selecting the Senate? It must be done by election. That's democracy, and democracy is what we're trying to achieve.

What about terms of office? I believe that the prime minister and deputy PM (and the premiers and vice premiers) should be elected for four year terms, *with a two-term restriction on the prime minister,* as should the House of Commons. I would have the Senate and the House of Commons elected for fixed four-year terms. After much thought and reading, I would not impose any term limits on senators or MPs. I have read with considerable interest and sympathy George Will's writings on term limitations (such as *Restoration*), and while he makes a persuasive case, I think it's wrong in a democracy to place undue restrictions on the right of the public to elect whomever they wish for as long as they wish. I make the same exception for the elected prime minister that the U.S. makes for its president. It has not been an undue hardship on American democracy to have a two-term limit for their president, and I believe this to be a reasonable restriction for a Canadian head of government.

In coming to these conclusions I have looked at the American system—which is really based upon elections to the House of Representatives every two years, so that there is an opportunity to elect one third of the Senate at least every two years. I don't believe two years is enough for the House of Commons. In the U.S. the congressperson starts working on re-election the moment he or she is elected in the first place. This is destabling and hugely expensive.

There is a movement in the States to limit senatorial terms to two, or a maximum of twelve years, because under the present system there is virtually no involuntary turnover. But that's not a problem with the system but with the voters—who can change their politicians at election time if they choose.

These are all arguable points. The important thing is that as Canadians, we make a commitment to change and then put in place a reformed system, after complete and thorough consultation. This leads to the question of process.

New Zealand showed the way when it changed its voting system from a strict "first past the post" to a combination of that system with proportional representation. The first step is to consult the people on whether or not they want a change and, if so, to what basic form. This requires a fair question, fairly put and widely debated.

I would suggest that each province nominate a commissioner—under the chair of someone agreeable to seven of the ten provinces representing at least fifty percent of the Canadian population (the present "Vancouver Amending Formula"). Again, the devil is in the details and it is not the purpose of this book to put flesh on all the bones of contention. I would suggest, however, that the provincial selections be made as B.C. selects its ombudsman—two thirds of the House based upon the unanimous consent of a select committee.

The House of Commons should then select ten representatives who, as with the provincial commissioners, would select a chairman. There would be, then, a commission of twenty-two members, with co-chairs. It would be the mandate of this commission to debate, then recommend, the basic possibilities to the public for vote by referendum.

I think there would be three basic propositions formulated. One would be the present system, untouched. Another would be the present system, changed. A third would be a new system such as I've proposed, or some variation thereof.

Once the matter has been deliberated and reported upon, one would think there would then be a good deal of national debate.

Once the public makes its decision as to which alternative it prefers (unless it prefers to preserve the status quo) it would be the duty of the commission to, for want of any other suitable word, thrash out the details for further approval by the public and subsequent implementation. That referendum would be so framed as to have the power of approving constitutional change.

I must quickly admit that there are bound to be refinements on this idea available, and it may be that there is a much better way of establishing a constituent assembly, an idea whose time has surely come.

A constituent assembly can take many forms in terms of appointment of members, and that is the trick. But essentially it is a group of citizens who deliberate and make constitutional recommendations to the "constituent" parts of the federation—that is, the provinces and federal government. Their recommendations are not binding but are bound to be persuasive, especially if they are unanimous. It was from just such an assembly that the United

States got its Constitution in 1787, and it has been used successfully in this century by Germany, Australia and South Africa, amongst others.

But what if we fail in these efforts? Well, so what?

It would be a shame, and it would say that Canadians are not able to agree upon a fair nationwide rebuilding of their system of governance. On the other hand, we would all learn a lot about our country: the things we have in common and the things that divide us. It could well fail, but still provide an important base for further efforts.

But I don't think it *would* fail. I believe that Canadians from coast to coast want to keep our country together and, even more importantly, re-establish it on a basis that will preserve it for our heirs. I believe that in a roundabout way the exercise would be like Samuel Johnson's "hanging in a fortnight"—it would concentrate the mind wonderfully.

There is already a deep sense of urgency now. All a constituent assembly will do is channel that urgency into an exercise that might just save the day. In short, a constituent assembly would give a process for change *legitimacy*, something all past efforts have badly lacked.

Whereas past efforts to obtain public involvement have mainly been exercises in fooling the public into thinking they have input, this would be an assembly of the public itself. It will be argued that this will all be time-consuming and expensive. But compared to what? Time-consuming compared to the endless and largely fruitless debates we have had for the past 130 years? Expensive when one considers national unity as the object of the exercise? Surely no one would seriously argue that.

These notions will be opposed by those who have a large and deeply entrenched stake in the present system continuing. The "higher-purpose persons," who have traditionally felt their views to be much wiser than those of the people, will object.

I expect no good reviews for these notions (nor for this book for that matter) from Central Canadian journalists who have prospered from the difficulties the current system poses. Certainly the present power structure will come up with masses of reasons why none of what I propose will work.

No one in power—be it a labour leader, a corporate CEO, or a prime minister—really trusts the judgment of those he rules. He knows best. The public are fools. Better the devil you know than the one you don't. Stick with the old ways that got you where you are, rather than putting in place something that might see you replaced.

The enormity of what I propose will put many people off. The reality is, however (if I'm right about the parlous state of national affairs), that radical restructuring will take place anyway. The only real questions are, when will this restructuring take place, and, will it be in response to tragic events rather than heading them off?

I can only say, with as much conviction as I can summon up, that if we *don't* make radical changes to the way we govern ourselves, we won't survive as a nation.

CHAPTER TWELVE

What Next?

As I write this, Jean Charest has taken over the provincial Liberal leader-ship in Quebec and is riding high in the polls. He could well parlay this pop-ularity into victory in the next Quebec election. If that happens, though, Canada's constitutional crisis will not be any closer to a solution.

Charest, who emphatically believes in the necessity of special status and a constitutional veto as a minimum for Quebec, will be taken by Quebeckers to have promised these things as a condition of his election, and will be expect-ed to see that these promises are redeemed—but they are not redeemable. For example, changing the amending formula and giving Quebec its precious veto would require the consent of *all* provinces. That won't be forthcoming—at least, not from British Columbia—so separatist discontent will only be aggra-vated. How will *that* make Canada's future more secure?

Some say Charest would bring a "friendly" (as in sympathetic to Canadian federalism) government to Quebec City. Really? Robert Bourassa was supposed to have headed a "friendly" government, and it was he who brokered the Charlottetown arrangement guaranteeing Quebec twenty-five percent of the House of Commons.

Jean Charest's arrival on the Quebec political scene will accomplish only one thing for Canadian unity: it will buy us a little time. How will Ottawa use that time? Not wisely, history tells us. Traditionally, Ottawa has done absolutely nothing during periods of constitutional "lull"—except in the case of Brian Mulroney, who, as already noted, used one to violently stir the constitutional pot.

Buying time, of course, is a time-honoured political strategy. Why take bold problem-solving initiatives when you can avoid the difficulties that inevitably accompany tough decisions? Why take potentially unpopular actions now, when you know that the underlying problems won't reach a crisis point for ten or fifteen years? We will, I fear, learn the sad answer to that question ere long.

We have no courageous leadership in Ottawa and none on the horizon, with the possible exception of Preston Manning. We have no will to defend what is ours—by that I mean what belongs to all Canadians. We continue to sleepwalk, in the hope that somehow the problems will go away.

Playing for time only aggravates national problems, and sets the stage for real political catastrophe. This will be particularly true in British Columbia, where the province's grievances against the federal government—over the Delgamuukw case, over federal fisheries policy as it relates to the West Coast, over Ottawa's habitual disregard for B.C.'s views, over the federal policy of Quebec appeasement—will very likely explode if the Quebec situation worsens.

Without decisive action, the Canadian dream of a nation of many regions—diverse in so many respects, yet Canadian throughout—seems doomed to disaster. Our government cannot deal with the very diversity that should be our greatest national strength.

I'm a Canadian first and foremost, but when I consider the possible ramifications of Quebec leaving the country, I become a Canadian who feels a sense of panic. I realize that panic in a crisis is not recommended, but I'm reminded of the cartoon that shows two explorers up to their necks in quicksand: One says to the other, "You know, Charles, I'm tempted to struggle."

I panic when I hear apparently knowledgable voices saying that if Quebec goes, we will partition Quebec—though without any violence, of course.

I panic when I hear people talk about creating a new Canada after Quebec goes, even though anyone with half a brain knows that British Columbia would never agree to a new union in which Ontario controls half the House of Commons.

I panic when I hear that there would be a "Western" federation formed, or that Alberta and British Columbia would form a new country.

Do these people not understand that with Quebec gone, the very essence of the great Canadian experiment would be gone, too? Whether you love her or hate her, Quebec is an integral part of Canada. What holds Canada together is the thrill of being part of a great experiment in making a multi-cultural society work. We may not all like multicultural policies, or where they're taking us. We may be annoyed at immigration policies old and new. But the multicultural ideal is a basic part of Canada. You can't remove Quebec from Canada, just as you can't remove the Ukrainians from the Prairies, the Scots from Nova Scotia or Chinatown from Vancouver. The country probably couldn't stand Toronto being popular either.

But the case of Quebec is especially unusual: from the beginning it has been national policy, not just an exercise in private tolerance, to support Quebec culture. For all the brave talk from some English-speaking Canadians, it's *not* going to be a good thing for the rest of Canada if Quebec goes—it will be the death of the country.

That's not to say that something might not be worked out between various regions. But to think that the country would just sail along as usual is crazy. For British Columbia, at any rate, Ontario would just replace Quebec as the national problem, and it would be a problem for which there would likely be only one solution—B.C. going it alone.

To keep a Canada together *without* Quebec would require far more effort than keeping the *present* country whole. But while this statement would be approved, I daresay, by Jean Chretien himself, there is one major difference between my position and the position of Chretien and the Canadian establishment: I am not prepared to sacrifice principle for, at best, a short-term, unprincipled solution.

If we retain Quebec's presence through appeasement, special treatment and continuing bribes, we will not gain her affection, respect or loyalty. We will simply whet her appetite for separation, and will pay the price later rather than sooner—and the price will be much higher for the delay.

If I'm right, there's only one way to proceed from here, and that is to lay it on the line.

What's the point of the House of Commons or the prime minister—or anyone else, for that matter—promising Quebec status as a "distinct" or "unique" society when most of the rest of the country will not agree? Why on earth promise Quebec a constitutional veto, when once again the notion will fail? And when we know that if a Quebec veto *did* somehow find its way into the Constitution, it would lead to certain disaster?

Since all past efforts at resolving the unity crisis have failed, why not finally speak plainly? Why not initiate discussions based on the bold truth? Whatever the law, Canada cannot survive unless the people from coast to coast and province to province accept that their country is indivisible. Court rulings one way or the other don't mean much in terms of political realities. We must come to a permanent understanding about what we are; if we persist with the notion that breakup is an option, it will always be a threat—and not necessarily from Quebec.

Granted, notwithstanding the views of courts or Parliament, if there is a "Yes" vote in a future Quebec referendum on separation—even if the question is loaded and the majority slim—the likelihood of a unilateral declaration of independence (UDI) is very strong. We must deal with this possibility.

Does this mean that we should prepare for the use of force? That violence might ensue? I don't believe that many Canadians would choose to keep Quebec in Canada by force. Certainly I wouldn't. So flooding Quebec with troops (many with mixed personal feelings) is not a sensible option.

Unhappily, there are complications to this issue. What about the Ungava region? What about the large anglophone pockets within Quebec who will not want to leave Canada?

If Quebec unilaterally declares independence, and the Native occupants of the Ungava region say, "We are Canadian citizens on Canadian land, and we demand protection," what do we do? Simply say, "Sorry, you may be Canadian citizens, but that doesn't mean that Canada will lift a finger to protect your rights"? This question is further complicated by the fact that while the Ungava Natives don't want to be part of Quebec, they may not be fussy about being part of what's left of Canada either.

As for those areas of Quebec inhabited by a huge majority of non-French-speaking Canadians, they too may demand protection of their birthright, which goes back two hundred years. Do we tell them that Canada hasn't the backbone to stand up for their rights either? If we do, history teaches us that there is a strong possibility of prolonged—and violent—civil strife in the areas affected.

If we do move to protect these groups and consider partitioning parts of Quebec (as strongly suggested by Intergovernmental Affairs Minister Stephane Dion in the fall of 1997), what will happen then? The creating of some Shankill Roads and Bogsides in Quebec, with a bit of Cyprus and Bosnia thrown in? Not much of a prospect, is it?

Many experts agree that there is no legal basis for partition and hold that international law permits a seceding country to maintain its existing borders. That may well be true, and in such matters I defer to the experts. But the problem is a practical one, not a legal one.

If the Inuit, the Cree, the anglophones and other Quebec minorities won't passively accept becoming citizens of the country of Quebec, what then?

Canadians are not a violent people, but this isn't because we've been blessed with more peace genes than everyone else in the world. Rather, because of our history and geography, we've had few real opportunities or sufficient provocation to be violent. But we're human beings and we must at least consider what's happened elsewhere when new countries are formed that contain within them large, unhappy minorities. Is Canada really different from other nations around the world that have faced this sort of thing? Let's hope so—but I somehow doubt it.

I raise the questions of force and violence because they are there. No one wants violence. We're talking about people with whom we have lived as fellow citizens for over 130 years. But can Canadians say, unequivocally and in advance, that under no circumstances will violence result from a Quebec UDI?

A stated policy of pacifism at all costs simply concedes all Quebec demands. Cannot it be argued that when a country abjures the use of force to protect its national integrity, it *sacrifices* that national integrity? I intend this not as a bellicose statement but as an object lesson of history. We can't remain in a state of denial fogged over by official reluctance to even discuss these issues.

There's a chance we can avoid the threat of violence, by convincing Quebeckers that their future rests with Canada. Obviously, that's what we are trying to do. But Jacques Parizeau is right: Quebec separatism won't go away and until the issue is resolved with some degree of finality, Canada is doomed to repeated periodic visits to the separatist dentist.

Even though I think the 1980 Quebec referendum was a desperately wrong idea, we have set the precedent, and then affirmed it with the 1995 vote. I believe we must now have "the mother of all referenda" in Quebec.

The key points, of course, are that the question be clear and unambiguous and that the voters be armed with all the facts.

Why another referendum? Two reasons.

First, it makes sense to have a "final showdown," if only to restore some sense of predictability and stability to this country. We simply cannot go on with a separation referendum or two each generation.

Secondly, I believe that if the "No" forces (that is, the federalist forces) are properly marshaled and armed, they will win the next Quebec referendum hands down and lay the ghosts of separation to rest—if not forever, long enough to finally work out a system of governance that we can all at least live with, if not love.

I say this not out of some dreamy optimism but because I strongly believe that, armed with all the facts, the vast majority of Quebeckers do not wish to leave Canada.

If Quebec voters believe that after a Quebec separation their new country will still send MPs to Ottawa; that as foreigners they will still work as Canadian public servants, members of the armed forces, and the RCMP; and that they will have dual-citizenship status; then they will probably vote to separate. If they believe that Quebec will still be protected by legislation requiring Ontario to purchase their dairy products; that separation will not bring a strong move for partition; that the breakup will be friendly, with nothing but goodwill from the remaining nine provinces; they will likely vote to separate.

If, on the other hand (and for the first time), Ottawa speaks not of bribes and appeasement but levels with Quebeckers about the harsh realities of separation, and combines this argument with a reasoned appeal that Quebec and Canada very much need one another, then I believe that unity will have a chance. Not much of one, but still a chance.

For the referendum, I would suggest a simple question along the lines of, "Do you wish Quebec to remain as part of Canada?" *Too* simple? Our own history of conscription questions and the last two "separation" questions in Quebec—all of which were needlessly tortuous—don't make much of a case for complicated questions. People must once and for all know what they're voting on.

I believe that the federal government should announce the referendum six months in advance, to give fair time for both sides to marshal arguments.

Any shorter would be unfair, and any longer would simply aggravate the economic consequences of the uncertainty caused by the pending vote.

Canada has an excellent pro-unity case to present to Quebec. We have a peaceful and overall a prosperous country. We have shared nearly 250 years of history. The advantages of the union have accrued to all regions, but especially to Quebec. For Quebec to break up this experiment in nation-building would be tragic. The province's own great leaders—Cartier, Laurier, Saint-Laurent and Trudeau—tried, in their own ways, to build *one* nation, not simply an accommodation between French-speaking and English-speaking Canadians. They saw, rightly, that this was ultimately in Quebec's interest. We must make Canada's case to Quebeckers and make them understand what being in Canada has meant for them—and for us.

There is an equally strong case to be made for the perils of a Quebec decision to separate. First, Quebeckers must know the consequences of a unilateral declaration of independence. They must know that there will be no "nice" divorce and that *there is no deal to be made if Quebec votes to leave.* As Brian Tobin, premier of Newfoundland, told me last year (and he's an appeaser), no one in "the rest of Canada" even has the authority to make a deal. Also, a Quebec separation will be seen in many parts of Canada, especially B.C., as anything but a friendly gesture. It will bring with it huge and irreparable ill will. Just how anyone thinks that some sort of a chummy family-themed deal can be put together with a newly separated Quebec is beyond comprehension.

No matter how politically incorrect it may seem, Quebeckers should also be told that a Quebec separation may be advantageous financially to the rest of Canada—particularly British Columbia—which will no longer have to dump tax dollars into the Quebec City coffers. Moreover, British Columbia dairy farmers and other industry leaders will welcome the disappearance of Quebec product quotas; they will surely, and rightly, demand to fill those orders themselves. And maybe some federal ships will be built again in B.C. shipyards! (All this presupposes, of course, that the "rest of Canada" will somehow survive losing Quebec.)

We must be sure that Quebeckers *know* all this. All the pollsters and many sage commentators have noted that in the 1995 referendum, a very significant number of voters thought that Quebec could vote "Yes" and still retain all the prerogatives of citizenship in Canada. Quebeckers thought that federal transfer payments would still be made, that pensions would be paid and that they would still be entitled to work for the federal government as if nothing had happened. Many thought that there was no *risk* in voting "Yes," because Canada would then yield to an independent Quebec nation still possessing all the rights of Canadian citizenship—that they could, as former B.C. Premier Bill Bennett once put it, have "divorce with bedroom privileges."

If there is a third referendum and Quebeckers are *not* fully informed by Ottawa as to the consequences of separation, we will deserve to lose our country. It's the tragic irony of Canada that while we've been so brave in fighting other people's wars, we have little stomach for the struggle to keep our own country intact.

Is it too late to prevent a "Yes" vote?

One is supposed to answer that question with a resounding "no"—on the theory, evidently, that denying a problem makes it go away. After all, isn't that the Canadian way? Muddle through and hope for the best? Maybe Jean Charest is the saviour on the white charger, and perhaps the falling birth rate of the *pure laine* (Quebecois French Canadians) will make a future "Yes" vote less and less likely.

When all is said and done, though, if the majority of Quebeckers still hold the view that they cannot tolerate a Canadian federation based on principles of equality, then Canada has three alternatives, as I see them.

First, we can stand firm on the principle of equality, and Quebeckers can learn to tolerate the situation and work within their country for changes—ones that the majority of their fellow citizens can live with. At the same time, Canada as a whole can seek better ways to govern itself, under a system of equality for all.

Second, Canada as a whole can counter the separatist mandate by deciding that it is *not* a country with ten juridically equal provinces, and that Quebec is a special case to be accommodated. This will ensure the eventual breakup of the country anyway, although that breakup will be slightly postponed.

Third, Quebec can, with all the terrors such a move would imply, unilaterally declare independence.

Because we have little in our history to which to refer, it's difficult to predict with any precision what will happen if Quebec secedes. Other nation-states have broken up, of course, but usually there's been a bilateral split, such as that of Czechoslovakia, or a splintering into many political units, as with the breakup of the Austro-Hungarian Empire in 1918, and the subsequent breakup of a former part of that empire, Yugoslavia. The fate of post-Quebec Canada is more difficult to foresee, because the country is so big, and because Quebec is such an integral part, both geographically and historically, of the existing country.

There is, of course, the chance—and, indeed, the hope—that we could keep the rest of Canada together. Perhaps some bold national or provincial leadership might emerge to save what remains of Canada. As the staggering events of the Second World War brought forth Winston Churchill, one or more Canadian leaders with vision, conviction and credibility might step forth.

But this hope is a thin straw to grasp. If he's still in power when Quebec secedes, Jean Chretien will be left with zero credibility and zero moral and political authority to helm a new Canada. Paul Martin? He's a Quebecker at heart, despite his Ontario roots. While he has, at this writing, more credibility than any other Liberal cabinet minister (faint praise indeed), he has given no hint of a political vision of Canada, and by the time Quebec is gone it will be pretty late to start developing one.

Preston Manning? Perhaps. Though chained to the West politically, he has obtained much popular support in Ontario. Manning has been a consistent booster of the "equality of provinces" philosophy, and certainly would go into the post-Quebec situation with the least baggage. He has no profile in Atlantic Canada, though, and he would have to gain a considerably wider public acceptance across Canada before having the capability to lead.

Newfoundland premier Brian Tobin, a first-class fellow, may have an enormous contribution to make, but he has been prominent in bribing and appeasing Quebec in recent years and was a supporter of Charlottetown—facts that a large number of Canadians will find hard to overlook.

There is always the possibility that someone we scarcely know of now will emerge to reunite what's left of Canada—but this is, let's face it, unlikely.

Besides strong leadership, a new Canada will require all citizens, especially those in Ontario, to accept a very different system of government. In many ways, Quebec has been a counter-balance to Ontario in Canada's body politic. When in government, I was astonished by the number of times Quebec and British Columbia were aligned against Ontario (though, admittedly, usually not for precisely the same reasons). With this counter-balance gone, Ontario would control about half of the House of Commons. The economic clout Ontario carries in Atlantic Canada, Saskatchewan and Manitoba would thus allow it to run the country absolutely. This would be unacceptable to British Columbia and, I daresay, Alberta.

One possible counter-balance would be a powerful new regionally based Senate. It would be difficult, though, for Ontario politicians to convince their people that they must concede on this point—even if that were critical to the cobbling together of a new Canada. It's especially hard to foresee this resolution when there has been no groundwork laid for it.

What if this doesn't happen?

It's not my purpose to set forth all the possibilities of a national regrouping subsequent to a Quebec secession, but the most likely result I foresee is British Columbia, after trying to put something together with all or some of the other provinces, and that failing—as surely it would—deciding to go it alone.

Many think B.C. would ally with Alberta, but I don't agree. While it might make sense economically, we're dealing here with two very different people. Moreover, from a practical point of view, what sort of government would you have? Certainly not strict "rep by pop"—Alberta would never stand still for B.C. having absolute control over the legislature. A bicameral house, with equal numbers in the upper house? British Columbia would look upon that arrangement as Ontario looks upon a powerful regional Senate for Canada as a whole. British Columbians are certainly no more self-sacrificing than anyone else, and would vastly prefer a B.C. they control entirely to constant squabbling over who controls what in a new nation where forty percent of the citizens have a much different history, ethnic mix, geography and economy.

For example, would Alberta want to make oil available to their new fellow countrymen at a discount from world prices? I somehow doubt it. Would B.C. charge Alberta less than Saskatchewan or Manitoba for port facilities? Don't bet on it.

If it would be difficult unto impossible to get Alberta and B.C. together, think of the problems in trying to form an alliance also including Saskatchewan and Manitoba. British Columbia would be to that "nation" as Ontario would be to a Quebec-less Canada.

As things now look, British Columbia will be an independent nation inside the first decade of the next century. Talks will fail and new political arrangements will result. One of them will be an independent British Columbia, probably calling itself Cascadia.

British Columbia, or Cascadia, will develop much closer relationships with the four adjacent American states, but will not join them politically. Such a union has never really been an option. We will, however, see new and increased trading patterns with U.S. partners. Much goodwill will exist between the former provinces of Canada, and they will likely continue to trade with one another as well.

I've spent the last twenty-five years publicly fighting to prevent this scenario—fighting for Canada. The problem has been that it's not the *same* Canada that the Canadian establishment has been fighting for. I see Canada through a very different prism. So do most British Columbians, though nuances will vary.

For Canada to survive, I believe that a revolution, a voluntary and peaceful one, is necessary. Revolution is not necessarily the enemy of tradition, though elites always plead tradition to avoid uncomfortable change. Revolution is the enemy of *outdated, unhelpful* and *divisive* tradition. The balance between tradition and progress is a delicate one; Canada's problem is that it simply refuses to change *anything*, and that will inevitably lead to catastrophe.

I wish I could hold out some rational hope for a united Canada to my children and grandchildren. Unhappily, I only have left the hope that comes with dreams. Even those reveries are contingent upon several things—some solution to the problems raised in the recent Delgamuukw decision that proves acceptable to B.C., a shift in Ottawa policy to include the concerns of B.C., a more inclusive attitude from the Central Canadian establishment— that seem highly unlikely.

But, in the words of Yogi Berra, the second-best catcher of his era (Roy Campanella being the best), "It ain't over till it's over." There are two available solutions to the Canadian-unity mess, but they require political courage of the highest order. They require far-sightedness and the ability to put the long-term welfare of our country ahead of short-term political agendas.

First, a constituent assembly must be set up, without the hedging of bets by putting safe, status-quo federalists in control. This assembly must start to operate as a mechanism by which Canadians can, for the very first time, decide what sort of country they want, or indeed, I suppose, whether they want one at all.

Second, there must be a legislated settlement of Native land claims. This solution may or may not accord with the Delgamuukw judgment, depending on who is reading the law. Mel Smith recommends a legislated settlement, not because it is a good idea in itself—it usually isn't—but because it seems so unlikely that appropriate deals can be reached with seventy-five or more separate Native bands.

These two things are far from easy to accomplish; and must happen with the consent of the provinces, especially the one most severely affected, British Columbia. I cannot see the likes of the present Canadian leadership, with the possible exception of Preston Manning, having the courage to instigate these things.

Still, as long as Canada has not yet reached political Armageddon, I will continue to hold onto faint hope for the country, hope that Canada will survive as a political entity. I'm bound to say, though, that I don't think it will.

CHAPTER THIRTEEN

On Sons of Bitches

Craig Jones is a law student at the University of British Columbia. He comes from very conservative stock and has no intention of overthrowing *anything* by force—not even his school's Law Undergraduate Society, much less the government.

When the Asia Pacific Economic Conference was held in Vancouver in November 1997 (with representatives from China, Indonesia and Singapore, amongst others) Jones concocted a sort of display: a coat rack supporting two cloth flags, painted with slogans. One said DEMOCRACY, the other FREE SPEECH. This device stood on the front lawn of the student residence in which Jones stays, which was alongside the road the APEC "dignitaries" were to travel.

The RCMP came to arrest Jones for his revolutionary sloganeering, so he held his arms out for what he thought would be handcuffs. Instead, two officers threw him face-down to the ground with his arms behind his back, while a third jumped up and down on the back of Jones' legs. He was then handcuffed, thrown in the back of a police car and driven to jail. The entire incident was filmed. Ironically, the policemen weren't from Vancouver and didn't know where the jail was, so Craig had to guide them.

Another young student—this one unquestionably a left-wing zealot, which last time I looked was a legitimate thing to be—was walking on the UBC campus the weekend *before* the conference was to start. A police car suddenly stopped and two policemen grabbed the student, threw him into the car and heaved him into the slammer. He had no signs, no weapons and was doing nothing wrong, not even disobeying a "don't walk on the lawn" sign.

The presidents of the great democracies of China, Singapore and Indonesia, so renowned for their tolerance of dissent, were protected from signs boosting the notions of democracy and free speech. And the two students? They were released—on the condition that they not demonstrate on this issue ever again!

This is what happens when you give the authorities—even here in Canada—a reason to restrict freedom. If society must err, mark me down for error on the side of free speech.

That great iconoclast-cum-cynic, H.L. Mencken, once said, "The trouble with fighting for human freedom is that you have to spend so much of your time defending sons of bitches." He's right—and we don't defend sons of bitches in this country. We never have and, as things look, never will.

It's all part of the national psyche. Canada was born out of a series of compromises intended to build not a *free* society, but one loyal to the British Crown and able to avoid absorption by those uppity Americans, with their notions of liberty. Citizens were either British subjects loyal to the Crown or captured aliens to be kept out of mischief, by judicious use of the carrot, stick and Roman Catholic Church. When the American Tories, called United Empire Loyalists here, came to Canada after the mass American *lese majeste*, we became even more loyal to imposed authority. As a result, English-speaking Canadians are now, with the possible exception of the German Swiss, the most tight-assed people in the world.

Francophone Quebeckers have just the opposite psyche. Thrown into captivity in 1759, they have, through great political and economic swings and roundabouts, always maintained a revolutionary zeal not far from the surface of their culture—especially since the Quiet Revolution in 1960.

English-speaking Canada, though, places law and order before all else. It's noteworthy that our constitutional "motto" is "Peace order and good government." No "Liberty! Equality! Fraternity!" for us. No cries of "Give me liberty or give me death!" No, for us it is peace (as in no absorption by Uncle Sam), order (as in a single Mountie escorting Sitting Bull and ten thousand braves across the border, deporting them to the U.S.) and good government (as in government by the upper classes, with only as much democracy as is absolutely necessary to keep that precious "order").

We in this country have always done what we've been told. Go to Flanders, rot in a rat-infested trench, then go over the top into withering machine-gun fire, because some European aristocracies couldn't keep their powers properly balanced? Right. Yes sir. Not a whimper.

Though I would be the last person in the world to say that we could have avoided the Second World War, it's interesting that at that time there was no real peace movement, even though we'd lost so many of our country's young people just twenty years earlier. There were a few conscientious objectors, but most Canadians not only did what they were told, they did it without complaint.

The implementation of the War Measures Act during the October Crisis in 1971 was probably the most outrageous act of tyranny ever passed by a so-called democracy, yet by and large the public applauded Pierre Trudeau for imposing martial law across the entire country—because in Quebec one person had been murdered and another kidnapped. When Trudeau told us that the events in Quebec threatened the security of the entire nation, we accepted this with almost no dissent. Only the federal NDP, under leader Tommy Douglas, asked questions. John Turner, then justice minister, promised Canadians a full explanation—which, twenty-seven years later, has yet to come.

After the October Crisis, when it appeared that we had thrown scores of people in jail and held them incommunicado, without right to counsel or bail, and that most of those people had never conspired with anyone to do anything, we simply overlooked it.

Canadians are tight-assed in how we govern ourselves too. We tolerate federal and provincial governments run by the first ministers, with no real constraints on their power. Because we hate to make waves, no one ever talks about changing the bloody system, only about getting *our* guy elected dictator instead of *their* guy. It's not considered appropriate to discuss fundamental change. Not Canadian, you know.

The media reflects all this. Just how we can call ourselves a nation when we have a muzzled press—muzzled because it is controlled utterly by those who have, for financial and control reasons, no interest in seeing change— is beyond me. Newspapers in this country are great at debating such issues as the need for a new sewer line or more law and order. However, when it comes to any real change to the status quo, however slight, they don't want to talk about it—and they don't think we should either.

"Up to Canadian standards" is often a phrase thrown about. In recent times it's been applied to Morton Downey, Jr., and more recently to Howard Stern. Both these broadcasters are abusive, abrasive, often ill-informed and American. Stern has done very well in the Toronto and Montreal markets.

Those whose incomes have been hurt by Stern's added competition have whinged to the CRTC that as an American who's a bit on the raw side, Stern is "not up to Canadian standards." While these losers prate on about Canadian standards, they are really on about the money, and their government-enforced monopoly. They're really saying, "We don't want free speech here if it's offensive."

"Canadian standards" are those of Peter Gzowski, who never said a controversial thing in his life and certainly didn't challenge the establishment on fundamental questions. In an interview, Gzowski once asked me why I didn't do some *good* for the country. The clear implication was that because I saw the country through a different prism than he and the Central Canadian establishment, my commitment—and even my loyalty—to Canada was suspect. Overall, I admit, broadcasting was well served by Peter Gzowski. But there is room for more feisty stuff too. Including Howard Stern—even in the Vancouver market, if that's what people want.

Our stuffy, elitist attitude prevails, though, because we are not truly a free country. For example, our humour is of the ironic sort, full of double entendre. I personally like that sort of humour, but it betrays a people afraid to speak out. It's a style that developed in England, where untrammelled free speech has still not yet arrived. The British have always suppressed the unpopular, from the religious dissenters of the seventeenth century to John Wilkes (the famous eighteenth-century pamphleteer) to Catholics and Jews (who were refused entry to the House of Commons until comparatively recent times). There are more recent stories of suppression, too: the abdication of King Edward in 1936; the refusal, that same year, to air Churchill's case for re-armament on the BBC; the Thatcher government's hugely embarrassing effort to suppress Peter Wright's book *Spycatcher* in the 1980s. In fact, until the 1970s, plays in London's West End were actively censored by Lord Chamberlain, a court-appointed beadle.

This national repression is a Canadian trait too. When anything likely to embarrass the government comes along, there is an establishment "harrumph" from coast to coast that "This isn't the Canadian way."

Compare this situation to that of the United States, a land of liberty where, from the days of Tom Paine, they've let it all hang out. Might we not have been a lot better off to expand notions of democracy rather than try, successfully I might add sadly, to contain it? I am scarcely an undiluted admirer of the U.S., but I do admire their political system, which allows for all manner of dissent. In fact, dissenting views often became orthodox thinking with the passage of time.

Admittedly, it's not been all peaches and cream in the States; the ability to speak out freely has ebbed and flowed. You wouldn't have wanted to be an abolitionist in the South in the 1850s, or a communist anywhere in the country in the 1950s. You still wouldn't want to be Black and raising hell in some parts of the country. However, the American people have always known that their country was spawned by revolution from which inalienable rights flowed. Even when rights were suppressed—as those of Japanese Americans, militant unionists like the "Wobblies," and anti-war activists have been in turn—in most cases the issue has come to a head and freedom has prevailed, the best modern example being the "Pentagon Papers" of the Vietnam era.

Mencken was right. When you fight for human freedom, you *do* have to defend some sons of bitches, and often you must give the finger to political correctness.

Until recently, *The North Shore News*, a community newspaper in North Vancouver, published a regular column by Doug Collins, one of the most unpleasant men I have ever known. He had a good reporting record, an unbelievable war record, and had once been a top media personality, as a national columnist for a number of papers and a CBC personality.

However, as the years passed Collins became a racist, progressing from mild to vicious. An Englishman by background who sounded more English as time passed, he believed, contrary to all evidence, that Canada was a British country. (Needless to say, he wasn't fussy about French Canadians.) An immigrant himself, he abhorred non-white immigration, and wanted to restrict Canadian immigration to backgrounds similar to his own.

Collins loved to wound. He was particularly hard on East Indians and Jews. He loved making fun of East Indian names, but toward the end, it was Jews who came in for most of it. A great admirer of neo-Nazi historian David Irving, Collins denied that the Holocaust had occurred. Actually, he did admit that the Nazis were a bit hard on the Jews and that excesses had no doubt taken place, but argued that at the very least, the Holocaust had been exaggerated. This matter came to a head with the release of the movie

Schindler's List, which Collins dubbed "Swindler's List," to the great distress of many Jews.

The issue divided Jewish opinion. The Canadian Jewish Congress took the strong view that Collins ought to be prosecuted criminally, and that he and his paper should be brought before the Human Rights Council, and they did just that. Other Jews felt that, as hurtful and odious as Collins' statements might be, millions of people had died for his right to be offensive.

I have stood against Collins for years. His writing on this subject was utterly repulsive. But I'm a free-speech man and I editorially supported, firmly and often, the unpopular view that he was entitled to say what he said. Even though Collins publicly and privately vilified me at every opportunity, I was called a racist by observers both inside and outside the Jewish community for defending his right to speak.

It's not hard to understand why. Thanks to Collins, "free speech" had come to be viewed as coded language for "anti-Semitism"—something I abhor. Because Collins had used free speech as a shield for spouting hurtful rubbish, those who supported his free-speech rights were also seen as anti-Semites.

Nor does the Canadian Jewish Congress's attitude stop there. If one criticizes the State of Israel, one runs the serious risk of being labelled an anti-Semite. It takes courage to say anything even remotely unflattering about Israel.

At the Human Rights Council hearing, Collins and his paper won their case, as well they should have. While it was nauseating to read their self-serving drivel about their courageous stand against censorship, the paper deserves credit for not listening to advertisers and well-meaning people who put convenience ahead of free speech.

What we're really talking about here is legislated politeness. One can call an Englishman a limey, a Scot parsimonious, and a German hard-headed, or allude to Irish affinity to whisky—and cause only a minor ripple. But you dare not say that Hong Kong immigrants can't drive (which they can't, mainly because they haven't done so until recently) or that Jews dominate the arts in the United States—which they clearly do. (Let me be clear, I'm supporting statements of fact, not hate-mongering: When people allude to Jewish domination of the arts, what is offensive is the inference that there is something sinister about it, and that it probably proves that there is an evil conspiracy that must be dealt with.) God help you if you call a Japanese person a "Jap," which everyone did during the Second World War, a Chinese person a Chinaman—as for so long was the fashion—or, now, an Afro-American a Negro. ("Black" became fashionable in the late 1960s, and it too is rapidly becoming a pejorative as fashions change.)

Let me be clear; it's wrong to call people any names. Obviously, pejorative terms, no matter who they are aimed at, are wrong. The question is how should society handle them: by suppression or societal disapproval? We have to go back to basics. Under our way of life, what is not expressly forbidden by democratically passed laws is permitted. In deciding what sort of conduct to proscribe, the state must consider, amongst other things, the enforceability of its proscriptions. That's not to say that if it can't catch even a tiny minority of transgressors it will forget passing laws and make their crime legal. It becomes an issue of harm done by the difficult-to-prosecute law-breaker—and common sense.

People have been calling each other names from the beginning of time. Efforts to curb this antisocial tendency have not been successful, except where the king was personally involved. You don't call the king in "The Wizard of Id" a fink, and you didn't call Henry VIII an adulterer, even though in both cases the statements are true. We've tortured, hanged, drawn and quartered and otherwise been pretty mean to people over the years who say naughty things about those in power, especially the church.

Over the centuries we slowly recognized that this was a bad idea—even if failure to enforce good manners permitted, and perhaps encouraged, very bad manners indeed. Eventually we went even further: If bad manners hurt people's feelings and exposed them to danger, that was still more acceptable than censorship. It was a matter of common sense and balance of rights.

Society does, of course, deal with bad manners. It holds bad-mannered people up to public contempt and ridicule. Leaders in the community set examples and society changes, albeit slowly. Public—and, more importantly, private—disapproval play a very important role in a free society. Over the past thirty years, terms that were common in private conversations, and often in public, now bring looks of horror. Jokes have, mercifully, changed. We're still far from perfect (who is?) but we're better by far.

We make a serious mistake in thinking that slights to races or people on account of their race (or religion, sexual persuasion, marital status, religion, etc.) must be dealt with by the state. Once that happens, freedom of speech becomes seriously curtailed generally. We are currently moving toward a society that officially disapproves of unpopular views and applies sanctions on inconvenient free speech. Not only is this philosophically unbearable to me and many other Canadians, it's impractical.

Take Ernst Zundel and Jim Keegstra. The former, a racist whacko who specializes in Holocaust-denial literature, became a fixture on the national news, with a hardhat on his head and a cross over his shoulder, because the government persisted in prosecuting him. There is no way in the world he could have *bought* this publicity. Thanks to the Criminal Code of Canada, Zundel became a media star, spewing out his vicious views for free across the nation. Here was a man prosecuted because his views, if widely disseminated, might bring harm to a minority, and thus given the widest possible circulation for those views.

Jim Keegstra, too, ought to have been a twenty-four-hour story. "Teacher fired for propagating anti-Semitism in school" should have been the 1984 headline to end the matter. Instead, almost fifteen years later, Keegstra is still getting publicity as he fights the government's case against him from tribunal to tribunal, from court to court. That's an intelligent way to fight intolerance?

Free speech can only exist if it is accepted that there will be rudeness and hurtfulness as a result. It's the insurance premium a free country pays for its liberty. Those who say that this is all very well coming from me, a middle-class WASP, should try being a lawyer, a politician and a public spectacle. They should talk to my grandchildren.

Are there any legitimate exceptions to untrammelled free speech?

It is said that you can't holler "Fire!" in a crowded theatre. True—but such an action is not an exercise in free speech. The man who does this is not offering an opinion but a falsehood, one designed not to offend the sensibilities of his audience, as Collins did, but to make people kill themselves. There is a world of difference between "kike" and "kill that Jew." It's as if one tried to defend a doctor who deliberately prescribes deadly poison; the doctor isn't trying to express an opinion, he's committing murder.

Treason has always been accepted as a legitimate reason to hamper free speech, but I have trouble with that. Perhaps the best example is that of William Joyce, the Irish American carrying a British passport who broadcast, as Lord Haw Haw, to Britain from Germany during the Second World War. He was convicted and hanged on the thin thread that his passport gave the English courts jurisdiction to try a naturalized German. But that was right after the war, a bad time for a person charged with treason to rely upon technicalities. Also charged was John Amery, a British-born Axis broadcaster. Amery's father was one of Churchill's oldest friends and a wartime cabinet colleague; Amery was hanged and, to his great credit, refused to ask his father for help in getting a commutation of his sentence.

Of course, Lord Haw Haw hardly destroyed British morale during the war, and in fact invariably provided amusement. It raises the question, who is a traitor? It's pretty easy for any government to agree that anyone who wants to change the system under which they exercise power is a traitor. Agitators of all sorts are traitors, in a strict interpretation of the word. (I've been called one, by no less than a prime minister.) That's fine—if all you're doing is calling them "traitors." It is quite another matter if you're about to hang them for their contrary views.

Libel laws are another widely accepted restriction on free speech. I have no trouble with the notion that if something untrue and harmful is uttered maliciously, there ought to be a penalty. But this should be very exceptional, especially with regards to public officials. Now, vigorous name calling or hard criticism brings out the writ. This is wrong, and helps those in authority keep a lid on what they don't want you and me as taxpayers to know about. Libel chill, for instance, is a technique whereby powerful figures dampen criticism by threatening or actually bringing costly court actions that most media outlets do not have the financial resources to defend against. This pernicious practice is encouraged by the enthusiasm with which courts awards damages against the media.

Should people be able to say hurtful and untrue things? Yes, subject to what I've just said. If the criterion for being prosecuted by the state is "hurtful," where do you stop? And by whose standards do we judge?

A recent case in Kelowna has underscored the complexities of living in a society that allows free speech. A number of physicians have claimed that as abortionists, their lives are endangered by a pro-life society that pickets them, "exposes" them, and badmouths them—thereby, so the argument goes, encouraging kooks to kill them. (One wonders a little at the "exposes" bit—is it now to be unlawful to say that a certain lawyer often takes un-popular cases, that a politician supports unpopular causes or—may I add—that talk-show hosts often render unpopular opinions?)

The extension of the argument that those who lawfully complain about your conduct must be punished because it might encourage a nutcase to be violent is pretty frightening.

The issue is simple. Free speech carries with it risks and plenty of unpleasantness. It can hurt, badly, and it can bring violence.

Moreover, as with the RCMP's actions at that Asia Pacific Economic Conference, authority can always claim a noble purpose for their deeds. In that case the stated purpose was the safeguarding of the thuggish heads of government who came to the conference. The real purpose was to spare the thugs embarrassment.

In extreme cases of free speech suppression, the consequences are extreme—as in Nazi Germany, or the USSR.

It's argued that in Canada we needn't go that far. We only need take a little free speech away in order to safeguard whomever it is we wish to safe-guard. Other countries have done it.

In Singapore, for example, any opposition to the government is subject to repression and jail, and spitting on the street can bring jail without a trial.

In Mexico, despite the trappings of free speech, the government has won every main election for over sixty years.

In Japan, you must get a permit to demonstrate, and Koreans kidnapped during Japan's brutal repression earlier in the century are still treated as third-class citizens at best.

The first decision to limit free speech begins a process that must, over time, lead to a system of governance similar to any of the above examples. It's a question of where you wish to err: on the side of the state's convenience, or on the side of the right of the populace to speak freely.

In this book, I have presented my case. I scarcely expect the echo of huzzahs from across the country to fill my ears. I am a non-violent revolutionary who, if I weren't bred into the Canadian passion for peace and order, might actually issue a call *aux barricades*. As such, my views are distinctly unsuit-able to those who have acquired and now maintain power in government or the community through the present system and its basic assumptions.

I expect no favourable views from media who, as the Charlottetown campaign proved, have lost their ability—if they ever had it—to question authority. Indeed, with a few honourable exceptions they have a stake in seeing as little as possible said about the Charlottetown issue. For that represented their greatest cave-in to authority, only holding the feet to the fire of those who had the temerity to question the establishment.

Nothing will probably come of this effort except this: I was true to myself and called it as I saw it.

Index